Urban Spaces

Urban Spaces

Edited by John Morris Dixon, FAIA

Visual Reference Publications, Inc., New York

Copyright © 1999 by Visual Reference Publications, Inc.

All rights reserved. No part of this book may be reproduced in any form or by any electronic or mechanical means, including information storage and retrieval systems, without permission in writing from the publisher.

Visual Reference Publications, Inc.
302 Fifth Avenue
New York, NY 10001

Distributors to the trade in the United States and Canada
Watson-Guptill
1515 Broadway
New York, NY 10036

Distributors outside the United States and Canada
Hearst Books International
1350 Avenue of the Americas
New York, NY 10019

Book Design: Harish Patel Design Associates, New York

Library of Congress Cataloging in Publication Data:
Urban Spaces

Printed in Hong Kong
ISBN 0-934590-32-X

CONTENTS

Introduction by John Morris Dixon, FAIA	6
Preface by Richard M. Rosan, President, Urban Land Institute	8
Altoon + Porter Architects	9
Arai / Jackson Architects and Planners	17
Brennan Beer Gorman / Architects	25
Callison Architecture, Inc.	33
Cooper Carry, Inc.	41
Duany Plater-Zyberk & Company	49
EDAW	57
EDSA, Edward D. Stone, Jr. and Associates	65
Elkus / Manfredi Architects Ltd	73
ELS / Elbasani & Logan Architects	81
A. Epstein & Sons International, Inc.	89
Gensler	97
Glatting Jackson Kercher Anglin Lopez Rinehart, Inc.	105
Goody, Clancy & Associates	113
The Harris Group / TBA² Architects	121
HDR Architecture, Inc.	129
Hellmuth, Obata + Kassabaum, Inc.	137
Jambhekar Strauss Architects PC	145
The Jerde Partnership International, Inc.	153
JJR Incorporated	161
Kohn Pedersen Fox Associates PC	169
MBT Architecture	177
The Planning Collaborative	185
ROMA Design Group	193
RTKL Associates Inc.	201
Sasaki Associates, Inc.	209
SITE	217
Skidmore, Owings & Merrill LLP	225
Smallwood, Reynolds, Stewart, Stewart & Associates, Inc.	233
The Stubbins Associates, Inc.	241
SWA Group	249
Torti Gallas & Partners • CHK	257
TVS / Thompson, Ventulett, Stainback & Associates, Inc.	265
Urban Design Associates	273
Van Tilburg, Banvard & Soderbergh, Architects, AIA	281
Ten Easy Lessons on Urban Development by Daniel A. Biederman	290
Project Credits	294
Index by Projects	304
Acknowledgements	308

Introduction: Urban Spaces with Public Appeal

There is justifiable concern these days that people in the modern world are withdrawing into private domains. Electronic wizardry has made it possible to work at home, shop at home, and be perpetually entertained at home. Increasingly, those homes are isolated behind guarded gates or segregated into developments for groups such as senior citizens or young professionals, each with its separate social and recreational facilities. Our local travel is overwhelmingly done in the isolation of the private car, increasingly in large SUVs with darkened windows. Little wonder that these citizens are reluctant to fund public facilities.

At the same time, there seems to be almost universal agreement, crossing political and economic lines, that steps must be taken to counteract this privatization and encourage people to meet in public. And notwithstanding electronic alternatives at home, today's people do crowd malls, cineplexes, fitness centers, and clubs — the whole array of public places that private enterprise provides. Where the public domain offers appealing streets, plazas, and parks, the populace flocks to them.

Of course, mere spaces are not enough. For decades, modern architects and planners naively maintained that open space, as such, was healthful and would stimulate community life. It took a lot of vacant office building plazas and deserted pedestrian malls to convince the design profession that the planning of urban spaces for public use is a very special art.

Starting in the 1960s, we benefited from the sage advice of urban theorists such as Jane Jacobs and William H. Whyte, who explained the human dynamics of the public realm. They stood modernist dogma on its ear by showing that "crass" elements such as shops, street vendors, and moderate amounts of automobile traffic make public spaces safer and more attractive. Their lessons are demonstrated in the festival marketplaces and mixed-use complexes that have flourished since the 1970s.

More recently, the proponents of the New Urbanism have been developing communities that demonstrate these principles, closely mixing a variety of residential and commercial types with carefully crafted community spaces. Their typical reliance on traditional architectural forms to make the public feel more comfortable has alienated designers who are dedicated modernists. But New Urbanism doesn't have to come with picket fences, Victorian lamp posts, and Georgian facades. Modernists who object to such nostalgic flourishes are challenged to develop alternatives for our own time, and many of them have. In this book, you will see a wide range of ways to make public spaces enticing and rewarding for the public.

In recent decades, the line between privately owned and publicly owned urban spaces has grown ever less clear. Historically, public spaces were usually limited to streets, squares, and parks, although churches, mosques, temple gardens, and such also played important public roles. In the 19th century, the many covered shopping arcades and galSleries were in effect public spaces, as were the ever-grander railroad stations and museums. With the spread of the enclosed shopping mall in recent decades, along with atriums in hotels and office buildings, more and more of our public space is in fact indoors. In places with climatic extremes, weather-protected spaces, usually privately built, have enhanced and promoted public life.

As the distinction between public and private urban spaces has become less clearcut, so has the question of who finances and makes crucial decisions about these spaces. We increasingly find private facilities on public land and publicly accessible spaces on private land. Today, major projects often entail negotiated zoning exceptions and design conditions tied to monetary considerations, whether tax abatement, direct subsidies, or special assessments. So basic decision-making on buildings and spaces are often made jointly by private owners and government agencies, often with community organizations involved as well. Public and private roles are also entwined in the ever more common Business Improvement Districts, in which owners in an area agree to assess themselves — with government supervision — to invest in improvements, some on private property, some on public.

Not all the "urban spaces" in this book are literally located in cities. The suburbs, which have expanded so vastly in this century, are often where the need for gathering places — other than shopping malls — is most severe. The suburban projects included here typically relieve the prevailing homogeneity by introducing greater density, along with distinctive and memorable shaping of buildings and open spaces. A few of the projects in the book are even sited in rural places, but nevertheless deal with concerns involving whole metropolitan areas or regions.

And where do these private owners and government officials turn for the design of urban spaces? They rely on architects, landscape architects, planners, and urban designers — any of them or, in many cases, several of them in collaboration. The sections of this book are identified with firms that have shown exceptional skill in the design of urban spaces, but the credit for shaping these spaces is inevitably shared with the clients who commissioned them, and generally with consultants and collaborating designers as well. Because the full credit lists for individual projects would have filled substantial (and unpredictable) amounts of our pages, these are found on the Credits pages at the back of the book.

Note that in two cases, the same project appears among the works of more than one firm. For example, information on Canal City Hakata is included under the firm that master planned the complex (pages 154-155) as well as the one in charge of the landscape architecture (pages 62-63). Arizona Center is covered under the firm that planned the entire complex (pages 254-256) and the one that designed the retail component (pages 82-83).

Collaboration is the watchword for really effective urban spaces. Nothing sets off more intense controversy than development proposals, and the work you see in this book required many constructive compromises and creative trade-offs. Good public spaces are never the products of unfettered individual inspiration, but of effective reconciliation between competing demands. Every example you will see here is in some sense a victory for the public realm over forces that tend to splinter our societies.

John Morris Dixon, FAIA

Preface

Richard M. Rosan
President, Urban Land Institute

Interest in the urban environment and urban spaces has increased greatly in the past several years. In cities of all sizes and in all regions, developers, designers, planners, and public officials have begun a dialogue about the need to create urban spaces that draw people, that establish a sense of place, that connect various components of the urban environment, and that are usable in addition to being beautiful. Urban "placemaking" is being approached with creativity and ingenuity, and has pushed developers and designers to create spaces that go beyond the ordinary. This book showcases some of those spaces.

Urban Spaces illustrates a wide variety of designs and project types, each distinctly urban spaces. From town centers to medical centers to streetscapes, the spaces presented in this book represent sophisticated design solutions. The 35 outstanding firms profiled share their insights on creating designs that enhance the urban environment while meeting clients' needs. The collection is also geographically diverse, with projects located in Cleveland, New York, Las Vegas, Rotterdam, Shanghai, and many other cities.

The Urban Land Institute was pleased to cooperate with the publishers of *Urban Spaces* because leading urban designers, planners, and architects, many of whom are associated with ULI, were looking for the opportunity to present their firm's projects and services in a high-quality publication. ULI represents more than 14,000 individuals dedicated to providing leadership in the use of land in order to enhance the total environment. Since 1936, ULI has promoted high-quality land use in all its forms. This new book, with its displays of top-notch urban spaces, is a worthy contribution to the mission of ULI, and the ULI is pleased to endorse it.

Altoon + Porter Architects

5700 Wilshire Boulevard
Suite 100
Los Angeles
California 90036
323.939.1900
323.939.1199 (Fax)

Altoon + Porter Architects

Fashion Valley Center
San Diego, California

Right: Lighting is ornamental, without detracting from shop fronts.
Below and below right: Walkways offer appealing views of both levels.
Photography: Erhard Pfeiffer.

Active urban spaces of the kind usually found only in downtown areas have been created in this expansion of a conventional edge-of-city shopping mall. The addition of a second floor to the open air center—expanding the complex to an area of 1.7 million square feet, had to be accomplished without disrupting business on the lower floor. The expansion was an opportunity to develop a number of different precincts, rather than one over-extended identity. Locations of stairs and escalators between floors are emphasized. Visual focal points in the center's diverse open spaces are not frivolous embellishments, but intrinsically practical elements such as structural supports, canopies, and light sources. Lighting is carefully designed to provide points of interest, as well as ample illumination, yet not to compete with brighter shop-front lighting. Because space is fairly confined, and an urban feeling is desired, planting is limited largely to

Right: Spare plantings and shopping kiosks lend urban feeling.
Below right: Canopies filter San Diego sunshine.

palm trees, potted plants, and climbing vines. In the year after the project's 1997 completion, daily visitors increased from 35,000 to 105,000.

Altoon + Porter Architects

Kaahumanu Center
Kahului, Maui, Hawaii

Below: *Rounded end of central concourse invites shoppers.*
Right and below right: *Elegantly simple steel framing supports layers of fiberglass.*
Photography: *Birdair (below), David Franzen (all others).*

Above: A circular skylight distinguishes the crossing of two principle axes.
Right: Lighting fixture recalls old village torches.

In this remodeled and expanded shopping center, primarily for island residents rather than tourists, the architects have created dramatic spatial spaces with a sense of community. Understated steel-frame structures are surmounted by Teflon-coated fiberglass canopies in striking, slightly mystifying configurations. Carefully arranged to admit island breezes while minimizing the impact of wind-driven rains, these canopies provide diffuse sunlight by day and soft indirect lighting by night. In their overlapping billows, there are also strong suggestions of the tall sailing ships that first brought commerce to these islands. Openings at ends of axes and between canopy layers assure views of sky, waterfront, and mountains.

Altoon + Porter Architects

Tower Place
Cincinnati, Ohio

Below: Canopied storefronts address the city street.
Below right: Limestone and grillework clad the parking levels above.
Facing page: Three levels of shopping connect with retail and offices in existing tower.
Photography: Rick Alexander, Greg Matulionis.

Compactness was the requirement in this downtown shopping center development, by Altoon + Porter with FWA Group, associated architects. The site is a quarter city block, adjoining one of America's earliest mixed-use complexes, the 1920s Carew Tower. The project had to provide parking for 500 cars and underground services for the entire block. The exterior had to acknowledge the urban street with storefronts along the sidewalk. Inside, a three-story shopping atrium is surmounted by a five-level parking garage, hollow in the center to admit daylight from a central skylight to the floor 100 feet below. On the atrium interior, a sense of urbanity is enhanced with marble floors, polished bronze handrails, and softly translucent lighting fixtures. Robert Kirschner was commissioned to create a central fountain and four 27-foot-long paintings for four sides of the atrium's light well. The exterior envelope above the storefronts is clad in limestone, with dark grilles admitting air and light to parking levels.

Left: Handrail detail underlines urbanity of atrium.
Below left: Lightwell above atrium features four vast paintings on its major walls.

Arai/Jackson
Architects and Planners

1601 East John
Seattle
Washington 98112
206.323.8800
206.323.8518 (Fax)
www.araijackson.com

Arai/Jackson

Seattle Central Community College Student Activities Center
Seattle, Washington

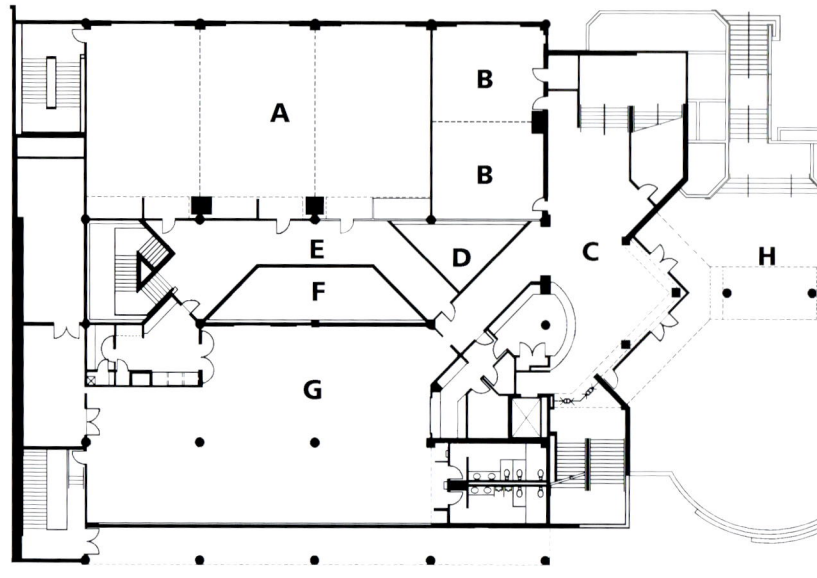

Above: The building is divided at street level by an entry plaza, which also serves as a gateway to the city park beyond.
Right: Canopy symbolizing gateway leads to main lobby entrance.
Photography: Steve Keating.

Housing the full range of student activity and recreational facilities, this building had to meet a variety of urban needs. Located along busy Broadway Avenue, the project was required to maintain pedestrian-oriented uses along the street front, with setbacks limited to 15 feet. As a component of the campus spanning the arterial street, it had to respect the scale and color of existing college buildings. Bordering a historic city park, the Bobby Morris Playfield, the new complex presented an opportunity to link this public open space to Broadway Avenue, from which it had been isolated. The

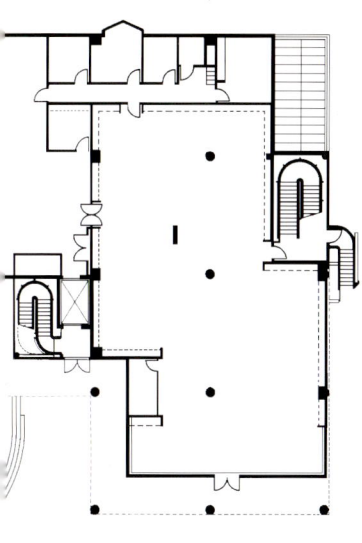

- **A** Multi-Purpose Dance Studio
- **B** Classroom
- **C** Foyer
- **D** Open to Below
- **E** Gallery
- **F** Open to Below
- **G** Student Lounge
- **H** Park Portal
- **I** Bookstore

Above right: Three interior levels are apparent to visitors.
Right: An urban gateway connects the historic park with the campus center.
Below: Patterns in tile cladding and concrete paving are elements of building's art program.

outcome of all these considerations is a two-part structure, connected below street level, with its main entrance located at an opening that acts as a portal to the playfield. The building's most pedestrian-compatible functions, the bookstore and the student lounge, are located along the street. The virtually windowless gym, ringed by a running track, is on the upper level of the larger building, student offices are above the bookstore. The swimming pool, racquet courts, fitness center, and locker rooms are below street level. Concrete and ceramic tile exterior cladding relate to the brick walls of the predominant 1960s campus buildings without mirroring them. Art by Cecelia Alvarez and Frank Video is integrated into the design in the form of ceramic tile patterns, sandblasted plaza concrete, etched windows and other elements, with motifs reflecting the cultural diversity of the student body.

Arai/Jackson

Tacoma Dome Transportation Station
Tacoma, Washington

Right: Transit island structure has transparent roof and identifying clock tower.
Below: Bridge from garage to transit island expresses project's industrial character.
Photography: Benjamin Benschneider.

Right: Steel canopies and bold graphics reflect industrial past, as well as present sports activities.
Below right: Complex is designed so it can be extended.

This phased facility (Phase I completed 1997; Phase II to be completed 2001) occupies a two block area in the heart of an emerging pedestrian district adjoining the Tacoma Dome Stadium. It provides parking and connections to local and intercity buses, plus future light rail and commuter rail systems. The architectural design reflects the historical industrial character of the district in its composition and in the use of industrial materials. Elements such as the garage elevator tower, the trussed bridge, and the transit island shelter are designed to admit ample natural light by day and to glow at night to create a well-lit and secure environment.

Arai/Jackson

Southwest Harbor Project, Terminal 5 Expansion Public Access
Seattle, Washington

Top right: Main gate, with reused timbers and delicate steel span.
Right: Skewed steel tower supports viewing platforms.
Left: Curved roof distinguishes utilitarian service structure.
Middle left: Bridge leads to harborside viewing platforms.
Bottom left: Tension-compression span at gateway suggests vertebrae.
Photography: Benjamin Benschneider.

As mitigation for the expansion of the Port of Seattle's Terminal 5, this project provides a landscaped pedestrian/bicycle path around the perimeter of the terminal and introduces new public access to the industrial south shore of Elliott Bay. Since the site lies over old landfill and a former wood treatment plant, regulations required barriers to separate the public from contaminated shorelines, thus challenging the notion of public access. In terms of design, the architects wanted to illustrate the environmental consequences of the site's industrial past, without making literal allusions to it. The elevated view deck offers a panorama of shipyards and the city skyline, while the cantilevered construction gives a sense of being out over the water. The skewed support columns and outward-projecting guardrails remind visitors of the delicate balance we must try to maintain with nature. Re-used timbers from the former factory's gantry crane support the vehicular gateway. The ribbed steel arc over this gate represents both the industrial past and the expected regrowth of nature.

Arai/Jackson

Angle Lake Park Improvements, Phase I
SeaTac, Washington

Right: Picnic shelter provides sturdy, hospitable protection from elements.
Below: Comfort station and picnic shelter flank central performance area.
Bottom right: Performance stage doubles as pergola.
Photography: Benjamin Benscheider.

The design challenge in adding structures to this municipal park was to convey a sense of warmth and enjoyment in construction that could withstand the abuse typical of public parks. Materials with textural qualities and a warm color range were used for the comfort station, performance stage, and picnic shelter, which are laid out in a rather formal grouping. Limestone veneer bases provide an image of richness and ruggedness, while serving the practical purpose of protecting the structures from rain run-off and splatter. Heavy timber framing provides a rustic quality along with durability. Metal gates on the restroom entries and wood louvers in end wall gables provide visual interest and allow for passive ventilation.

Arai/Jackson

Meadowbrook Community Center
Seattle, Washington

Above: Center's multi-purpose room faces baseball field.
Left: Entry admits ample daylight and acts as lantern by night.
Below left: Hovering over lobby are artist Mark Calderon's salmon, in cast plaster with copper finish.
Bottom right: Building mass is broken into smaller, contrasting volumes.
Photography: Kevin Haas, left and below left; Benjamin Benschneider, above and bottom.

One role a community center can play is in teaching the community about the preservation and management of our increasingly constricted natural environment. This recent community center by Arai/Jackson is in Meadowbrook Playfield, a large open area in northeast Seattle. Through intensive discussions with the community, it was decided to site the facility between the high school baseball field, an arterial road, a community-based wetlands project, and an existing pool facility. The center's multipurpose room is glazed to form an indoor-outdoor space that opens toward the ballfield. Other facilities in the building include a gym, shower and rest rooms, offices, and activity rooms. A "daylighted" stream (formerly underground) runs through the complex, visibly connecting the wetlands with a creek adjoining the site and serving as an object lesson in the restoration of natural landscape features.

24

Brennan Beer Gorman / Architects

515 Madison Avenue
New York
New York 10022
212.888.7663
212.935.3868 (Fax)
www.bbg-bbgm.com

1030 15th Street, NW
Suite 900
Washington, DC 20005
202.452.1644
202.452.1647 (Fax)

13F Lyndhurst Tower
1 Lyndhurst Terrace
Central, Hong Kong
852.2525.9766
852.2525.9850 (Fax)

Brennan Beer Gorman/ Architects

Sudirman Central Business District, Gateway Precinct Jakarta, Indonesia

Below: Model of Gateway Precinct shows Jakarta Financial Tower, left, Conrad International Center, center, and Jakarta Stock Exchange Building, right.
Right: Jakarta Stock Exchange Building, with walls of gray granite and silver-gray reflective glass.
Photography: Roy Wright (below); Eric Niemy (right).

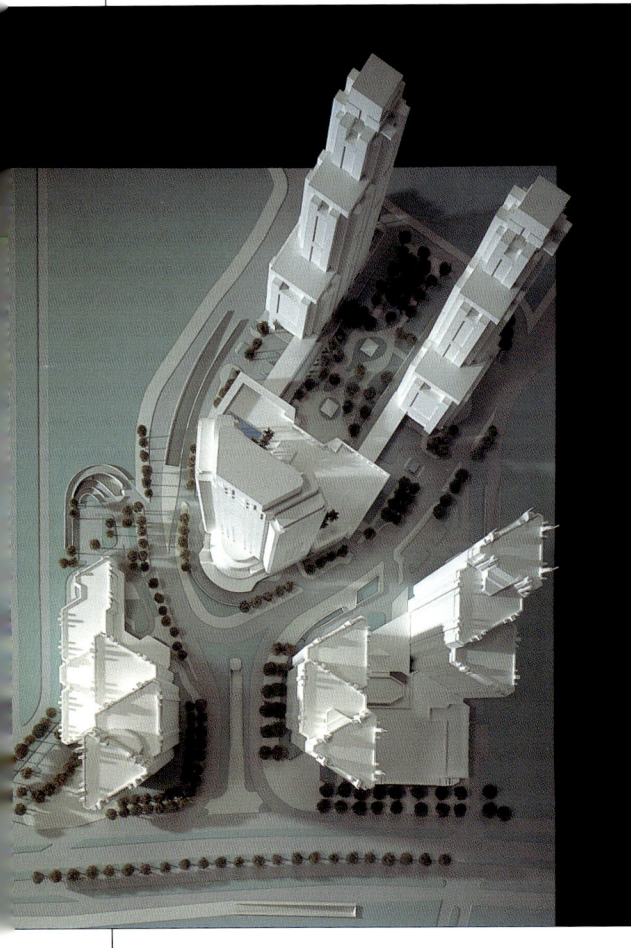

Right: Jakarta Financial Tower, with reflective glass corners emphasizing verticality and providing dramatic offices.
Below: Conrad International Hotel has complex geometry and terraces at numerous setbacks.
Photography: BBG/A.

Jakarta Stock Exchange Building
Conrad International Center
Jakarta Financial Tower

Development in Jakarta arrived at a new scale in the 7.5-million-square-foot mixed-use Gateway Precinct, which constitutes the first three parcels of the planned 100-acre Sudirman Central Business District. BBG/A adapted the master plan for the precinct and is the design architect for the three complementary projects. The Conrad International project, on the central parcel, is a 3.6-million-square-foot complex, anchored by a 42-story, 700-room hotel, with 154 extended-stay service flats, 567,000 square feet of retail, and 64,600 square feet of landscaped public open space. Setbacks at the tower's lower levels provide terraces for the hotel's public spaces. At the top of the tower, setbacks

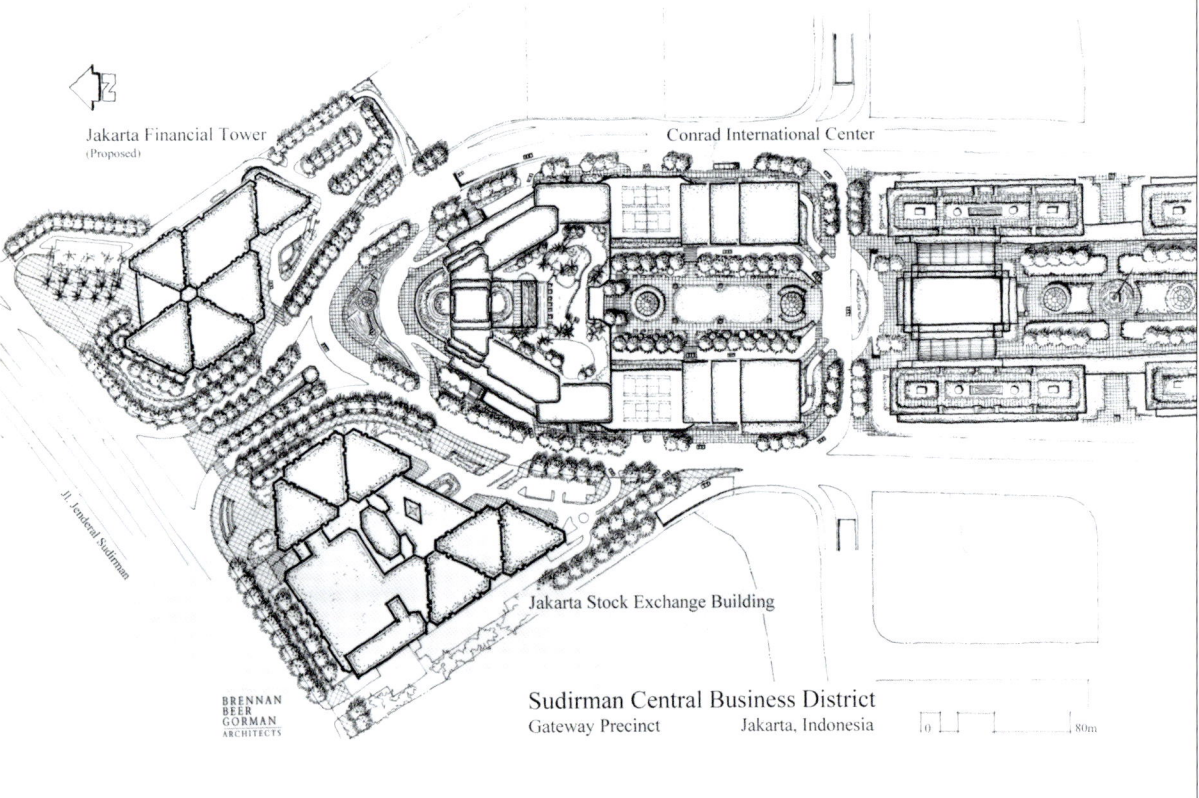

Above left: Jakarta Stock Exchange Building lobby.
Left: Site plan.
Above: Triangular exterior forms of Jakarta Stock Exchange Building.
Photography: Eric Niemy.

allow for terraced suites. A three-story entrance lobby is glazed at the north and south to permit sweeping through views. The Jakarta Stock Exchange Building and the Jakarta Financial Tower are similarly planned, each consisting of towers of three equilateral triangles, clustered atop a multi-story podium. Each triangular block rises to a different height, with the Financial Tower's tallest rising 34 stories above a seven-story podium. The two form a balanced gateway to the Sudirman Central Business District. The Stock Exchange tower is a privately developed 2,050,000-square-foot structure, consisting of two 32-story towers linked by a four-story podium housing a common lobby and a 27,000-square-foot trading floor. Each tower plan consists of a cluster of three equilateral triangles, designed so that the height of each could be adjusted at the time of construction, depending on floor area needs, without extensive redesign.

Above left: Jakarta Stock Exchange Building.
Bottom Left: Porte-cochere at base of building.
Above: Typical elevator doors.
Photography: Justin van Soest (above left and bottom left); Louis Hedgecock (above).

Brennan Beer Gorman/Architects

The Colgate Center
Jersey City, New Jersey

Directly across the Hudson River from downtown Manhattan, a 42-acre tract is being transformed from Colgate-Palmolive's former factory site into an urban downtown. As master planners, Brennan Beer Gorman/Architects were careful to integrate planning for 7.5 million square feet of new development with the street grid of the adjoining historic Paulus Hook district. Emphasis in the plan is on opening views from the community to the river and taking maximum advantage of the waterfront. Low office buildings along the water and taller office buildings and residential on the inland blocks all enjoy the site's extraordinary views. In addition to 1,500 residential units and five to six million square feet of offices, the plan provides for 250,000 square feet of retail use, a 400-room hotel, a 400-slip marina, and extensive areas of park and riverfront esplanade. Design guidelines cover massing, density, parking, off-street loading, etc., and include a requirement for 40-foot-high masonry-clad bases to maintain the

Above left: Model representing master plan, showing parks and espanades, with 101 Hudson building rendered in detail, at right in photo.
Left: Water-level view of model shows landmark Colgate clock at left.
Below: Overhead view of model shows continuity of streets with existing city grid.
Photography: Roy Wright.

scale of the adjacent rowhouse areas. Brennan Beer Gorman/Architects was also the architect for 101 Hudson, the first project constructed under the Colgate Center master plan. At 42 stories, it is the tallest building in New Jersey, with a floor area of 1,506,000 square feet. The structure was designed to meet the needs of Merrill Lynch, its primary tenant, for back office space only a few minutes by mass transit from Manhattan. The building's architectural details, recalling New York towers of the Art Deco period, are executed in precast concrete, with black granite cladding portions of the lower six floors. Sculptural setbacks at the top of the building are dramatized with night lighting, giving the structure a strong identity in views from either side of the river.

Above: View corridors exploit extraordinary views of Lower Manhattan.
Left: Waterfront promenade links residents and office employees to river.

Above: 101 Hudson tower recalls forms of 1930s skyscrapers.
Above right: Entry area features angular ornament in black granite and precast concrete.
Right: Stone detail continues into lobby.
Photography: Robert D. Golding/b&h photographics (above); ESTO/Peter Mauss (above right); Lenscape Incorporated (right).

# Callison Architecture, Inc.

1420 Fifth Avenue
Suite 2400
Seattle
Washington 98101.2343
206.623.4646
206.623.4625 (Fax)

Callison Architecture, Inc.

U.S. Bank Centre
Seattle, Washington

Above left: Tower in downtown Seattle.
Above: Retail level on first floor.
Left: Office lobby on second level, which includes some retail.
Facing page: Entrance rotunda.
Photography: Above left and facing page, Fred Housel; above and left, Robert Pisano.

The U.S. Bank Centre (formerly Pacific First Centre) is a 44-story, 1.5-million-square-foot, $200-million mixed-use structure in the heart of downtown Seattle. The building was designed to reflect both historical and contemporary architectural elements of the surrounding urban context and to provide a dynamic and compatible combination of public and private indoor spaces. A three-story retail atrium at the base invites pedestrians to circulate on all levels. Here shoppers explore the offerings of national retailers, workers from the area bring their lunches to enjoy the hospitable environment, tourists view a premier glass sculpture collection, and evening visitors enjoy drinks or dinner before a show. Retail tenant turnover is among the lowest in Seattle's downtown core. The complex includes 41 floors of offices, along with a restaurant, cinemas, day-care facilities, and parking.

Callison Architecture, Inc.

Harbor Steps - Phase I
Seattle, Washington

This mixed-use development incorporates residential, retail, parking, and hotel components. Callison's master plan for the site takes maximum advantage of its location where a major east-west axis slopes sharply down to the harbor, ensuring optimal views out and an appealing water-to-land view. Callison was the architect for the master plan and 16-story residential tower, with retail functions at its base, the first of four structures proposed for the site. Phase 1 of the project, now completed, includes 169 living units in 307,000 square feet.

Right and facing page: Lower retail floors follow steps down slope, with residential floors above.
Below: Model of Phases I and II build-out shows two of the four buildings designed in the master plan.
Below right: 16-story tower displays double-scale structural grid.
Photography: Right facing page and below right, Patrick Barta.

Callison Architecture, Inc.

Carillon Point
Kirkland, Washington

Located on the shore of Lake Washington, this 31-acre development includes a 100,000-square-foot luxury hotel, 450,000 square feet of office space in five buildings, 20,000 square feet of retail, two restaurants, condominiums and apartments, a 201-slip marina, and 1,750 parking spaces in four garages. The design goal was to create an environment bustling with the activity of office workers, hotel guests, shoppers, diners, people arriving and departing by boat, and pedestrians attracted to the waterfront. The buildings are organized around a central plaza, open to the water and framed by two buildings. Six contemporary carillons, or bell towers, surround a platform that can be used for performances and public events. Chiming every hour, they provide a focal point for the plaza and strong identifying elements for the entire complex. Two grand staircases connect the project to a public esplanade along the waterfront. Buildings are positioned to maximize lake views, while maintaining view corridors from Lake Washington Boulevard.

Top: Carillons on lakefront, seen between two office structure in foreground.
Above left: Lakeside building includes restaurant, retail, and offices.
Bottom left: Carillons surround platform at top of grand stairs.
Photography: Top, Fred Housel; above left and bottom left, Doug Etheridge.

Callison Architecture, Inc.

Wells Fargo + Starbucks New Store Prototype

Top photo: Sign combining the two tenants' logos.
Right: Hearthside setting for coffee, bank counter in background.
Below right: Coffee and food area.
Photography: Callison Architecture/Chris Eden.

Wells Fargo Bank and Starbucks Coffee teamed up to provide customer convenience on a small scale. This new co-retailing concept combines banking, coffee, food, express office services, and laundry in the hospitable setting of a neighborhood meeting place. The project explores the possibilities of "the third place," between office and home, which provides essential services and a social gathering place. Tenants expand their businesses and benefit from the others' peak hours. The concept is being premiered at four California locations: two in San Francisco, one each in Pasadena and Orange County.

Callison Architecture, Inc.

Fashion Show Mall
Las Vegas, Nevada

The redesign of this 818,000-square-foot shopping center was carried out to reposition it in a growing urban market. The center's exterior has been enhanced with new signage, new entries, and pedestrian pathways under striking new trellises. A new logo and environmental graphics establish the project's revised identity. Interior updating and upgrading includes new marble flooring and other finishes throughout, new lighting, and improved circulations. The interior court features a new landscaping, a fountain, and customer seating. Callison's services included architecture, interior design, and environmental graphics.

Above right: New trellises are supported on pylons that combine planters and lighting.
Right: Intended to respond to Las Vegas' entertainment atmosphere, Callison's master plan created a streetscape that encourages imaginative store fronts including Dive Restaurant and Sfuzzi.
Photography: Fred Housel.

Cooper Carry, Inc.

3520 Piedmont Rd., N.E.
Suite 200
Atlanta
Georgia 30305-1595
404.237.2000
404.237.0276 (Fax)

112 South Alfred Street
Suite 100
Alexandria
Virginia 22314
703.519.6152
703.519.7127 (Fax)

Cooper Carry, Inc.

**SunTrust Financial Centre
Tampa, Florida**

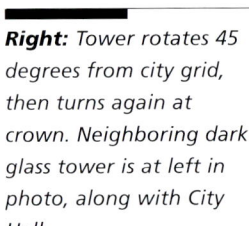

Right: *Tower rotates 45 degrees from city grid, then turns again at crown. Neighboring dark glass tower is at left in photo, along with City Hall.*
Photography: *E. Alan McGhee.*

The location of this mixed-use tower in downtown Tampa did much to determine its distinctive form. The main shaft of the building, housing the office floors, is rotated 45 degrees to the street grid to ease confrontation with a 40-story, property-line-to-property-line tower across the street and to improve views of the bay and city from the offices. The design also responds to the classical base-shaft-and-cap configuration of the City Hall, diagonally opposite this tower in another direction. The lower portion of the building is aligned with

Above: Well modulated night lighting can be tinted with filters for special occasions.
Right: Lobby features sculpture "Don Quixote Segunda Parte" by Izhar Patkin.
Below: Torcheres flank pedestrian entry between two groves of trees.

the streets to reinforce the downtown character of the location. The first two floors accommodate the main lobby, a bank, a restaurant, services, and access to parking. Floors three through nine provide over 500 parking spaces behind office-building-quality walls, and the top floor of the base houses a 30,000-square-foot data operations center. The tower floors above include 525,000 square feet of office space. A corner landscaped plaza mediates between this tower and the City Hall and provides seating under a bosque of live oaks for outdoor lunches.

Cooper Carry, Inc.

Bethesda Retail District
Bethesda, Maryland

Right: Sidewalk seating outside new building housing anchor bookstore.
Below: Pedestrian walk passes between storefronts and seating.
Below right: Seating alternates with landscaping along curbside.
Photography: Eric Taylor

The sidewalk is the focus of Cooper Carry's project to revitalize 42 acres of downtown Bethesda. The firm's pivotal contribution was to rearrange the conventional layers of public space outside retail frontages. The usual sequence – seating/pedestrian way/landscaping – is altered by placing the pedestrian path up against the storefronts, and organizing seating in "outdoor rooms" interspersed with landscaping along the curbside. The total extent of the commission from a private client included master planning and architectural design for new and remodeled buildings, including 121,000 square feet of specialty retail, 200,000 square feet of anchor retail, and 68,000 square feet of restaurant space, plus about four acres of public space, primarily sidewalk. The scheme

Right: Major retail building is configured to create small plaza, with fountain and seating around planters.
Below right: Brick paving defines primary pedestrian route along storefronts.

had to meet the city's Streetscape Plan Standards, and it has won so much local approval that the architects are now drawing up revised streetscape design guidelines for Bethesda. The final phase of this project is scheduled for completion in September 2000.

45

Cooper Carry, Inc.

Mizner Park, Boca Raton, Florida

Right: New buildings with offices above stores front two-block-long park.
Below: Molds from workshop of architect Addison Mizner were used to produce fountain.
Photography: Right and facing page, Cooper Carry, Inc.; below, Tom Knibbs.

Mizner Park was a major public-private effort to revitalize a fading downtown by replacing a failed shopping mall, dating from 1974, with a new mix of uses. The architects' proposal was to create an "instant downtown" organized around a major public space. The design was inspired by Addison Mizner, the architect-entrepreneur who created the Palm Beach style of the 1910s and 1920s, then worked on an unrealized dream of Boca Raton as the ultimate resort city. Mizner's influence is visible in the continuous arcades lining the streets, the incremental massing of buildings in 30-foot bays, and the stucco walls in shades of pink. The five phases (out of six) completed from 1989 to 1998 include 272 residential units, 230,000 square feet of retail and cinema, and 281,000 square feet of offices. The two-block long park at the center of the development has become the city's major civic space.

Above right: Dining court between restaurant buildings, residential building in background.
Right: Buildings with apartments above retail on one side of park.

Right and below: *Plantings, fountains, and lighting underscore feeling of traditional subtropical city.*

Below right: *Building fronts broken up by setbacks, columns, and awnings sustain modest scale in this large development.*

Photography: *Right and below, Cooper Carry, Inc.; below right, Stephen Traves.*

Duany Plater-Zyberk & Company

1023 Southwest 25th Avenue
Miami
Florida 33135
305.644.1023
305.644.1021 (Fax)
www.dpz.com

Washington
Charlotte

Duany Plater-Zyberk & Company
Kentlands
Gaithersburg, Maryland

The 352-acre Kentlands Farm was rezoned for mixed use in the late 1980s. The zoning permitted a regional shopping mall that was eventually downscaled to a regional shopping center. A series of designs drawn up over a two-and-a-half-year period was intended to reconcile the inflexible shopping center type with a traditional downtown. One constant feature was a seamless attachment of this commercial component to the Kentlands street grid so that residents could conveniently walk to the retail center from each of its five neighborhoods. To encourage future urban continuity, the parking lot of the shopping center was dimensioned to accommodate its gradual redevelopment as urban blocks. The town square, at the heart of the Midtown neighborhood, is bordered by the shopping center entrance, three-story live/work buildings that contain shops and offices, and four-story senior apartments. The town's cultural center is in Old

Top left: Old Farm neighborhood mixes new houses and adapted farm buildings.
Above: Rowhouses face comparably-scaled single-family houses across an attached green.
Photography: Mike Watkins (top), Alex S. MacLean (above), Lewellyn (right).

Right: The architectural code ensures that homes reflect Maryland and Mid-Atlantic precedents.

50

Left: Houses close to street and each other foster sense of place and community.
Top left: Town plan.
Below: Transitions in building type and massing occur along mid-block alleys maintaining street harmony.
Bottom: Old Farm neighborhood demonstrates how rowhouses, garage apartments and large mansions can be located in close proximity.
Photography: Lewellyn (left), Alex S. MacLean (below), Harry Connolly (bottom).

Farm neighborhood, centered on the original Kent homestead and farm buildings. The Lake District is planned around a wooded green, and the Hill District, which overlooks the community, is focused on the Clubhouse. The development's 1,500 residential units range from $500,000 mansions to $600-per-month garage apartments. Residential structures also include rowhouses and apartment buildings. The town has an elementary school, a church, a child-care center and an athletic facility, and prominent sites have been reserved for future civic buildings. A design code guides homebuilders to provide authentic traditional exteriors.

Duany Plater-Zyberk & Company

Town of Seaside
Walton County, Florida

Located on the Gulf of Mexico in the Florida panhandle, Seaside is an 80-acre resort community that has been developing since 1980. The Seaside plan proposed a traditional American settlement pattern, approximating the size and components of a historic Southern town, as an alternative to the usual suburban configuration. Streets are designed to encourage walking. Pedestrian paths along back lot lines offer alternative walking routes. The retail district is designed as a civic downtown, with a green, a conference center doubling as a town hall, a post office, and a small inn. The beach is accessible by boardwalks over the protected dunes, each with a distinctive pavilion by a different designer. The intention throughout the town is to encourage structures by a variety of architects. Public buildings have been designed by architects chosen for their sympathy with the regional vernacular. Designs for private buildings are reviewed for their adherence to the Master Plan and Zoning Code, which is meant to

Above: Aerial view shows development radiating from town center.
Right: Turrets and widow's walks appear on many of the sheet metal house roofs. Beach entry pavilions provide each street with its own entry to the waterfront. Small beachfront buildings allow view corridors between them.
Photography: Alex S. MacLean.

generate an environment similar to a pre-1940 Southern town. Private lots are required to have native landscaping and lawns are prohibited. Today, Seaside is almost entirely built out and financially successful. It has become exemplary of the principles underlying the New Urbanism, which can be applied to communities of all types and scales.

Top right: Beach and other community spaces are within a short walk of every house.
Center right: Private houses are closely spaced, with front porches set back a uniformly short distance from the street.
Right: Ruskin Square is a small plaza lined by three-story live/work units with ground-floor shops, including several art galleries and a café.
Photography: Alex S. MacLean (top and above right), Andres Duany (right).

Duany Plater-Zyberk & Company

Village of Windsor
Vero Beach, Florida

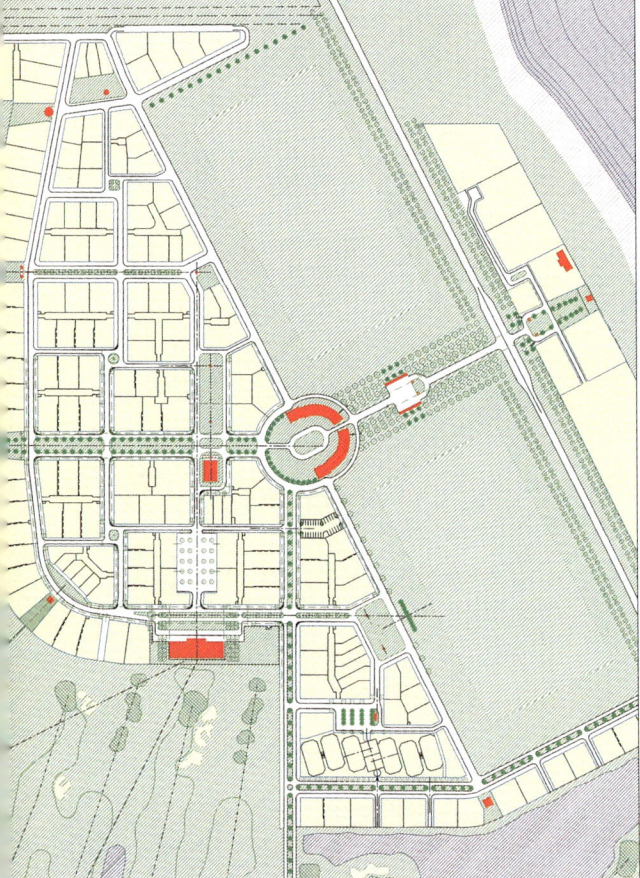

Top: Projecting balcony on a house by DPZ overlooks palm-lined Windsor Boulevard.
Above: Characteristic courtyard pool and two-story garage/guest quarters at DPZ house.
Photography: Thomas Delbeck (below left, above); Carlos Morales (top).

Top left: Plan, showing polo fields along oceanfront highway.
Above left: Multifamily rowhouse structure exemplifies design rules.

Located on Florida's East Coast, the resort town of Windsor contrasts a dense village with a golf course and two polo fields. The village neighborhood is of intimate scale, in the urban tradition of the Caribbean. Designed to function as a real community, Windsor includes at its center a general store, a post office, office space, apartments, an inn, and a bistro. The town's urban regulations require houses and continuous garden walls to be built at the property line, defining the public streets and squares while forming private gardens. Architectural regulations mandate a vernacular architecture responding to the climate, with masonry at the first floor, porches, balconies, and roof overhangs. With the exception of the code for Poundbury in England, this is the most prescriptive design code drawn up by Duany Plater-Zyberk. Streets vary in size and are flanked by single or multiple rows of trees.

Right: Village and ocean are linked by a broad tree-lined boulevard that offers an appealing pedestrian route from the golfcourse, between the polo fields and on to the beach.
Below: Overview illustrates subtle variety of house design permitted by town code.

Duany Plater-Zyberk & Company

Riverside by Post
Atlanta, Georgia

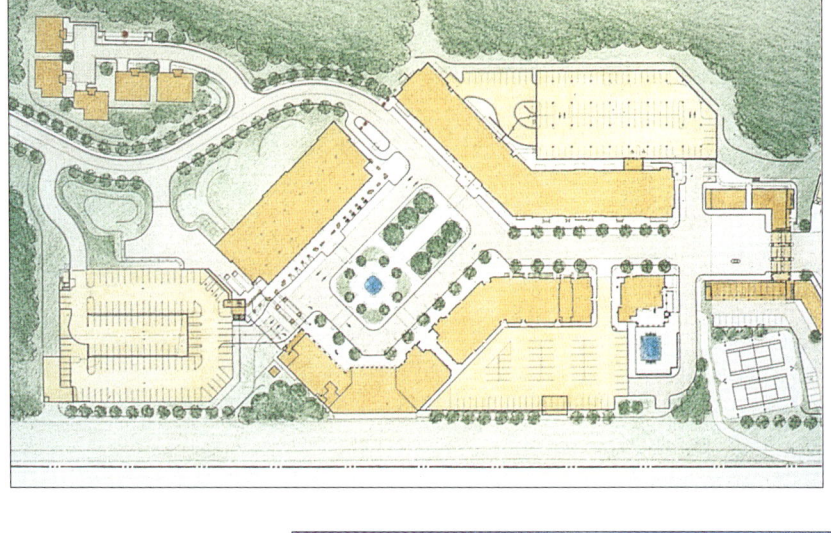

Located in the archetypal edge city at the intersection of I-75 and I-285, Riverside offers a new option for residents of the Atlanta suburbs. With one of the country's largest concentrations of office space, this area has a decidedly suburban land-use pattern, sprawling for miles along both interstates and generating severe traffic problems. Post Properties chose a site here for a new model of high-density apartment development. DPZ designed a master plan that includes Post's own headquarters, along with other offices, retail space, and multifamily, attached, and single-family residential units. Riverside residents have the rare option of walking to work. A site with severe topographical limitations, only 60 percent buildable, reinforced the rationale for high-density construction surrounded by natural landscape. The developers and the several architectural firms involved in this project expect Riverside to set a pattern for other neo-traditional developments in suburban situations.

Top: Plan of Riverside's core.
Above: Mixed-use, medium-rise buildings around the central square.
Left: Consistently scaled structures frame the approach to a tall office/retail tower located at the central square.
Photography: Post Properties (above); Steve Hinds (left).

EDAW

753 Davis Street
San Francisco
California 94111
415.433.1484
415.788.4875 (Fax)
www.edaw.com

Alexandria
703.836.1414
Atlanta
404.365.1110
Denver
303.595.4522
Irvine
949.660.8044
London
441.71.674.0700
Sydney
612.9906.6899
Hong Kong
852.2833.5595

EDAW

**Centennial Olympic Park
Atlanta, Georgia**

Left and bottom: Fountain represents five-ring Olympic symbol with 251 water jets.
Below left: Park offers variety of experiences on downtown site.
Photography: Dixi Carrillo, EDAW, Inc.

One of the most valuable legacies of Atlanta's 1996 Olympic Games is this 21-acre park at the city's very center. Although located directly between the downtown business core on one side and Atlanta's convention center and sports arenas on the other, the area had been largely vacant and dilapidated. On a schedule of only 18 months for design and construction, the site was transformed into the central Olympic gathering place, focused on Centennial Plaza, with its Fountain of Rings, 65-foot light towers, and 1,200-seat amphitheater. Phase 2 of the park, completed after the Olympics, includes five distinct landscaped and paved plazas, a multi-level water garden, two garden pavilions, restrooms, picnic shelters, and a visitor center. One area of the Phase 2 park is dedicated to those affected by the explosion during the Games, including a single illuminated glass brick for the one woman who lost her life.

Above left: Phase 2 of park includes variety of environments.
Above: Centennial Plaza, 100 meters square, was focus of Olympic festivities.
Below: Park provides Atlanta's first major downtown oasis.

EDAW

Washington Harbour
Washington, DC

Top of page: Curvilinear buildings define oval plaza and other open spaces.
Above: Fountains animate central plaza, where diners on two levels enjoy views of river and Kennedy Center.
Photography: Dixi Carrillo, EDAW, Inc.

A two-acre open space in a private, mixed-use commercial development reconnects this Georgetown neighborhood with the Potomac River. Completed in 1985 on the site of a former concrete plant, the development overcomes the barrier of an elevated highway by drawing the public through a generous pedestrian promenade, extending the line of an existing street to a new waterside plaza. Built atop parking and below flood level, the plaza demanded technical ingenuity. When the Potomac floods, a wall of steel panels rises between concrete columns, which double as light stanchions, to protect the plaza and the retail spaces fronting it. Along the waterside boardwalk, passenger boats can tie up, recalling Georgetown's origin as a port that predates the founding of Washington.

Above: Separated from Georgetown by an elevated highway, complex continues line of key street to riverfront plaza.
Right: Boardwalk offers views of Watergate, an earlier curvilinear mixed-use complex.
Below: Concrete columns support flood wall that comes up when river rises.

EDAW

Canal City Hakata
Fukuoka, Japan

Above: Grand Hyatt rooftop garden provides bucolic view for surrounding rooms.
Above right: Along canal, greenery appears in pots and in vines on balconies.
Right: Where canal widens, a rocky pool and featured tree.
Photography: Dixi Carrillo, EDAW, Inc.

As designers of all open spaces in this $1.4-billion mixed-use project, EDAW worked closely with prime architect, The Jerde Partnership, to produce memorable landscape and hardscape under severe constraints. Along the canal promenade, use of plantings was limited by the high levels of pedestrian traffic and the need for visibility of storefronts. To reflect differences in adjacent retail, the promenade was divided into five distinct zones, representing the stars, moon, sun, earth, and sea, with lighting, paving, planting, graphics, and water features responding to these metaphors. For the streets bordering the site, EDAW developed a distinctive treatment, involving lighting, graphics, and banners, which has been adopted by the city for adjoining streets. For the club level of the project's Grand Hyatt Hotel, a rooftop garden was designed, combining Eastern and Western design inspirations. Structural considerations dictated the shallow pebble-lined pool and the location of large plantings over key supporting members.

Below left: At its approaches, project is identified by distinctive graphics and street treatment.
Below right: Paving patterns identify sections of canal walkway.

EDAW

Coors Field
Denver, Colorado

EDAW worked with HOK Sport, architects, to relate this major league baseball stadium to Denver's downtown urban fabric. Main entries are aligned with existing street grids, and site details reflect the historic character of the surrounding district. Many hours of meetings with local agencies and neighborhood advisory groups lie behind the design. Architectural and site design had to minimize the obtrusiveness of an elevated highway adjoining the site. One major design strategy was to develop a strong axial promenade to lead pedestrian traffic toward the stadium, with the bold gateway sculpture, "Evolution of the Ball" by Lonnie Hanson, complementing the stadium and deflecting attention from the highway ramp that rises in between.

Above: Stadium is sited at edge of downtown Denver.
Left: Sculpture "Evolution of the Ball" stands astride main walk from parking areas.
Below: Walkway paving and framework of sculpture tie site development to stadium.
Photography: Dixi Carrillo, EDAW, Inc.

EDSA
Edward D. Stone, Jr. and Associates

1512 E. Broward Boulevard
Suite 110
Fort Lauderdale
Florida 33301
954.524.3330
954.524.0177 (Fax)
www.edsaplan.com

500 S. Magnolia Avenue
Orlando
Florida 32801
407.425.3330
407.425.8058 (Fax)

3232 A Nebraska Avenue
Santa Monica
California 90404
310.315.1066
310.315.0916 (Fax)

EDSA

**Fort Lauderdale Beach
Revitalization
Fort Lauderdale, Florida**

Left: *New beach wall invites sitting and lounging.*
Below left: *Pedestrian activity attracts beachfront cafes.*
Photography: *Below left, Patricia Riddle Franklin; bottom right, Dan Forer; others, EDSA.*

Top right: *Generous planting enhances resort atmosphere.*
Second from top, right: *Broad plaza at terminus of Las Olas Boulevard.*
Third from top, right: *Traditional light standards and banners add flavor.*
Bottom right: *Paving meets beach in wave-like steps.*

After years of college Spring Break gatherings on its beaches, with the attendant deterioration of public and private facilities bordering them, the city of Fort Lauderdale decided to make improvements that would attract a broader range of vacationers. EDSA was retained to create a new urban image, encourage pedestrian circulation, and stimulate private sector redevelopment. Traffic along 1.8 miles of beachfront highway A1A was reduced by moving two lanes of southbound traffic one block inland. All beachfront parking was removed and replaced by landscaped parking bay medians on designated "People Streets" running toward the beachfront. Roadway area was recaptured for a broad "Beachwalk" with generous plantings of coconut palms and other plants that thrive at the edge of the sand. The existing concrete-block sand barrier was transformed into a sculptural wall that invites sitting and sunbathing, and vibrant paving patterns enhance the area's tropical resort atmosphere. Columned openings in the beach wall mark the People Street intersections. All plans had to meet stringent state guidelines for traffic and coastal conservation. Lighting had to be carefully adjusted so as not to discourage nesting sea turtles during their June-to-November season.

EDSA

Broward County Library
Fort Lauderdale, Florida

Below: Pool separates library from street.
Right: Upper terrace with geometrical paving overlooks main plaza.
Photography: EDSA.

Situated in the heart of downtown Fort Lauderdale, the 256,000-square-foot library by architects Marcel Breuer Associates (with Miller & Meier and Associates) was completed in 1983 as a major component of the city's downtown renewal. EDSA's mission was to develop the 32,500 square feet of usable public space around the structure to provide an inviting entry and a comfortable, shady dining area. Generous plantings were used as baffles against the streets on three

Top right: Library plaza serves as mini-park.
Middle and bottom right: Gentle steps around still water form downtown oasis.

sides. The main library plaza serves as a major urban space where workers from nearby buildings gather at lunch time and as a convenient location for city-sponsored events such as noon-hour concerts and arts festivals. Still and splashing water help to provide an effective transition from street to library, and plantings soften the rectangular geometry of the building's façades.

EDSA

Riverwalk
Fort Lauderdale, Florida

In a city known previously for its beach alone, the Riverwalk provides a new 28-acre urban park that is heavily used by a growing downtown working population and is the location of attractions including the Performing Arts Center, Museum of Discovery and Science, Las Olas Riverfront entertainment center, and premium office space. Residential development is also planned. Boaters had docked along the New River for decades, but the riverbanks had been underutilized and inaccessible to the public. The city's goal was to make downtown attractive to development by investing in municipal infrastructure. EDSA's goal in the master planning and design of Riverwalk was to create a public "yard" along the river, where none had existed before, responding to the city's maritime tradition. Traditionally styled paving, lighting, and seating is surrounded by lush, subtropical landscaping in a flowing pattern juxtaposed to the rigid street grid that predominates in the downtown. EDSA's design guidelines have been adopted to cover future linear parks and improvement of adjacent streets, as well as landscaping of private development within the Riverwalk District.

Facing page, top: *Public and private office development is attracted to downtown's Riverwalk District.*
Facing page, bottom: *Performing Arts Center seen from Riverwalk.*
Above: *Active and passive use is encouraged.*
Left: *Gazebo and clock recall Florida of a century ago.*
Photography: *Dan Forer, above; EDSA, all others.*

EDSA

Barnett Plaza
Tampa, Florida

Left: Night lighting picks out key elements of plaza.
Below left: Plaza design responds to rectangular motifs of building.
Below right: Charles Perry sculpture "Solstice" seems to be supported on pool surface.
Bottom: Sunken pool is animated by 74 water jets.
Photography: EDSA.

"A living room for downtown Tampa," is the way landscape architect Edward D. Stone, Jr., has described the 1.5-acre public space at the base of the 42-story Barnett Plaza building. Completed in 1986, the open plaza set a pattern for the design of paving, street furniture and plantings for six city blocks developed by the Paragon Group. Major design elements include a bosque of 55 live oak trees and a 28-foot-high sculpture by Charles Perry that appears to float on a reflecting pool, one of a series of pools and water features. The rectangular patterns of Italian granite steps and paving used throughout the space complement the building's grids of marble and reflective glass.

**Elkus/Manfredi
Architects Ltd**

530 Atlantic Avenue
Boston
Massachusetts 02210
617.426.1300
617.426.7502 (Fax)

Elkus/Manfredi Architects Ltd   28 State Street Boston, Massachusetts

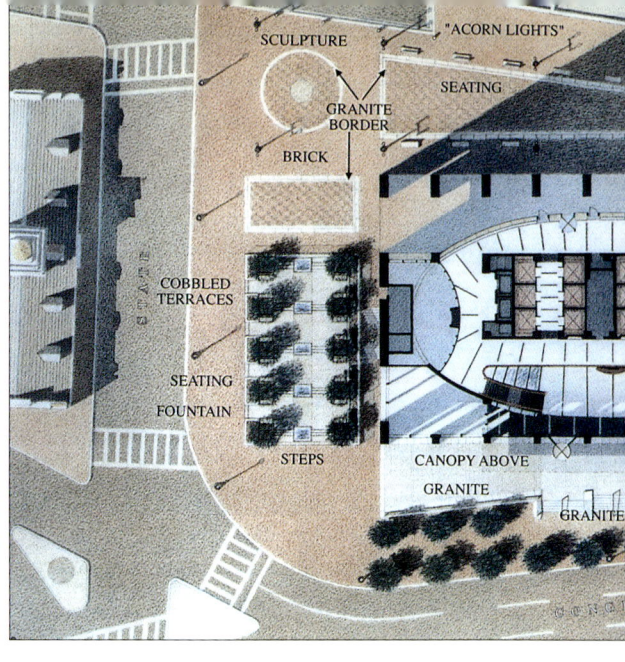

Above: Upper level of lobby, much expanded, with 39-foot-high clear glass.
Above left: 28 State towers above plaza of Boston City Hall (left in photo).
Left: Stairwell to new lower lobby entrances.
Right: Stair rail detail.
Photography: Bruce T. Martin.

Left: Site and building plan shows elliptical glazed lobby, with upper-level entries at top, lower-level access toward bottom at foot of curved stairs, State Street Steps at left.
Right: State Street Steps, with view of Faneuil Hall cupola.
Below right: State Street Steps from lower end, with landmark Old State House beyond.
Bottom right: State Street Steps, with cobbled water feature on a fair day.

Completed in 1968 in the heart of Boston's Financial District, 28 State occupies the 100% corner in the Financial District. One of the first private structures to go up around the newly completed Government Center, the office tower held itself aloof from its still-gritty surroundings. Designed by Edward Larrabee Barnes, the building took the form of a stone-clad monolith, with one understated entrance on its uphill side and a small corner entrance into a lower-level bank branch on its downhill side. The site offered little amenity, with massive raised planters denying much of it to public use. In carrying out a full remodeling that included asbestos removal, structural stiffening, improved mechanical and lighting systems, new windows, and other upgrading, the architects were charged to make the building much more accessible and to develop the site as usable open space and to connect all four facades to the surrounding pedestrian ways. The goal was to link the building with its surroundings, which include some of the city's most prized landmarks. The upper lobby was expanded into an elliptical space, bounded by 39-foot-high clear glass curtain walls. A spacious new lower lobby was created in the former branch bank location by adding a major new entry to the building from Congress Street. A new three-level underground garage was located in the basement area, replacing former bank vaults and the central mechanical system. The potential of the 35,300-square-foot area around the building was developed with the "State Street Steps," a series of terraces with seating, planting, and cascading water that have become a popular meeting spot since opening in May 1997.

Elkus/Manfredi Architects Ltd

Sansom Common
Philadelphia, Pennsylvania

While the University of Pennsylvania has one of the country's most attractive urban campuses, it has become an inward-looking pedestrian environment, turning its back on the city streets to the north. The goal for Sansom Common is to establish a critical mass of commercial activity, associated with Penn but drawing on the wider community and remaining active into the night. Anchors of the project are a 56,000-square-foot bookstore (managed by Barnes & Noble) and a 190,000-square-foot, six-story hotel (The Inn at Penn), both in a commercial block completed in 1998. These and other structures will hold the street edges and conceal the back sides of other buildings now visible from the streets. The sitewalk of 30th Street from Walnut to Sansom has been widened to form a 50-foot wide plaza, which not only provides a

Above: Retail shops along Walnut Street.
Right: Shops and restaurants in new buildings along 36th Street, Inn at Penn in background.

forum for commercial and public uses, but also provides a forecourt for the existing Institute of Contemporary Art at its North End. Exterior materials, appropriate to commercial street fronts yet compatible with campus buildings, include molded Pennsylvania brick, cast stone trim, red granite bases, and aluminum storefronts. To make the area attractive after dark, the exterior lighting scheme includes generous window and interior display lighting, decorative sconces on buildings, illuminated glass canopies, up-lighting on the accent tower, and historically inspired street lighting, all with warm-colored sources to render a natural appearance.

Top right: Hotel rooms rise above two-story bookstore.
Above right: Main entrance to hotel is through auto court at end of new street.
Right: Principal portion of development area includes: south block of retail and hotel lobbies, with guest rooms spreading over upper floors; north block split by new street on axis of main hotel entry, with interim landscaping on either side awaiting infill buildings lining sidewalks.

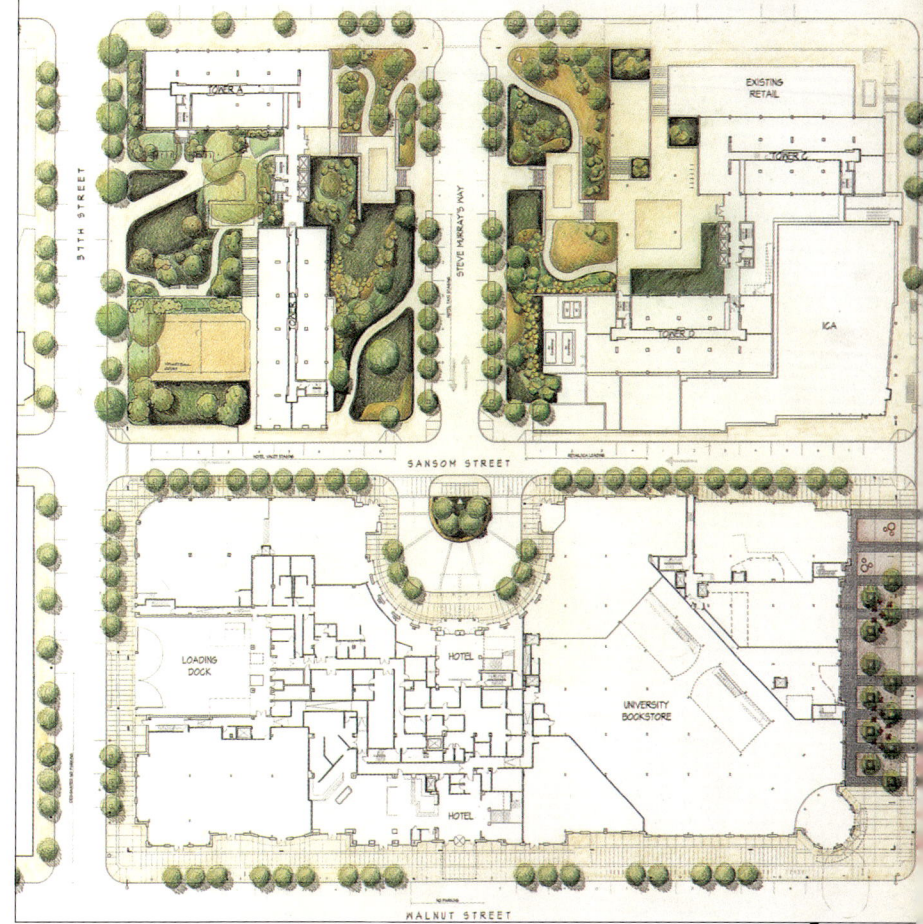

77

Elkus/Manfredi Architects Ltd

730 North Michigan Avenue
Chicago, Illinois

Above: Site plan of full city block development and hotel lobby at upper left.
Left: Michigan Avenue frontage, showing (left to right) Tiffany, Pottery Barn, Banana Republic, Polo Ralph Lauren.
Photography: Bob Shimer, Hedrich Blessing.

Situated on the prestigious Magnificent Mile of North Michigan Avenue, this project creates a streetscape of apparently separate "buildings" for prominent retailers. Working with individual tenants, including Tiffany & Company, Pottery Barn, Banana Republic, Polo Ralph Lauren, and Comp USA and their designers, the architects designed individual building segments, with distinct floor-to-floor heights, column spacing, and façade treatment expressing their identities. In contrast to nearby large-scale projects that have produced uniform block fronts and inward-turning retail malls, this one reinforces the tradition of modestly scaled three-to-four-story buildings that have given North Michigan its special cachet. It also maximizes rental potential by giving six major retailers prominent flagship locations. Comprising a whole city block, the complex provides 235,000 square feet of shopping and restaurant space. A second phase of construction is planned to include a 350-room, five-star hotel, currently in design by Elkus/Manfredi, to rise above the retail base, using air rights above the Phase One development.

Right: Stores at night.
Below: Stores as completed as of 1997.

Elkus/Manfredi Architects Ltd

CityPlace
West Palm Beach, Florida

While it will radically alter a ten-city-block (72.9-acre) area of downtown West Palm Beach, CityPlace is designed to be an integral part of the existing city, not a discreet development. Its first phase, scheduled for completion in 2000, will include 1,424,000 square feet of retail, restaurants, cinemas, residential (510 units), and a performance hall converted from an existing church. The 1,430,000 square feet of Phase II, scheduled for 2002 completion, will include a 400,000-square-foot convention hall, a 375-room hotel, and 750,000 square feet of office space. In addition, there will be 1,200,000 square feet of parking (4,200 spaces) in Phase I, 1,700,000 (5,000 spaces) in Phase II. A series of memorable public plazas will occur around the revamped church and at the entries to the hotel and the convention center. The architectural treatment of buildings throughout the area will maintain the area's Mediterranean architectural heritage, with numerous arcades, balconies, and upper-level gardened terraces.

Top right: Retail frontage, with apartments above, facing Church Plaza.
Above left: Plan of plaza at center of site, surrounding existing church converted into performance hall.
Above right: Arcaded retail fronts face plaza, with major fountain at back of converted church.
Right: Retail façades near Church Plaza.

ELS/Elbasani & Logan Architects

2040 Addison Street
Berkeley
California 94704
510.549.2929
510.843.3304 (Fax)
els@elsarch.com

ELS/Elbasani & Logan Architects
The Shops at Arizona Center
Phoenix, Arizona

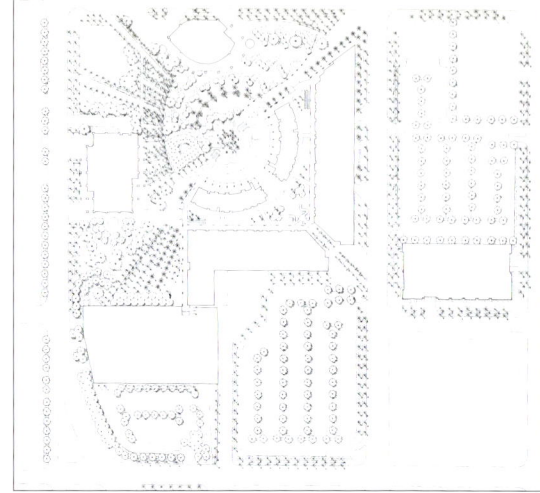

Above: Fan-like canopies cast partial shade and reflect night lighting on walkways.
Right, top and bottom: Site plan and aerial view show retail and dining structures complementing center's lush garden.
Right, middle: Two levels of dining overlook central palm grove.
Photography: Greg Hursley, except aerial, Timothy Hursley.

Right: Custom lighting display identifies shops on outer facades.
Below right: Passages between curved dining pavilion and linear shop structures are enlivened with stairs and bridges.
Photography: Timothy Hursley, this page.

Retailing is a major component of the mixed-use Arizona Center, designed for Rouse-Arizona Center, Inc. to bring new life to downtown Phoenix. Wrapped around two sides of a three-acre oasis-like garden, the shopping and dining portions of the development are in two distinct layers. A fan-shaped two-story structure features a second-story food court overlooking the gardens. Two linear buildings, aligned with the city's grid, form an L embracing this curved pavilion. Each linear building has two levels of shops and a top floor of offices. Circulation is outdoors, rather than in an air-conditioned mall. Shade from the desert sun is provided by canopies and overhangs, and louvers at the edges often ease the transition between bright sun and shade. Arizona sandstone paving integrates retail circulation, open spaces, and garden surfaces throughout the complex. Recognizing that the retail development's roofs would be prominent in views from Arizona Center's office towers, the architects made these complement the central gardens with clean forms almost equally appealing to the eye. Rooftop courts provide greenery, and mechanical equipment is either hidden or screened. A lively array of circular lighting fixtures on one of the perimeter structures, identifying the complex from the parking areas, was allowable under local codes that usually prohibit signs or logos of this size.

ELS/Elbasani & Logan Architects   Pioneer Place
Portland, Oregon

This four-city-block mixed-use development for Rouse-Portland, Inc., reconciles the scale of Portland's office core to the south with that of the historic Pioneer Courthouse to the west. The architects and their client, The Rouse Company won an architect-developer competition for the project. Two blocks were developed in the first phase. The three-story Pavilion Building, adjacent to the courthouse, is well below allowable density for its block. Three floors of retail above grade and one below are ranged around a central atrium. On the other block a two-story department store is at the base of a 16-story office tower. A below-grade concourse connects the basement-level retail of the Pavilion Building with a food court under the department store, and a third-level bridge across the street links retail on the two blocks. Particular attention was given to creating lively store windows at street level and in having all three stories of the Pavilion brightly lighted at night to provide visual interest from the street. The second phase contains street level retail and a city owned parking structure (by others) on the third block. ELS is designing the final phase on the fourth block which includes retail and cinemas.

Above: Food court below department store.
Right: Project includes Pavilion Building (foreground) and office tower (to right).
Photography: Timothy Hursley.

Above: Bridge linking project's two blocks; Pioneer Courthouse cupola beyond.
Right, above: Pavilion Building's central atrium brings daylight to retail on three stories plus basement level.
Right, below: Glazed canopies at corner entrances stretch along street frontage to encourage pedestrian traffic.

ELS/Elbasani & Logan Architects

Clarke Quay
Singapore

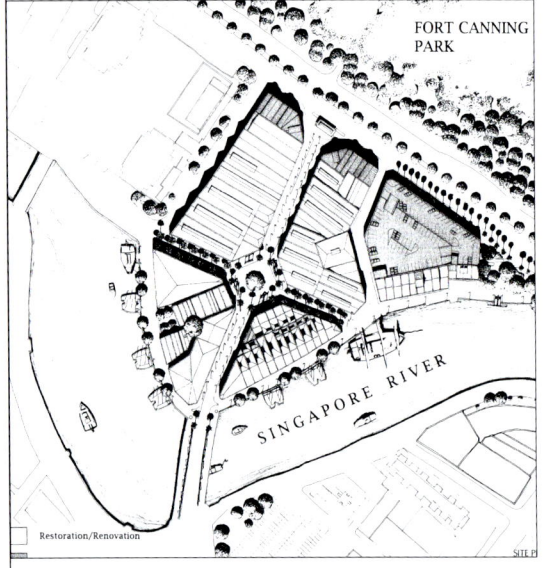

Left, above: On area plan, darker tone indicates new construction.
Above: Before and after views of shophouses along river.
Below: Dining outside renovated structures.

Facing page: Shophouse row.
Photography: Trends Publishing International (above and facing); Dixi Carrillo (below).

At Clarke Quay, five blocks of abandoned buildings on the Singapore River were adapted for re-use as a retail and cultural district. The area was built up in the 1800s, combining both European and East Asian traditions. Shophouses (retail shops with living quarters above) and godowns (warehouses) lined the streets, and tongkangs (barges) moved goods to and from seagoing ships. Most of the buildings have covered "five foot ways" along their fronts to protect the pedestrians from tropical sun and rain, as required by an 1822 ordinance. Historically, the surviving buildings represent the years 1880 to 1930. Many of the structures, abandoned by the late 1980s, required extensive rehabilitation or reconstruction. Fortunately, the building techniques of brick and plaster, wood windows and doors, and terra cotta roofing were still in widespread use. Sixty craftsmen were brought from China to restore the area's Chinese-style mansion, which operates as the River House, a private function facility. For the district's more typical buildings, details and variegated, muted colors were selected to avoid the "new" look so common in restorations. A 500-car garage and two new infill structures feature recessed walkways and other traditional

Above: Renovated waterfront buildings, flanking Chinese-style mansion, restored as private function center.
Left: Restaurants in riverfront shophouses and on restored barges.
Photography: Trends Publishing International (above); Dixi Carrillo (left).

elements. Details are modern interpretations that respect the scale and character of neighboring buildings. Streets were closed to traffic to encourage use by pedestrians, pushcarts, food vendors, and street performers. Period gas lamps and street trees emphasize the historical setting and festive character of the project. Along the river, waterfront dining can be found in the buildings, on the promenade, and on the restored tongkangs. Clients for the project were DBS Land/Raffles International, Ltd. and local architects were RSP Architects Planners & Engineers.

A. Epstein and Sons International, Inc.

600 West Fulton Street   Los Angeles
Chicago   New York
Illinois 60661.1199   Tel Aviv
312.454.9100   Tokyo
312.559.1217 (Fax)   Warsaw

A. Epstein and Sons International, Inc.

Chicago Urban Entertainment District
Chicago, Illinois

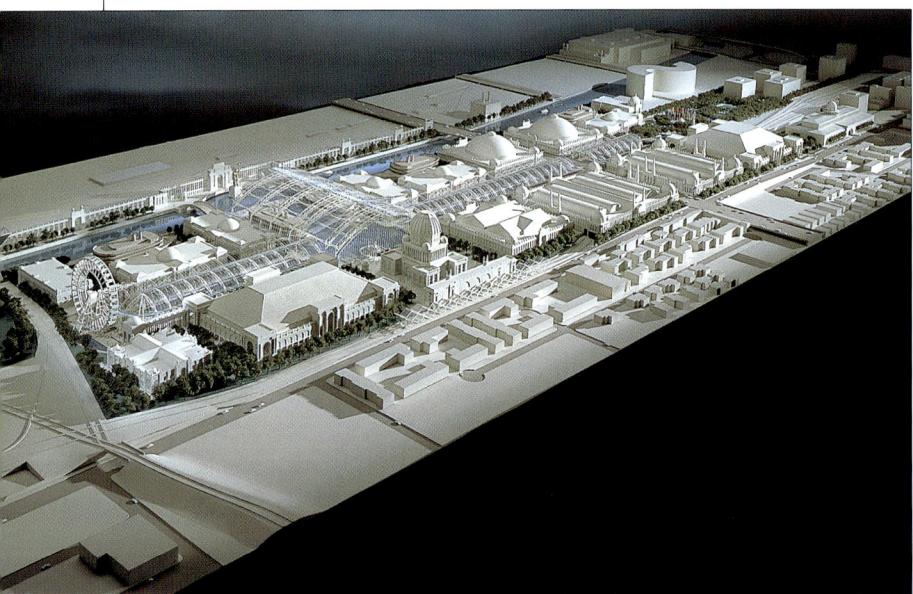

A 100-acre site bordering the South Branch of the Chicago River is envisioned in this master plan as a major attraction at the edge of the city core. A tract of abandoned rail yards, the land is largely cleared and under unified ownership, so that construction can proceed without significant relocation or demolition. The plan proposes a wide range of entertainment, cultural, and retail activities focused on a grand, fully enclosed midway. The master plan proposes three million square feet of cultural and entertainment facilities on two levels, with 220,000 square feet of retail fronting the midway at pedestrian level. Below ground will be 3,800,000 square feet of parking and service spaces. Five casino boats of 90,000 square feet each could be anchored in river inlets. The development will fill a present gap between Printers Row to the north and Chinatown to the south, thus joining two important existing retail and entertainment areas. The district's master plan would extend Chicago's historic street grid, yet provide adequate buffers from adjoining communities. The Metra track embankment and the river provide existing buffers to the east and west. With its central midway, lagoons, and domed pavilions, the district will be reminiscent of the Chicago's 1893 World Columbian Exposition, but it would also include vast steel-and-glass vaulted canopies of late 20th-Century character.

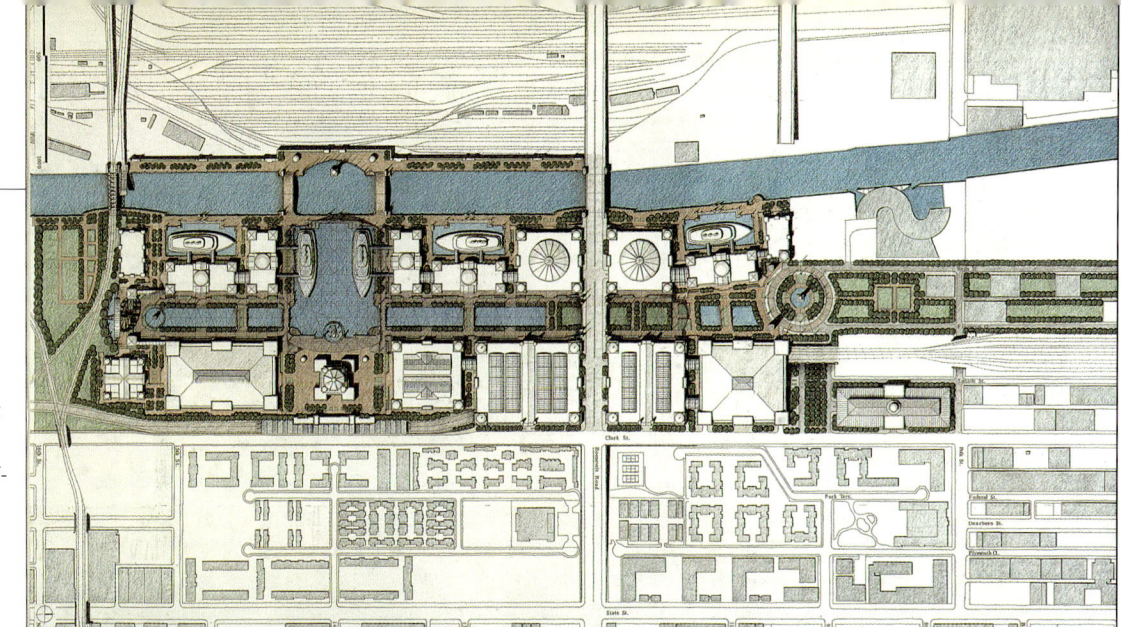

Facing page, top: View from north.
Facing page, left: View from southeast.
Right: Master plan, with north to the right.
Below: Vast covered public spaces would link pavilions and ferris wheel reminiscent of the 1893 Chicago fair.
Photography: James Steinkamp, Steinkamp/Ballogg.

A. Epstein and Sons
International, Inc.

**Museum of Science
and Industry
Chicago, Illinois**

Chicago's Museum of Science and Industry has been ingeniously enhanced by the addition of a 1,500-car garage. By placing the parking on three levels extending 45 feet underground, the architects were able to restore seven acres of park area around the building to its original Olmsted plan. A new arrival hall and lobby bring visitors from the new garage into expansive, well-lighted spaces that reinforce the museum's mission to present achievements of modern science and technology. Post-tensioned concrete and steel were used in the garage construction. A very high level of lighting in the garage and the new lobby create an open, secure atmosphere that counteracts the negative connotations of underground facilities. The restored landscape properly sets off the landmark museum, originally constructed as the Fine Arts Building for the World Columbian Exposition of 1893. A. Epstein and Sons carried out the structural engineering, as well as architectural and interior design for the $45-million project.

Facing page, top: Restored landscape around 1893 landmark.
Facing page, bottom: Extensive space and floating ceiling panels greet visitors approaching museum from garage.
Above: Levels of exhibits are visible to arriving visitors.
Above right: Streamlined locomotive is focal attraction seen from entry lobby.
Photography: Steve Hall/Hedrich Blessing.

A. Epstein and Sons International, Inc.

Midway Airport
Chicago, Illinois

Above and below:
Monument representing Chicago would include abstract references to city, lake, industry, and The Prairies.
Left: *Overall view of proposed new passenger terminal.*
Model photography:
Steinkamp/Ballogg

The Midway Airport Terminal Development Program proposes a new 980,000-square-foot terminal with double the number of gates and concession area of the current one. Once the world's busiest airport, Midway became the city's secondary gateway in 1960, with the opening of O'Hare. Since airline deregulation in 1978, new airlines have taken advantage of Midway's close-to-downtown location. High, open structural bays will admit ample natural light to buildings that acknowledge Midway's "budget flyer" role. For the new airport, the architects have also designed the "Four Elements" monument, a public art installation symbolizing four essential aspects of the city as a "Welcome to Chicago." Tall granite piers, representing urban buildings, would front a water feature representing the lake. Industry would be represented by stainless steel pipes emitting steam and The Prairies by a stand of native, flowering plant material.

A. Epstein and Sons International, Inc.

Auto Transportation

**South Wells Self Park
Chicago, Illinois**
A mid-block site, adjacent to the El tracks, is the location of this 850-car, 168,000-square-foot garage. In lieu of retail space on the ground floor, 25 percent of the site has been set aside as a small urban park. The structure is cast-in-place concrete, with ornamental metal screens. Lighting is designed to produce a pleasing glow, with no light sources visible from the street or the El.

Top right: Canopy strongly identifies Midway toll gate.
Above right: Pedestrian canopy has vinyl fabric with turnbuckle supports.
Right: Auto canopy has tapered steel members, with pipe outriggers.
Below: Detail and overall views of South Wells Street garage.
Photography: Barbara Karant (toll plaza); Steinkamp/Ballogg (garage).

**Midway Airport Exit Toll Plaza
Chicago, Illinois**
Refined design has been applied here to a simple set of elements: toll booths, staff service spaces, a car-scaled canopy, a pedestrian canopy, and a garden wall. Located at the airport's main entrance, the canopy acts as both weather protection and a gateway symbol. The scale difference between the two canopies is expressed in the tapered steel frame of the large one and the tensioned fabric of the small one. At night, the main canopy serves as a large light reflector.

A. Epstein and Sons International, Inc.

Master Planning

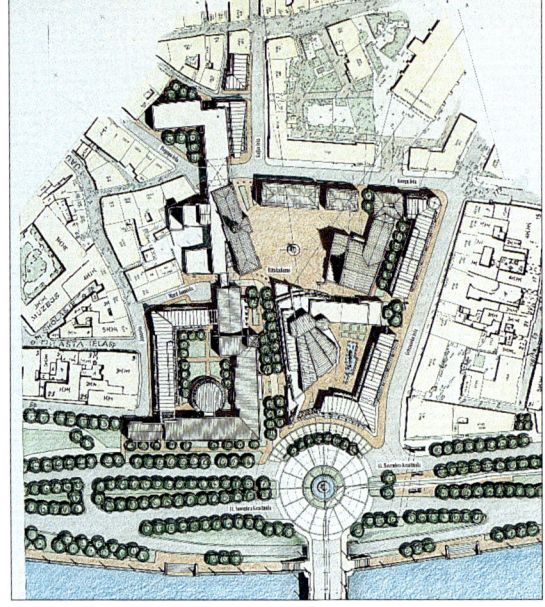

Quest International
Hoffman Estates, Illinois

A 15-acre site in a Chicago-area office park has been planned for the American headquarters of a European-owned producer of food flavorings and preservatives. Layout and building plans are based on the European principle that no worker should be more than six meters from a window. The plan makes a transition from largely rectangular near the roads to irregular near the wetlands tract to the east.

Riga "Ratsnams" District
Riga, Latvia

Drawn up for a major developer and the city of Riga, this plan will guide redevelopment of a key site in the "old city." One objective is to recreate the square that was the setting for the former City Council building (Ratsnams) before World War II. A new performing arts center will link the restored square to an improved riverfront promenade.

Moscow Botanical Garden
Moscow, Russia

This joint public/private venture calls for the rehabilitation of Russia's oldest botanical garden in exchange for development rights to adjacent land. Buffer spaces between the garden and the new development include three formal gardens to the east, residential gardens to the north, and a landscaped setting for retail pavilions to the south.

Left: Riga plan shows new circle at end of bridge, performing arts center (middle of plan) and restored square (upper middle) recreating pre-World War II open space.
Below left: Quest International site plan shows covered walkways linking buildings, pedestrian "street" along wetlands border, taking advantage of views.
Below right: Plan for Moscow shows 10-acre restored garden within 31-acre public/private development.

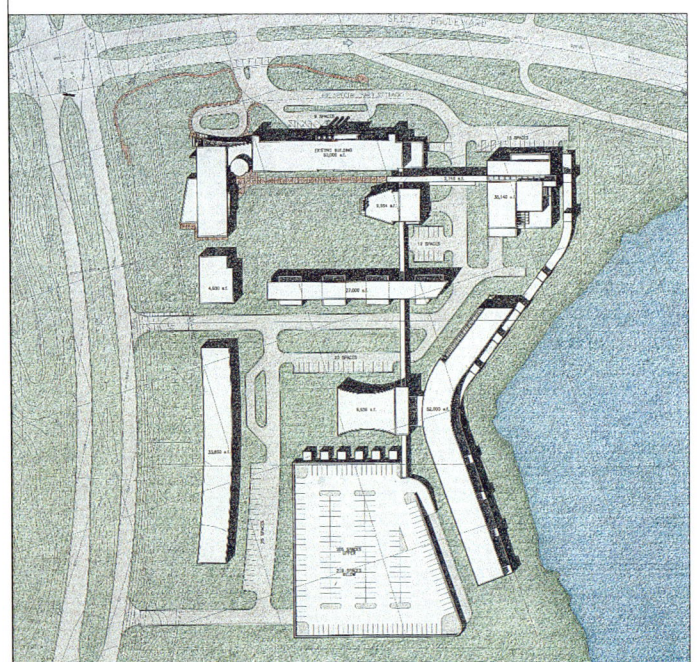

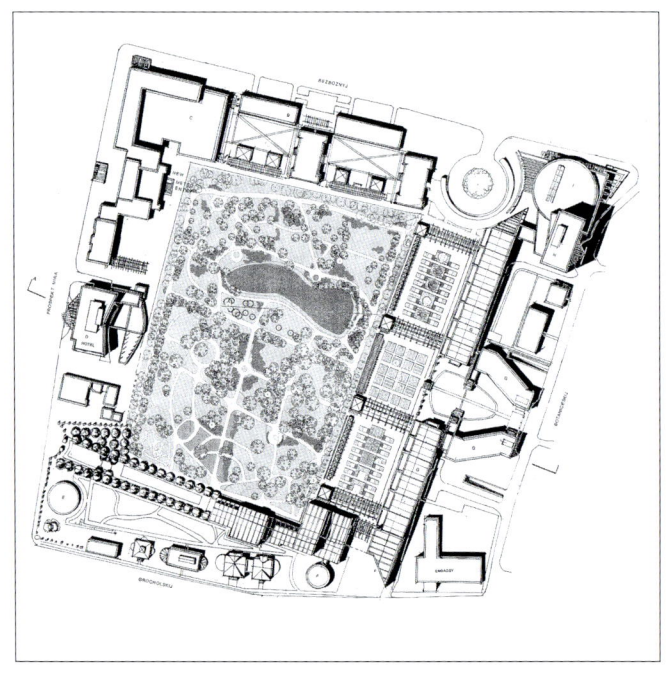

Gensler

600 California Street
San Francisco
California 94108
415.433.3700
415.627.3737 (Fax)
www.gensler.com

Atlanta
Boston
Chicago
Dallas
Denver
Detroit
Hong Kong
Houston
London
Los Angeles
New York
Newport Beach
Parsippany, NJ
San Francisco
Tokyo
Washington, DC

Gensler

**Oracle Corporate Campus
Redwood Shores, California**

Below: Executive office building, left in photo, is one of six structures of related form and consistent wall treatment arrayed along a lagoon.
Below right: One of four similar towers with trapezoid-plus-cylinder massing.
Photography: Timothy Hursley.

Can a 1.6-million-square-foot suburban office development be a community amenity? Yes, that's what the Oracle campus has accomplished. The public driving by the 65-acre development sees a broad lagoon along the road, surrounded by generous plantings, with office towers shimmering beyond. Instead of the casually dispersed structures typical of office parks, this campus offers the viewer a bold and consistent set of urban-scaled forms and spaces. For those who wish to enjoy the project more personally, the site offers waterside public space, as well as running and biking trails linked into a regional system.

Gensler began planning what is now the Oracle campus back in the mid-1980s, after the Canadian developer Campeau bought the site of the popular tourist attraction, Marine World Africa/USA. Shortly after the firm completed its master plan, in 1988, William Wilson & Associates bought the property, commissioned Gensler to design the first office building, and began marketing the site to leading Silicon Valley companies. Oracle Corporation, a producer of database software, was sufficiently impressed to buy into the project, relying on Wilson to carry out subsequent construction. Now, eleven years later, construction is being completed on a complex that includes six office buildings, a conference/media center, a fitness facility, and four parking garages.

Gensler's first step in developing the master plan was to relocate the 11-acre lagoon – required for environmental reasons – to extend along Marine World Parkway, the main access road. An earlier plan by others had placed the lagoon at the center of the property, with buildings facing inward around it, so that the complex turned its back on neighboring development. The new plan organized the site in bands extending outward from the lagoon: a pedestrian zone, an array of office buildings, a ring of parking, and a more rustic zone at the edge of the surrounding wetlands.

During the review process for the plan, the extensive open spaces and trails were very favorably viewed by the community. To enhance the park's usefulness, William Wilson has built facilities, including an amphitheater, exercise stations, and restrooms. Employee support facilities — the conference/media center and the fitness center — have been deliberately placed in a more informal setting along the ring drive, near the wetlands, as a change from the office environment.

Facing page: Towers are placed to be seen from neighboring buildings yet permit maximum uninterrupted views from each one.
Right: Glass and precast concrete curtain walls are detailed to emphasize interpenetration of cylindrical and trapezoidal volumes.
Photography: Timothy Hursley.
Below: Site plan shows office buildings laid out between lagoon and parking zone, with executive offices in the distinctive double-cylinder structure. Fitness Center and Conference Center are at top left of plan, on far side of parking structures, facing out toward wetlands.

101

Right: Four towers stand in echelon along the lagoon.
Facing page, top: Conference Center is structure of related but distinctive design.
Facing page middle: Lobby of one tower.
Facing page, lower middle: Diagrammatic elevation of project, including design response to FAA height limits.
Bottom: In panorama of entire complex; executive office building second from right. Glazing is slightly reflective on upper floors, slightly tinted but non-reflective on lower two floors to allow views in and out. Height of towers steps down toward either end of complex as required by flight paths of nearby airport.
Photography: right: Timothy Hursley; facing page, top: Chas McGrath; facing page, middle: S. Takata; below: George Soo, Ken Ong.

Gensler's plan allowed for either single or multiple tenancy, establishing design guidelines for each parcel, covering building massing and exterior appearance. As they step across the site, the buildings follow a sloping height limit imposed by the flight path of nearby San Carlos Airport. As closely related as the buildings are in design, some distinctions express their individual roles. The first building completed, which houses Oracle's executive offices, is not the largest, but takes the unique "gateway" form of a rectangular block, flanked by two cylinders, broadside to the lagoon. The building between this one and the main road has also been given a distinctive form, with a gently curved main block that defers visibly to the self-contained, symmetrical volume of the "gateway" building.

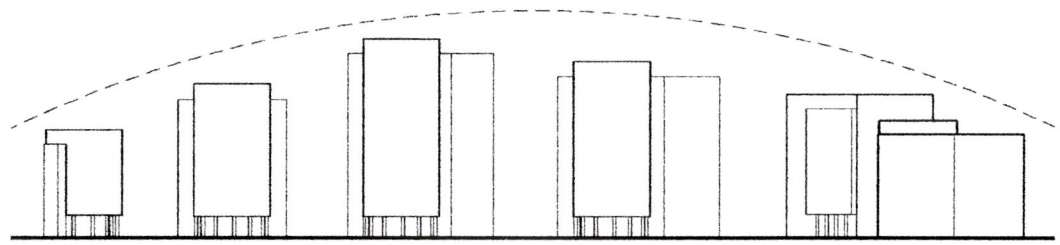

Above: View of the towers from executive office building.
Photography: Timothy Hursley.

The Oracle campus is unusual in that it was carried out over an 11-year period by the same team of owner, developer, architect/ designer, and contractor from master plan to final implementation, with a consistent standard of quality.

Glatting Jackson Kercher Anglin Lopez Rinehart, Inc.

33 East Pine Street
The Ellis Building
Orlando
Florida 32801
407.843.6552
407.839.1789 (Fax)
www.glatting.com

222 Clematis Street
Suite 200
West Palm Beach
Florida 33401
561.659.6552
561.833.1790 (Fax)

Glatting Jackson Kercher
Anglin Lopez Rinehart, Inc.

West Orange Trail
Orange County, Florida

Urban spaces can have very unusual dimensions. This one is conceived as a 17-mile-long, 14-foot-wide asphalt "rail-trail" for hikers, skaters, bicyclists, and horseback riders. Passing through a variety of communities and rural areas, it has been designed to harmonize with its natural surroundings and to connect with existing pathways, school yards, parks, and other facilities in the communities it passes through. Extensive coordination was required to satisfy the several governmental jurisdictions along its route. The project's five-mile-long, $2.1-million first phase, now completed, includes three distinctive trailheads. The County Line Station at the western end of the trail is reminiscent of an old Florida homestead, with a main house (for restrooms and concessions), a maintenance barn, and picnic pavilions. Both the main building and the maintenance barn have porches, and rocking chairs are provided to set a relaxed tone and

Left and below: Bridge that carried railroad over Florida Turnpike has been redesigned to resemble old-time trestles, with weathering steel superstructure and green vinyl-coated mesh that protect trail users.
Photography: left, Eschbach; others, architects.

Above: Grand opening of trail.
Left: Long-unused railroad tracks, uncovered during construction.

Above: Wooded areas were preserved and simple wood safety barriers installed.
Left: Trail runs through Winter Garden, where trains run along street median.
Below: One portion of trail parallels tracks through Winter Garden.

encourage people-watching. In the community of Oakland, an old house was moved from the outskirts of town to the trail corridor to serve as a historical museum. In Winter Garden, the trail's 40,000 users per month have brought an infusion of business activity to the recently struggling downtown district. The old railroad bridge that carries the trail over the Florida Turnpike has been redesigned to resemble a trestle of earlier times, at the same time providing a safety enclosure for trail users.

Above: Main building at County Line Station Trailhead includes restrooms and concessions, and is designed to recall area's old farmsteads.
Left: Simple signs inform users about trail itself and community facilities along way.

Glatting Jackson Kercher Anglin Lopez Rinehart, Inc.

Primera
Lake Mary, Florida

Top: *Primera entry sign by Shaughnessy Hart & Associates.*
Above: *Office building beyond lake.*
Photography: *Phil Germano.*

Now a highly touted mixed-use office park, Primera did not start out as a success. The original development floundered, leaving the property under the ownership of the Insurance Commissioner of North Carolina. The turnaround began with a reorientation of Primera from a retail project to a mixed-use office park. Design standards incorporating landscaping and new signage gave the development a fresh image, reversing the community's perception of failure. This strategy was followed by the recruitment of quality national developers to bring office, restaurant, and hotel uses to the 188-acre site. The success of the project resulted from high design standards, a flexible market approach, and a cooperative relationship with the local jurisdiction.

Left and left below: Lakes provide settings for buildings constructed to date.
Below: Street signage and sidewalks are designed to enhance the pedestrian environment.

Above: Developments such as a Pizzeria Uno restaurant were required to preserve existing trees.
Below: Aerial view of partially completed project.

Primera's new design standards placed a strong emphasis on quality landscaping, pedestrian amenities, and materials that are compatible from tract to tract. Close coordination with each developer during the design phase and speedy design reviews contributed to a well-designed, cohesive project. Primera's development benefited from a flexible framework that permitted the market to determine the amount of various uses. As an example, the initial plan included one hotel, but two hotels were ultimately included without significant alterations in the project's plans. The ability to be flexible resulted from the high level of trust between the development team and the City of Lake Mary. The city would not accept for review a tract within Primera without a letter from the master developer affirming consistency with Primera's design standards. The close working relationship allowed difficult issues to be resolved in a partnership fashion.

Goody, Clancy & Associates
Architecture and Planning

334 Boylston Street
Boston
Massachusetts 02116.3866
617.262.2760
617.262.9512 (Fax)
arch@gcassoc.com

Goody, Clancy & Associates

Massachusetts Transportation Building
Boston, Massachusetts

Left: Atrium, lighted and warmed by tiers of glazing, is bounded by brick-paved indoor streets.
Photography: Anton Grassl.

Starting with a program for a 900,000-square-foot state office building, the architects created a mixed-use structure integrated into the fabric of downtown Boston. Instead of an isolated monument, they gave the city an eight-story structure that fills out a city block of lowrise and midrise structures, right to the sidewalks. Special legislation was required to permit ground-floor retail uses in a state building. While the retail lines two blocks of streetfront, several of the commercial spaces also face the dramatically daylighted atrium that rises through the building's office floors. A formerly deadend alley has been redesigned as a pedestrian street that is extended through the block by way of the atrium. Another indoor pedestrian route cuts diagonally along the edge of the atrium, linking two street entrances. Heat from the people and light fixtures is collected and stored for use in sub-basement water tanks. This innovative approach to heating the building has won awards for energy conservation.

Above: After photo shows improved alley leading to atrium entry, with stepped glazing above it.
Top right: Boylston Alley before building construction.
Right: Public and state office workers mix in atrium.
Photography: Anton Grassl, right; Goody, Clancy & Associates, others.

Goody, Clancy & Associates

Harbor Point
Boston, Massachusetts

Once the site of a failed public housing project that was largely abandoned by the early 1980s, Harbor Point has been transformed into a 50-acre mixed-income residential community. It includes a pool and athletic facility, a daycare center, and other community amenities. A central greenway with tennis courts at one end leads to a linear park running along the harborfront that the earlier project virtually ignored. One-third of the original brick residential buildings were retained, with radical remodeling. They have been joined by new apartment and townhouse structures arranged on a grid of streets recalling traditional city layouts, rather than the disorienting cul de sacs and remote parking lots of the preceding project. Residents of the project at the time of its conversion to a private development have been integrated into the resident mix. With its exceptional views and open spaces in a near-downtown location, the project has been an economic success. National recognition includes a 1993 Rudy Bruner Award in Urban Excellence and a 1992 Urban Land Institute Special Award for Excellence.

Top: Site plan, showing central greenway and waterfront park.
Above: Townhouses and apartment mix; cars park along streets.
Right: Aerial view shows mix of buildings, scattered parking.
Photography: Anton Grassl, above; Alex MacLean, Landslides, right.

Right: Gabled rooftops help create a vertical rhythm and reduce the scale of block-long midrise buildings.
Far right: Sidewalk outside townhouses.
Photography: Goody, Clancy & Associates.

Goody, Clancy & Associates

The Freedom Trail
Boston, Massachusetts

Above: Old State House, 1712.
Above right: Faneuil Hall, 1742, with Faneuil Hall Marketplace and waterfront in background.
Photography: Peter Vanderwarker, above; Steve Rosenthal, above right.

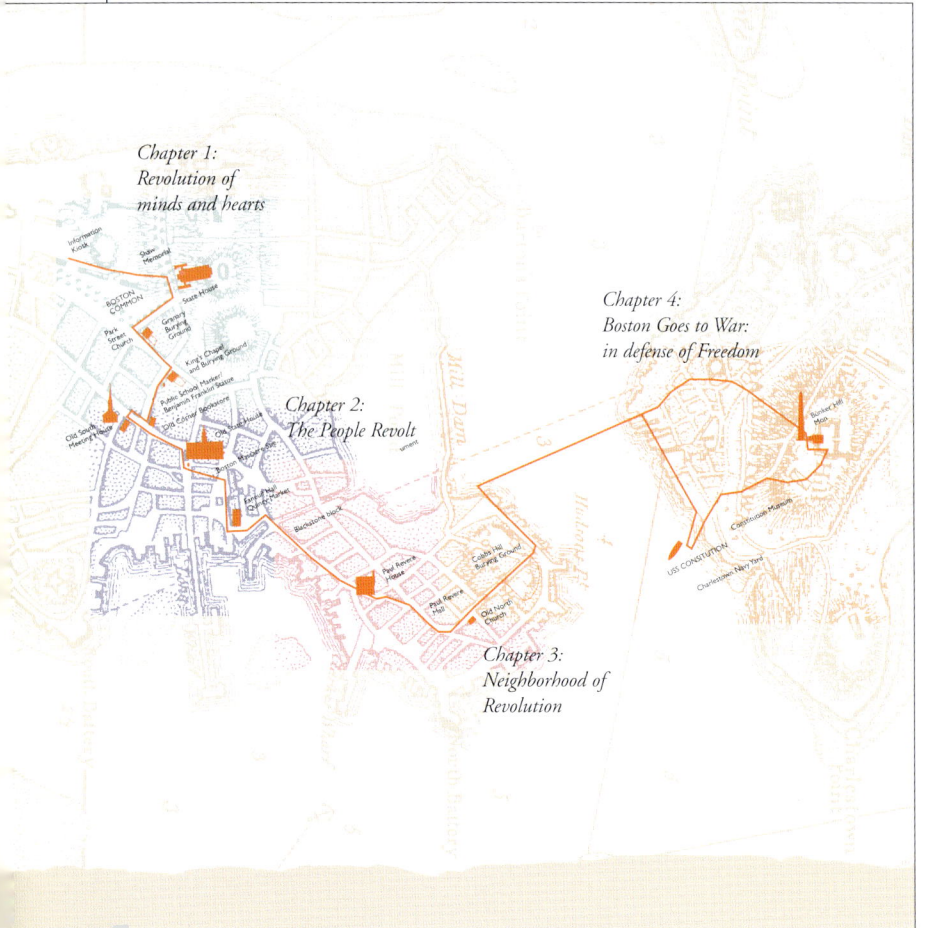

Boston's Freedom Trail has long been established as means to guide visitors through a series of landmarks from the Revolutionary War period and the early republic. With funding from the National Parks Service, Goody, Clancy & Associates carried out an analysis and master plan for the trail. To make the trail more appealing and informative, the plan called for adding interpretive elements and programs and for restoring historic sites along the route. Goody Clancy & Associates served as architect for the renovations of two of the city's most venerable sites – the Old State House and Faneuil Hall – with combined project costs totaling $10 million.

Goody, Clancy & Associates

Tent City
Boston, Massachusetts

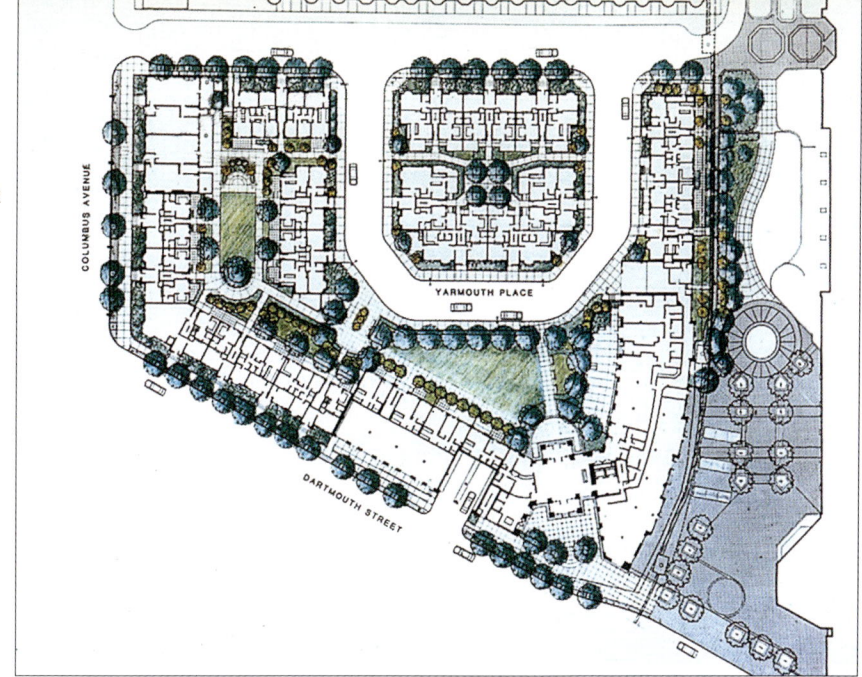

For a mixed-income residential complex in the shadow of Back Bay's prime office towers, the architects established a new street and open space pattern in scale with those of the adjacent historic South End. A series of landscaped courtyards opens from this street. Four-story brick structures on the portions of the site adjoining the South End neighborhood recall the townhouses of this historic district with their bay windows and mansarded top floors. At the corner of the site closest to Copley Square's commercial structures, the buildings rise in stages to 12 stories. Two floors of below-grade parking cover the entire site. At grade level there are community facilities, a childcare center and (facing the commercial streets) retail shops. A community based nonprofit development corporation financed the project with a combination of city, state and federal programs. Tent City has received awards from ULI, The Boston Society of Architects and the United Nations Habitat Award.

Top: *A new internal street provides frontage and separate entries for all the lowrise units. One and two bedroom units are located in a midrise building which steps up from four to twelve stories, adjacent to the massive Copley Place.*
Right: *Lowrise portion of project reflects forms of existing South End townhouse (background in photo).*
Photography: Steve Rosenthal.

Goody, Clancy & Associates

Langham Court
Boston, Massachusetts

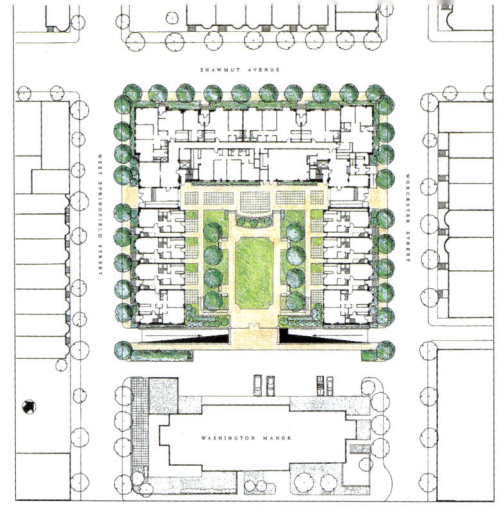

Top: Residential buildings hug the sidewalks, leaving common court at center of block.
Left: Four-story duplex-over-duplex units adjoin midrise apartment building.
Bottom: Project respects scale and texture of South End neighborhood.
Photography: Steve Rosenthal.

Filling a one-acre city block in the city's historic South End, this 84-unit residential development consists of duplexes stacked in four-story townhouse configurations, plus a five-story elevator apartment structure. The 12,000-square-foot courtyard at the center of the block is shared by all residents and is often used for neighborhood events. Parking is below grade. This community sponsored non-profit development is a limited equity cooperative. Financing involved a variety of city, state and federal programs. Langham Court won a national AIA Honor Award in 1992.

The Harris Group/
TBA² Architects

THE HARRIS GROUP
The Rotunda, Suite 175
4201 Congress Street
Charlotte
North Carolina 28209
704.556.1717
704.552.9944 (Fax)

TBA² ARCHITECTS
112 South Tryon Street
Suite 200
Charlotte
North Carolina 28284
704.333.6686
704.333.2926 (Fax)

The Harris Group/ TBA² Architects

Phillips Place
Charlotte, North Carolina

Phillips Place is an innovative mixed-use development, incorporating residential units over retail along a "main street" that is appealing to pedestrians but does not exclude cars. The project demonstrates that integrated mixed use can work in a suburban environment – in this case 15 to 20 minutes from downtown Charlotte – and be accepted by adjoining, well-established residential neighborhoods. The rezoning plan required that the project dictate extreme sensitivity to the surrounding land uses, while permitting residential densities higher than had previously been approved in the area in order to ensure economic viability. The inclusion of residential over retail required an amendment to local zoning. Since this type of development had never before taken place anywhere in the Charlotte area, numerous plan interpretations and changes were required to satisfy codes. The 35-acre development includes 130,000 square feet of retail, restaurants, and movie theater; 402 residential units (48 of them over retail), and an inn with 124 rooms and suites. Two of its three parking garages are shared between retail

Left: Lighted fountains at both ends of retail/residential street feature rampant lions derived from the projects logo, which is based on the family crest of the Phillips family, original owners of site.
Photography: All Phillips Place photos by Rick Alexander unless otherwise noted.

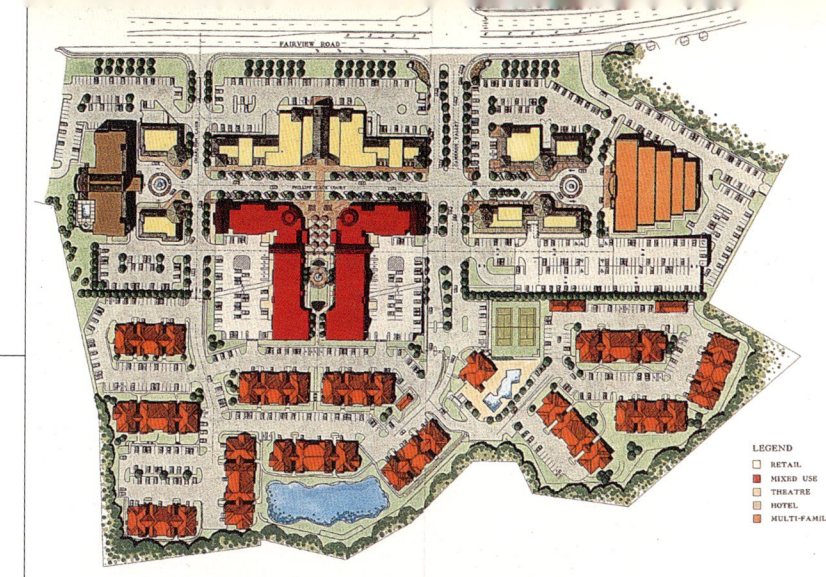

and residential users. The project team was challenged to create a pedestrian-scaled environment on a site fronting on a heavily traveled six-lane highway bordered by high-tension power lines. The internalization of the "main street" provided a controlled environment befitting a destination retail experience. The street is anchored at one end by the movie theater, with a prominent marquee, and at the other end by the inn, with its porte-cochere. The retail, entertainment, lodging, and residential components all reinforce each other. Most of the storefronts along the main street have generous windows, and several spaces 24 to 26 feet high create opportunities for exceptional shopping or dining environments.

Facing page: *Pavilions offer dramatic high retail spaces.*
Top right: *Plan shows mixed retail/residential at center, inn at left, cinema at right, residential in lower portion.*
Right: *Sign kiosk at entry, in keeping with architectural style, identifies tenants for approaching visitors.*
Below: *Inn at one end of "main street" is convenient to Palm restaurant. Seasonal flower plantings add to pedestrian appeal.*
Photography: *Facing page by Larry Harwell, Carolina Photo Group.*

Below and facing page bottom: Domed corner pavilions mark key intersection. Façades recalling historic Charleston or Savannah are clad with synthetic stucco above Mexican sandstone bases.

Emphasis was placed on landscaping and lighting to ensure a pleasant, safe pedestrian experience by day or in the evening. Continuity of design between residential and commercial areas was also stressed. The project's unique appearance, mix of uses, and affluent demographics have attracted several exclusive specialty retailers and restaurants not previously in the Charlotte market (among them Dean and Deluca, Via Veneto, and Restoration Hardware and The Palm restaurant). The project team was carefully organized to meet exceptional needs. The Harris Group, which had extensive experience with retail and hotel development, formed a partnership with Post Properties, which had more residential experience and was interested in pursuing higher-density projects. TBA[2] Architects of Charlotte, the prime designers, collaborated with LandDesign, Inc., for site planning and with Post Landscaping for site development. The team employed

Right: Pedimented cinema façade, generously lighted, anchors opposite end of "main street" from inn. Signage is carefully controlled.

essentially one contractor for all buildings, regardless of type, ensuring coordinated, on-time project delivery. The project received necessary public approvals at the end of 1994 and was substantially completed in April 1998. By July 1, 1998, 95 percent of retail space had been leased (with 90 percent already occupied) and over 98 percent of residential units had been leased. Total construction value is $78 million.

Above: Residences adjacent to and over retail enjoy landscaped private courtyard.

HDR Architecture, Inc.

8404 Indian Hills Drive
Omaha
Nebraska 68114
402.399.1000
402.399.1238 (Fax)

HDR Architecture, Inc.

Centro Medico Integral Hospital Los Angeles
Torreon, Mexico

Above: On the quiet side of the hospital, away from the street, a series of interconnected courtyards can be reached directly from patient rooms.
Right: The doctors' office wing rises above the entry courtyard, with its stone paving and extensive trellis-like canopy.
Photography: Mark Trew.

On a site in an emerging suburb of Torreon, a tower was created as a focal point at the end of a major boulevard leading out from the city center. From there, vehicles and pedestrians are directed to an arrival court that provides direct access to the lobby, the chapel, the cafeteria, the outdoor dining plaza, and the children's play area. Reflecting Torreon's mild climate and Mexican culture's attitude that hospital stays for loved ones are family affairs, the patient rooms are designed around generous outdoor healing courtyards that can accommodate large family gatherings. Completed in 1994, the Torreon hospital is the first of several that HDR is designing for a company building private hospitals to U.S. standards in various Mexican cities. The $16-million Torreon complex combines women's hospital rooms and medical treatment facilities with doctors' offices, parking, and other services mentioned above. This range of facilities and services responds to the needs and culture of the patients and their families, making their hospital stay a positive experience.

HDR Architecture, Inc.

Centro Medico Integral Hospital Santa Engracia
Monterrey, Mexico

Situated off a boulevard serving a prosperous suburb of Monterrey, the hillside site offered challenges (a large, unattractive electrical substation and other undistinguished developments as neighbors) and opportunities (excellent views of adjacent mountains) to HDR's designers. The irregularly shaped 1.6-hectare (about four-acre) sloping site and building code limitations made it challenging to accommodate the numerous program elements, including parking for 400 cars. The required parking was used to wrap two edges of the site, buffering the hospital from the substation. The layout creates three entry/egress points to the garage, each off different street levels, eliminating the expense of interior ramps. A combination of outward-looking and inward-focused urban spaces was established in the design. The arrival plaza is wrapped by the building complex on three sides, with the open side oriented to striking mountain views. A simple but elegant fountain is centered in this plaza, serving as a hub for pedestrian and vehicular movement. Patient room wings overlooking quiet courtyards ring the plaza. These courtyards break the hospital mass into smaller elements. The courtyard plantings also serve to enrich the plaza. Elsewhere, a contained exterior courtyard

Above: Dining patio outside cafeteria overlooks large gardened courtyard.
Right: Undulating walls provide interest and integrate structure into landscape.
Photography: Mark Trew.

with water features provides landscape relief and natural light to the hospital interior. The courtyard includes a patio for the hospital cafeteria and serves as an open-air passageway between the garage and the main building.

Right: Gardened courtyard between hospital and garage includes dining terrace.
Below Right: Generous loggia at main entry.

HDR Architecture, Inc.

Aire Plex
Cass County, Nebraska

Above right: Plan of 175-acre site.
Right: Restaurant structure rises in center of amphitheater.
Below: Amphitheater seen from entry pavilion.
Facing page: Aerial view of amphitheater.
Photography: Tom Kessler.

A 175-acre tract between Nebraska's primary urban centers, Omaha and Lincoln, will accommodate a set of attractions to provide accessible weekend recreation and leisure time activities for residents and visitors. The Strategic Air Command (SAC) museum, Mahoney State Park, the Nebraska Wildlife Safari, and Quarry Oaks golf course will complement this privately developed music and performance center. The dream of Chip Davis, founder of the Mannheim Steamroller music group, the complex will include several family-oriented attractions organized around a central amphitheater. While accommodating up to 17,000 people, the amphitheater is designed to feel comfortable for an audience as small as 5,000. A Center Stage Restaurant will occupy the middle of the lawn seating area, reinforcing the enclosure for the amphitheater bowl. Outdoor dining terraces step down the bowl, paralleling the lawn seating, providing 300 guests with prime views of the stage. A canopied picnic area patterned after a Munich biergarten, a night sky observatory, a children's music camp, residences for performing artists, and a 100-room hotel are also included in the master plan.

HDR Architecture, Inc.

Durham Western Heritage Museum
Omaha, Nebraska

The Durham Western Heritage Museum occupies the Union Station in downtown Omaha. Its renovation is part of Omaha's efforts to restore and enhance the city's urban core and create activities to bring people downtown. The station was built in 1931. Its restored and elegant Main Waiting Room is reflected on the exterior with two-story window bays, creating a monumental scale. The building was built directly on the sidewalk without setbacks. The train tracks and platforms were on the lower level, and were converted by HDR's design into a 500-foot-long enclosure displaying restored locomotives and other rolling stock. The sidewalk at street level above is part of the roof deck over the tracks. HDR Architecture's renovation respected this multilevel urban condition, presenting the building to the city in a direct and unadorned manner.

Above: The former Union Station's terra cotta exterior.
Below Left: Restored Main Waiting Room provides grand entry and exhibit space.
Below Right: Toplighted extension over tracks houses historical railroad exhibits.
Photography: Tom Kessler.

Hellmuth, Obata + Kassabaum, Inc

One Metropolitan Square
211 North Broadway
Suite 600
St. Louis
Missouri 63102.2733
314.421.2000
314.621.0944 (Fax)
contact@corp.hok.com

Atlanta
Berlin
Brisbane
Chicago
Dallas
Greenville, SC
Hong Kong
Houston
Kansas City
London
Los Angeles
Mexico City
Moscow
New York
Newport Beach, CA
Orlando
Ottawa
San Francisco
Seattle
Shanghai
St. Louis
Sydney
Tampa
Tokyo
Toronto
Warsaw
Washington, DC

Hellmuth, Obata + Kassabaum, Inc

Hellmuth, Obata + Kassabaum, Inc.

Federal Reserve Bank of Minneapolis
Minneapolis, Minnesota

The 9.4-acre site of the Federal Reserve Bank is pivotal in several respects: It is the location of the city's original settlement and first public square; it adjoins a present-day major bridge across the Mississippi; it is situated between the present downtown, the 19th-century warehouse district, and a riverfront park. The 618,000-square-foot building, integrated with its site, is divided into two distinct portions housing different functions. The tower portion contains regulatory and policy-making functions in technically up-to-the-minute office spaces. The low-rise operations center, handling vast

Top: Bank complex from across Mississippi.
Middle: Bridgehead Square reinstates city's original public square.
Right: Bridgehead Square includes documentation of site's history
Photography: Top, middle and right, Don F. Wong.

quantities of check, cash, and electronic transfers, requires exceptional operational and security features.

Pedestrian connections between downtown and the river have been re-established by providing links across the site at both ends and in the center. Bridgehead Square re-establishes a public square at the bridge end of the site and leads to a greensward sloping towards the river edge, where an overlook offers dramatic views of the Mississippi River, the bridge, and the city skyline. The passage at the center of the site occurs between the office tower and the operations wing, passing through an auto court and down stairs toward the river. At the far end of the site, a meandering path winds through an area of native trees, grasses, and wildflowers.

Top: *Private seating in Bridgehead Square.*
Middle right: *View toward downtown, with axis of Nicollet Mall marked by pylons and stairsteps in greensward.*
Right: *Canopies shelter overlook on riverbank.*
Photography: *Top, Don F. Wong; middle, David Amalong, HOK; right, Jim Fetterman, HOK.*

Hellmuth, Obata + Kassabaum, Inc.

St. Louis Union Station
St. Louis, Missouri

Above right: Union Station's façade faces public plaza with Carl Milles fountains.
Below: Outdoor dining in train shed.
Facing page: One-acre lake under train shed canopy.
Photography: Above and facing page, Bill Mathis; below, Robert Pettus.

The redevelopment of St. Louis Union Station transformed a 100-year-old train station into a successful mixed-use development. The 61.5-acre site includes a steel-framed train shed spanning a space 600 feet wide and 810 feet long (covering about 11 acres) plus a massive Romanesque headhouse that is the station's prominent urban face. Completed in 1892, the complex had been abandoned years before this project was initiated in 1981. The redevelopment includes 172,000 square feet of festival retail space, plus a 550-room hotel, reusing the elegant headhouse interiors, with guest room wings under the train shed. Also under the vast train shed are public plazas, gardens, a lake, fountains, and a beer garden. Parking for 2,000 cars is included on the site. The design challenge was to integrate a variety of new structures and landscape elements, inside and outside the train shed, without compromising the station's extraordinary architectural qualities. The design solution involved treating the train shed area as a "town center," with a retail pedestrian "street" running along the headhouse, then along one side of the shed, linked at the end to tree-lined extensions leading to parking facilities. Some railroad features such as signal bridges and butterfly sheds were retained to reflect the site's historical identity.

Hellmuth, Obata + Kassabaum, Inc.

Apple Computer, Inc. Research and Development Campus Cupertino, California

This 32-acre corporate campus is conceived much like a university campus, with five four-story R&D buildings and a two-story structure for common functions, including conference rooms, auditorium, library, and indoor-outdoor dining areas. Though initially occupied solely by Apple, the complex is designed so that buildings can be leased or sold separately in the future. Lobbies are designed with this possibility in mind, and parking is planned for subdivision by individual tenant. The buildings stand inside a loop road, facing a central quadrangle. This quadrangle is the "heart" of the campus with an amphitheater-like lawn that is used for picnics, concerts, and celebrations. Smaller, semi-enclosed courtyards adjacent to the entrances are ideal for impromptu meetings, an important goal of Apple's. The lush landscaping was created within the city's strict xeriscape ordinance, limiting watered plantings. While the buildings have similar exteriors of precast concrete with granite accents, their varied configurations and lobbies lend them individuality.

Top: Main entrance to center.
Above left: Paths in quadrangle define circulation desire lines and link the amphitheater with the entire campus.
Left: Dining area facing quadrangle.
Photography: John Sutton.

Hellmuth, Obata + Kassabaum, Inc.

Kellogg Company Corporate Headquarters
Battle Creek, Michigan

On a severely blighted 17-acre industrial site in downtown Battle Creek, Kellogg has built a new headquarters and contributed a riverfront park to the city. The grounds, sloping down to the Battle Creek River, include a 10-acre public park, five acres of gardens for employees, a garden of ornamental grasses, a perennial garden, and a woodland garden with azaleas under shade trees. At the building entrance, formal rows of trees line the axis linking the headquarters to the city's McCamly Square. On the side toward the river, the building overlooks a terraced garden, with sculptured retaining walls that create interesting patterns after snowfalls. The building itself is divided into two matching blocks, with an atrium between them that is planted with large trees and tropical plants around a fountain. Terraces overlooking the atrium accommodate seating areas and planters.

Top: Garden front of building, with terraced lawn.
Right: View toward river includes reflecting pool, terraced lawn, and ornamental grass garden along stream.
Far right: Entry, with rows of trees, and patterned paving.
Photography: Balthazar Korab.

Hellmuth, Obata + Kassabaum, Inc.

Hong Kong Stadium
Hong Kong

This new stadium was built to accommodate 40,000 for sporting events and 50,000 for concerts on the confined site of its 28,000-seat predecessor. What's more, it includes modern amenities such as 50 air-conditioned corporate suites, a 300-seat restaurant, ample concession areas, and deluxe player and media facilities. The design fits its site, the bowl formed by a former granite quarry, which offers impressive views in one direction. A strikingly lyrical character is established by the translucent roofs, supported on soaring arches. The stadium won a 1995 AIA Honor Award.

Top photo: Stadium with city and harbor beyond.
Above: Cable-supported canopies glow at night.
Right: Stairs at entrance form platform for viewing sports fields and city.
Photography: Kerun Ip.

**Jambhekar Strauss
Architects PC**

15 West 36th Street
New York
New York 10018
212.279.1536
212.279.1535 (Fax)
jspc@jspc.com

Jambhekar Strauss Architects PC
Buffalo Inner Harbor Project
Buffalo, New York

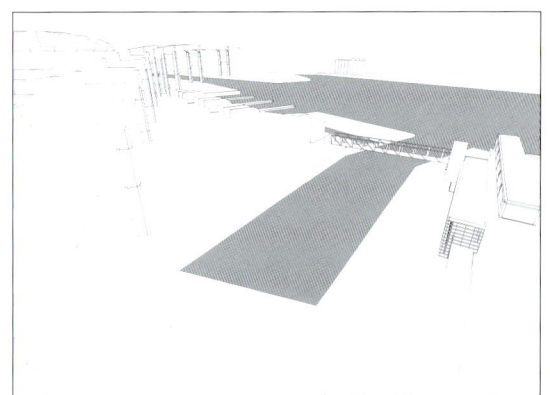

Located where the Erie Canal once met the Great Lakes, Buffalo was the nation's largest inland grain port and the gateway for tens of thousands of westbound immigrants. On this 13.5 acre site at the heart of the old port, few remnants of earlier maritime uses survive. Twentieth-century additions include an auditorium (1939), a public housing project (1953), and a sports arena (1991), none of them oriented to waterfront uses. The Empire State Development Corporation commissioned the architects to reconfigure the site to restore the old connection of the city's downtown to the waterfront. The project includes extending city streets into the site, redesigning the existing Veterans' Park, creating a waterfront promenade and creating new gathering space on the waterfront, as well as dredging three harbor basins. A 14,000-square-foot Naval Museum and Maritime Center, designed by Jambhekar Strauss, will serve both park users and maritime activities. In addition to exhibition spaces, the building will include the harbor master's office, a café, and public restrooms. The building's massing will establish a varied street wall, intended to relate to proposed commercial development on the opposite side of the canal slip. The construction of the project is scheduled for completion in 2001.

Top left: Elevated highway sweeps over site.
Above: Project site, in center, is surrounded by housing project, auditorium, and arena.
Left: Site model shows new waterfront promenade and boat slips, with Naval Museum at center.

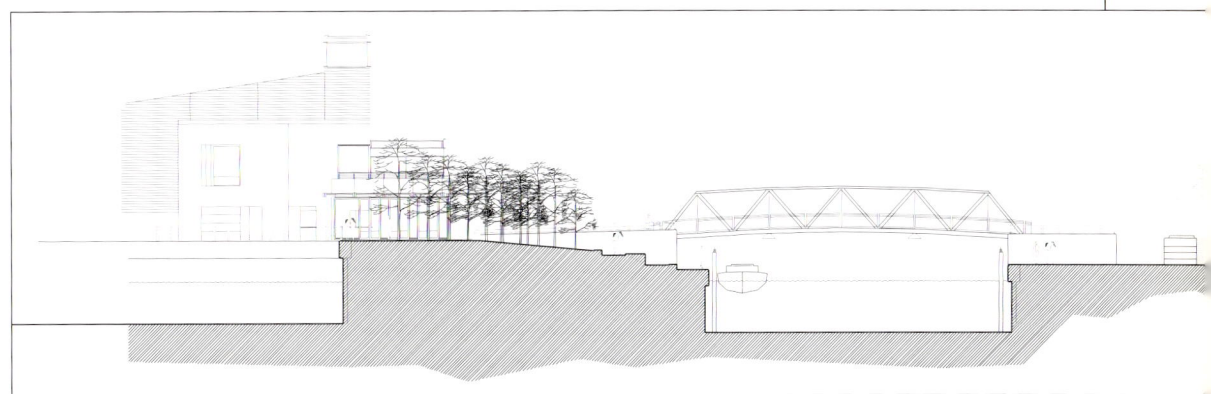

Above right:
Section/elevation through site showing relationship between newly dredged canal slip and Maritime Museum.
Right: Model and wireframe diagram of new Naval Museum and Maritime Center, located at the center of public activity.

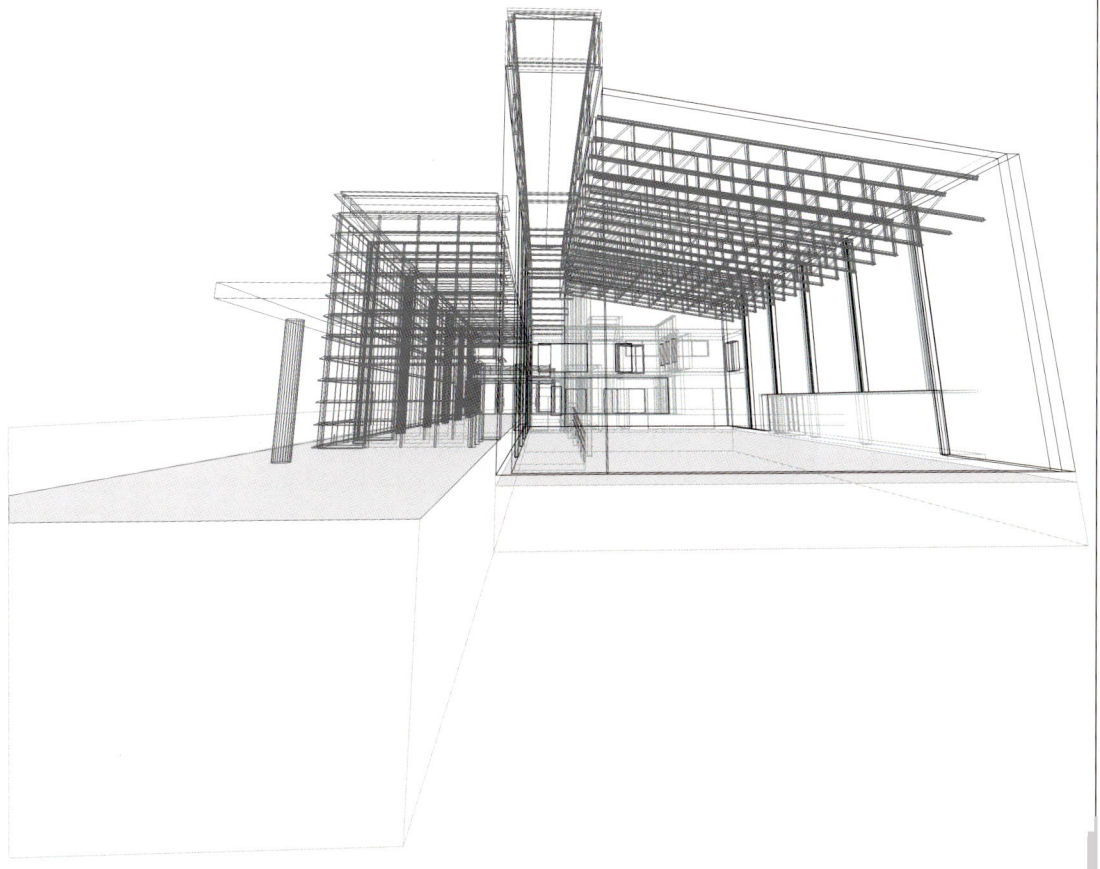

Jambhekar Strauss Architects PC

NJT Hudson-Bergen Light Rail Transit System, SOS Phase
Hudson and Bergen Counties, New Jersey

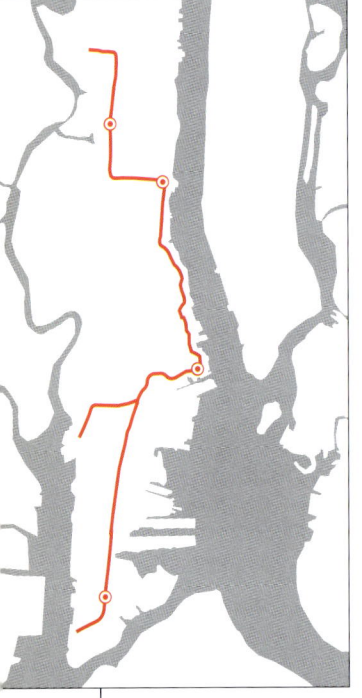

For a new light rail transit system in New Jersey that will run parallel to the Hudson River, the architects have designed 12 passenger stations plus support facilities. The need to establish an identity for the new transit line suggested an approach that unifies the system while reflecting the local context of each structure. As primarily outdoor facilities, the stations tend to blend into their urban or natural settings, a goal supported by the work of artists and landscape architects. The design of the 22nd Street Station

Left: Route map of light rail transit system.
Below left: Sculptural form tops elevator tower at Port Imperial Ferry Station.
Bottom left: Detail of tensile fabric canopies at Port Imperial Ferry Station.
Below: Model of 22nd Street Station.

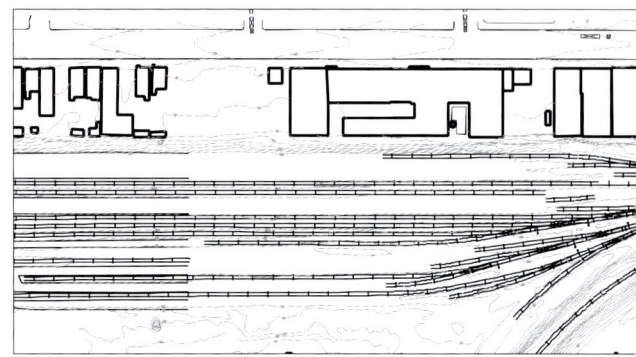

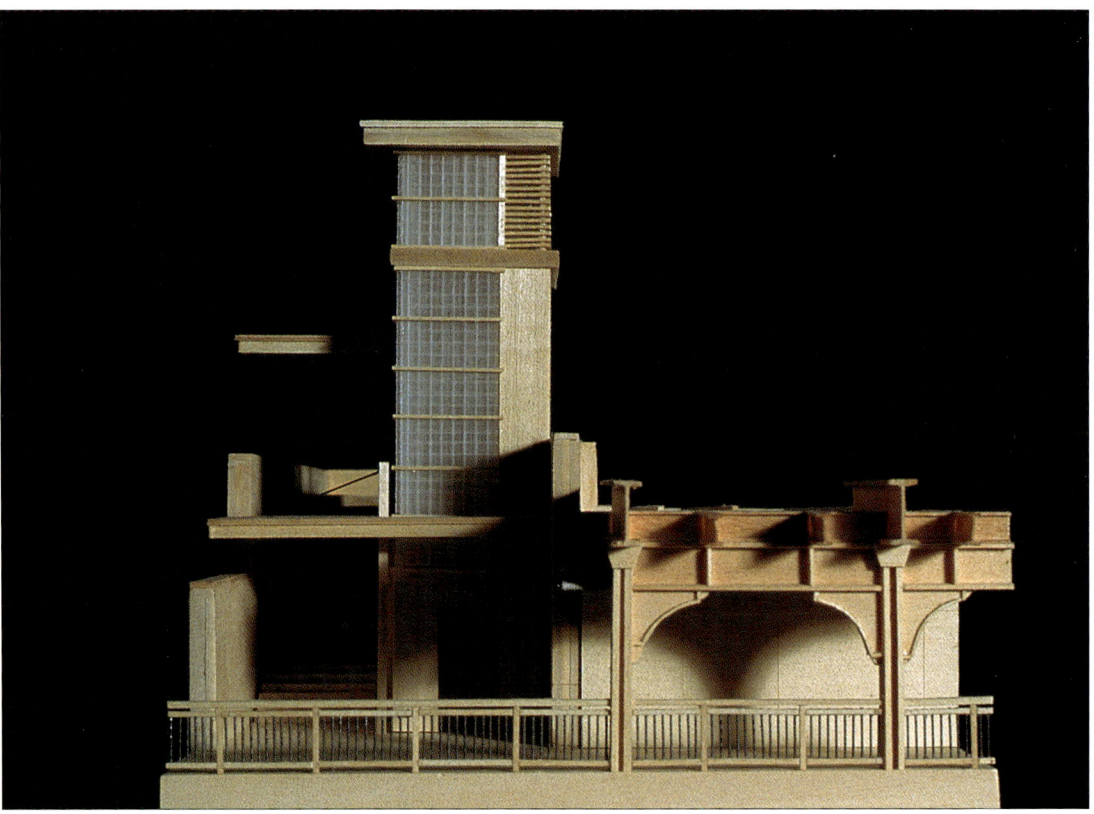

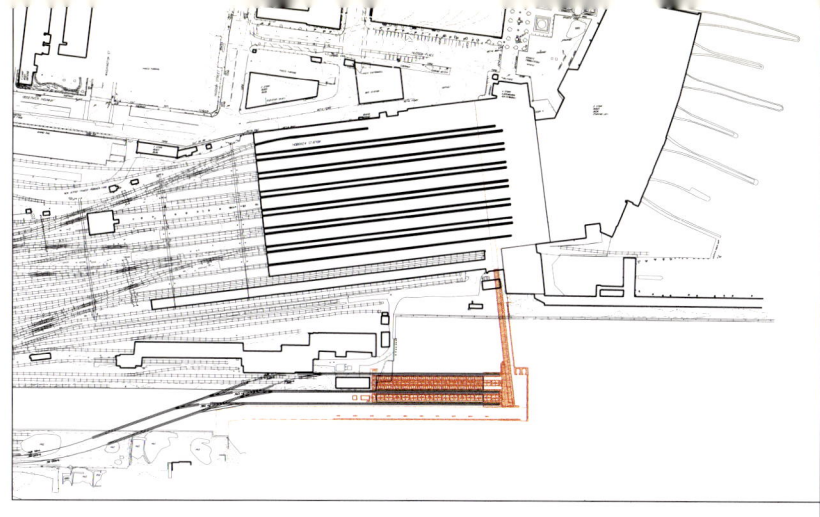
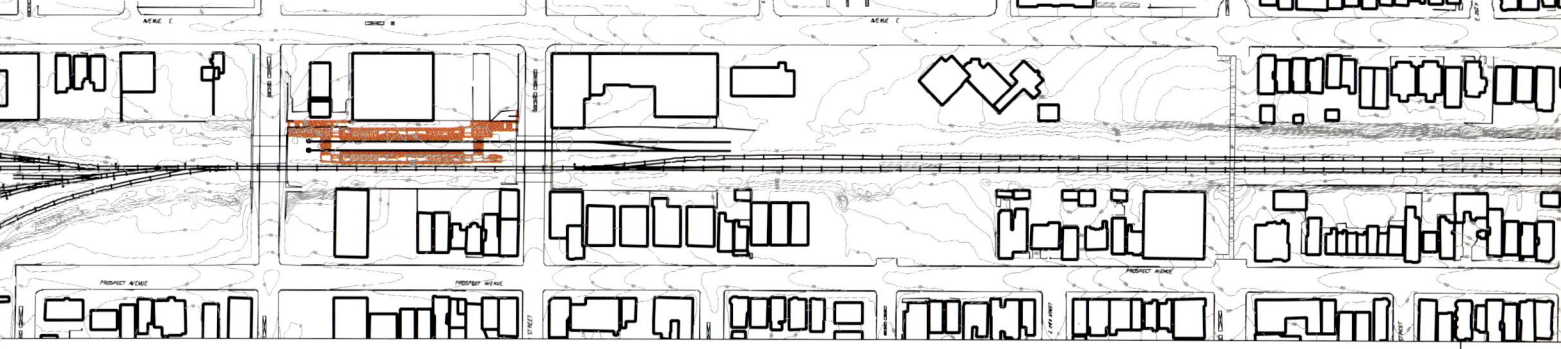

Top left: Model of tensile fabric canopies at Port Imperial Ferry Station, designed to be moved when station is moved.
Top right: Plan of Hoboken Station, with light rail platforms at bottom, commuter lines adjacent to ferry slips above.
Above: Plan of 22nd Street Station.
Far right: Detail of 69th Street Station model.
Bottom right: Front view of employee facility along new Light Rail Transit System.

in Bayonne reflects the historic nature of its downtown location. Materials and details reflect both the residential neighborhood to one side and the industrial area to the other. At the Port Imperial Ferry Station, cable-supported canopies offer nautical gestures toward the ferry and recognize sweeping views of the river and Manhattan, while facilitating an eventual move to a final alignment a few hundred feet away. In an industrial corridor of North Bergen, the 69th Street Station has generous lighting of its overpass, its glass block elevator tower, and the sculpture that crowns it, helping to create a lively and secure environment for passengers. At the Hoboken Station, located at the confluence of commuter trains, PATH transit to Manhattan, and ferry lines, canopies, paving, and a pedestrian plaza are designed to clarify connections.

Jambhekar Strauss Architects PC

Williamsburg Community Center
Brooklyn, New York

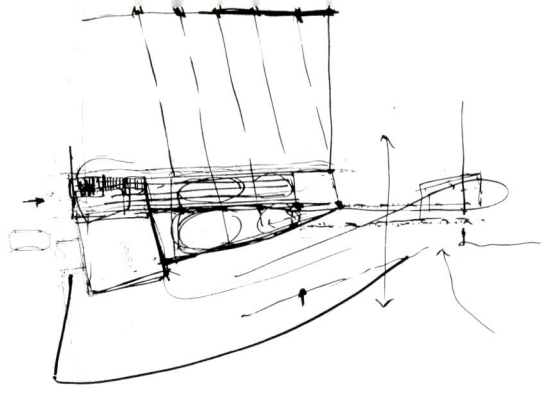

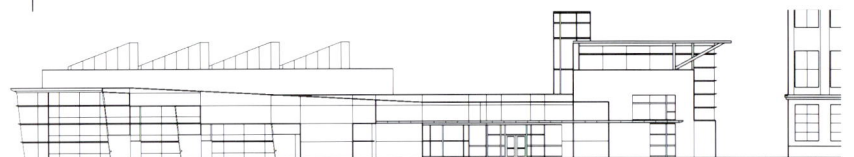

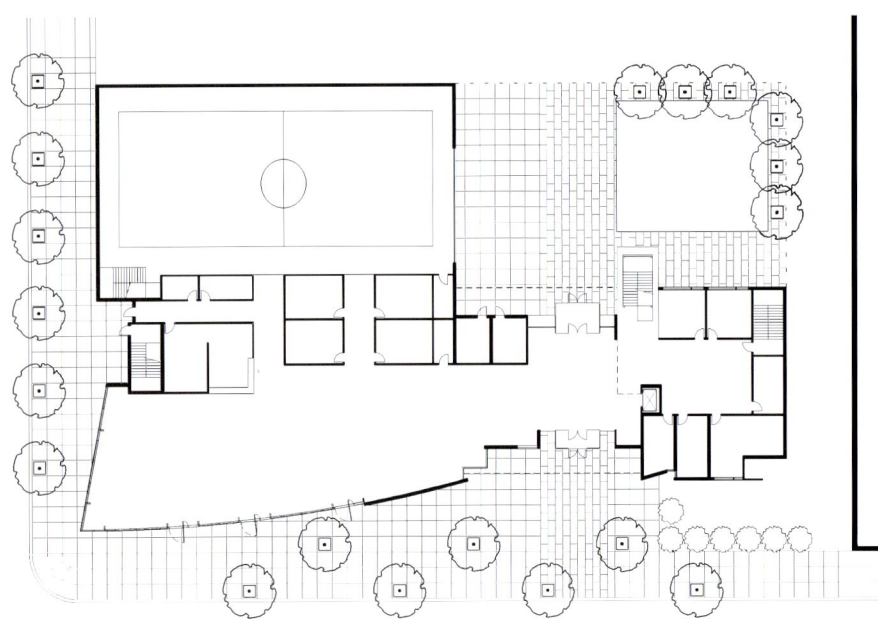

Above: Early conceptual sketch.
Right: Neighborhood plan showing center to left of large school, within repetitive public housing tract, which is flanked by blocks of rowhouses.
Left, top to bottom: Front elevation, plan and model of building.
Below right: East façade.

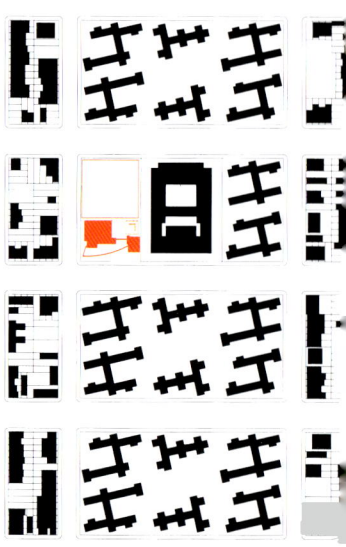

This public community center is designed to serve a diverse urban neighborhood that includes brownstone rowhouses and low-rise public housing. A large elementary school adjoins this site, and these two community buildings are embedded in Williamsburg Houses, a pioneering public project (by William Lescaze and others, 1937), comprising well-kept four-story brick structures with mature trees and grass courtyards. The new center responds to the respected precedent of Williamsburg Houses with a large, column-free glazed gathering space as a kind of "front porch," facing a generous plaza. The two major volumes house the top-lighted gymnasium and two floors of arts classrooms and studios.

The center includes a commercial kitchen, community conference rooms, offices, locker rooms, and other ancillary facilities.

Jambhekar Strauss Architects PC

Lehman College Communication Station
Bronx, New York

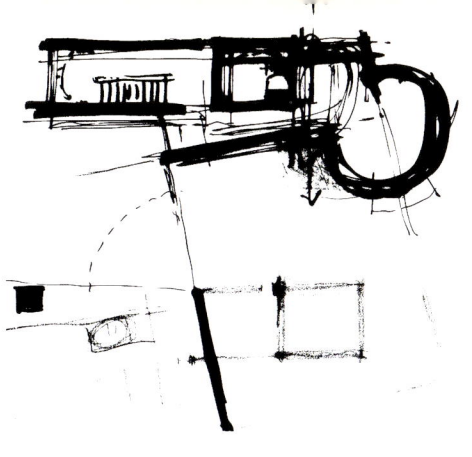

The 30-acre campus of Lehman College, a component of New York's City University, comprises four original Neo-Gothic buildings, plus more modern facilities by such noted architects as Marcel Breuer and Rafael Viñoly. The new communication station will serve as both a prominent campus entrance and a 24-hour security and emergency response headquarters. The design integrates functional and technical requirements with other considerations such as pedestrian movement and visual relationships to buildings of various eras. A metal-clad cylinder forms the core monitoring station and pushes outside the campus edge, becoming a focal point for those approaching. The plaza just inside the campus edge invites public entry and connects to the main internal walkways.

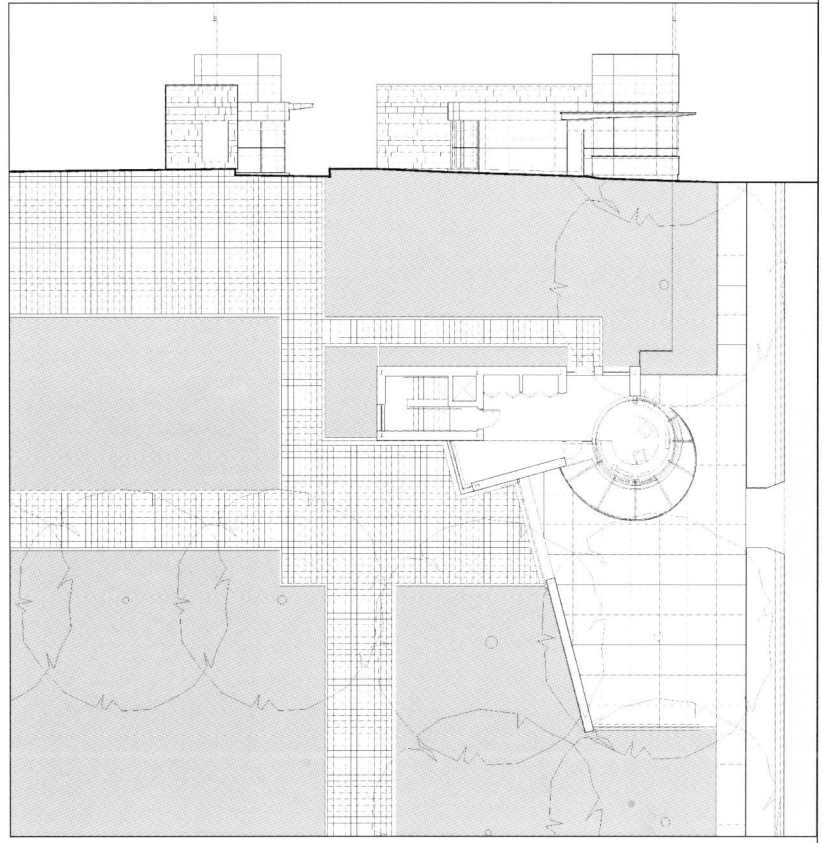

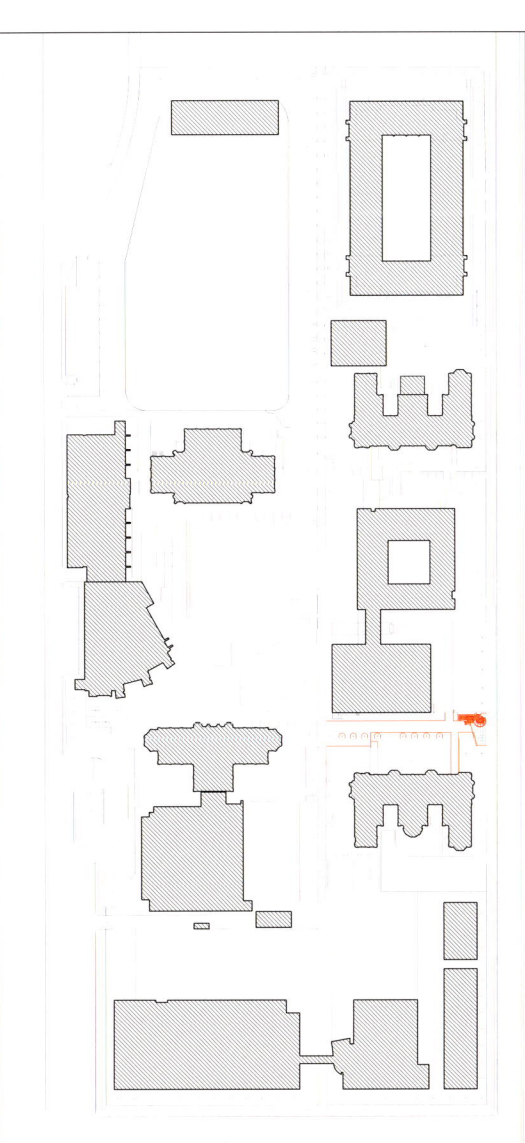

Top: *Early conceptual sketch.*
Top right: *Plan and elevations.*
Left: *Campus plan, with re-landscaped area adjoining the building.*
Right: *Model of the building seen from outside campus.*

Jambhekar Strauss Architects PC

Transit Hub Development
Queens, New York

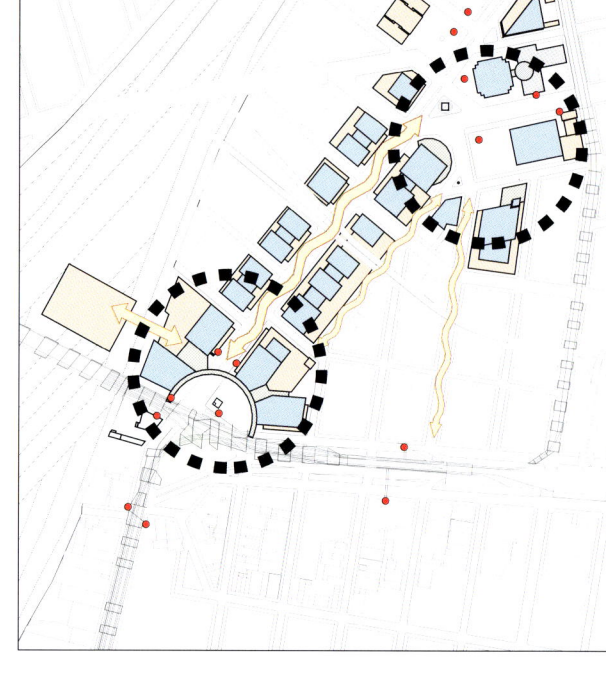

The project involves the rezoning and commercial redevelopment of an industrial area between two major subway stations only a few minutes from midtown Manhattan. The objective is to create a viable office and transportation center that can be accomplished in phases, integrating with the neighborhood's existing scale and mix of uses. The area is now occupied by 10-to-12-story loft buildings, interspersed with such elements as subway viaducts and highway ramps. The proposal explores the possibility of three million square feet of commercial development organized around pedestrian nodes at the transit stations. Pedestrian plazas would be developed at these stations, with atrium-like office building lobbies fronting on them.

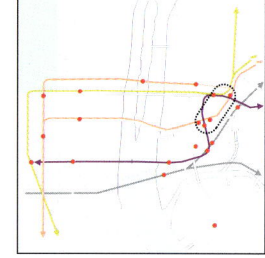

Above left: Location plan showing connection to Manhattan subway system.
Above right: Plan shows office spine, pedestrian plazas at subway stations.
Left: New pedestrian area would be ringed by a glazed arcade leading into atrium-like building lobbies.
Right: Model showing potential office buildings in white. Tallest tower in background is existing.

The Jerde Partnership International, Inc.

913 Ocean Front Walk
Venice
California 90291
310.399.1987
310.392.1316 (Fax)

The Jerde Partnership International, Inc. **Canal City Hakata Fukuoka, Japan**

Above: Components of the complex arrayed along its canal.
Above Right: Vividly striated Sun Plaza is a setting for public events.
Right: Walkways and bridges on several levels link project components.
Photography: Hiroyuki Kawano.

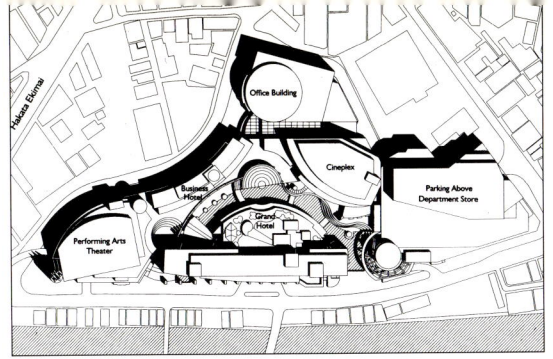

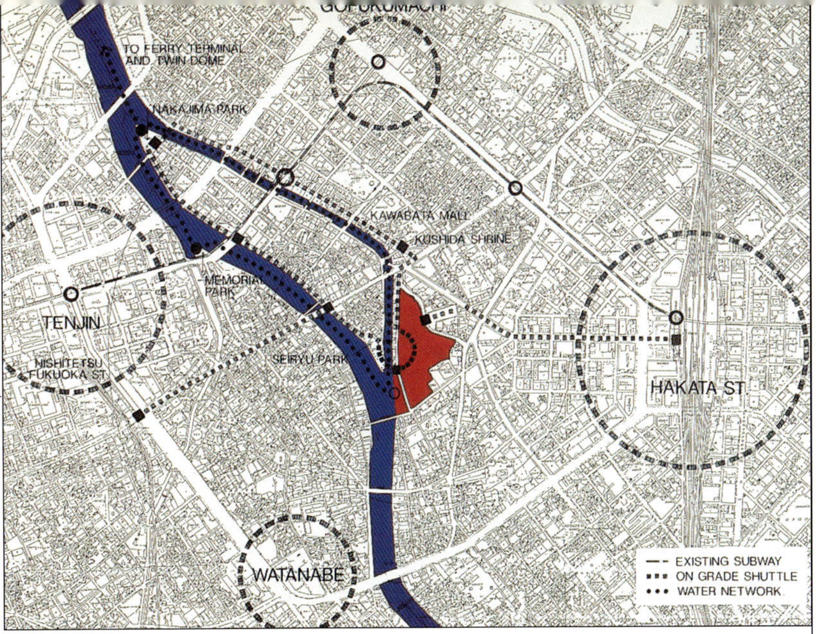

Above: Site plan.
Right: District map.
Below Right: View along canal from Sun Plaza, hotel on right, retail districts in background.

Developed at a cost of $1.4 billion, the 2.5-million-square-foot Canal City Hakata is the largest real estate project in Japan's history. Recapturing an abandoned waterfront factory site at the core of the city, the project relates to the active areas around it by combining shopping, entertainment, cultural, educational, hotel, and office uses. Deliberately responding to the dislocations of rapid urbanization, the project reintegrates economic and social functions by developing space along its canal spine for festive events, community gatherings, and open markets. Construction along the canal is shaped by the metaphor of a canyon, with hard-surfaced "cliff faces," as well as softer, interactive spaces inspired by meandering streams. Paving echoes the geologic patterns of sand, stone, or mineral deposits, with embedded sea life fossils and shells. The flanking buildings rise in horizontal bands like natural strata, with rugged stone at the base and lighter, more refined surfaces toward the top. Portions of the public space along the canal are identified with parts of the universe: Star Court, Moon Walk, Earth Walk, and Sea Court. The centerpiece of the canal passage and the entire complex is the hollow hemisphere rising above the Sun Plaza.

The Jerde Partnership International, Inc.

Beursplein
Rotterdam, The Netherlands

The Beursplein project reunites a fractured urban core that has been split by a major traffic artery, Coolsingel Boulevard, which has become increasingly busy as an approach to a major bridge that opened in 1997. Rotterdam's central core, destroyed by carpet bombing in World War II, includes notable examples of late-1940s planning, including Europe's first all-pedestrian street, the Lijnbaan shopping promenade. But the broad postwar boulevard separating the Lijnbaan from the active retail and market area was depressing economic activities on both sides. The Jerde firm and their Dutch collaborators restored the connection with a below-grade pedestrian street, the 300-meter-long Beursplein Promenade, which passes under the roadway and provides a new connection to a key metro station. Gentle ramps, sloping stairs, escalators, and elevators ease the transition between levels. In a metaphorical reference to the modern city vs. the traditional city, one side of the new promenade is lined with shops with stone portals and planters, the other side with metal and glass fronts. Atop the stone walls, gently curving clear glass canopies provide shelter at both

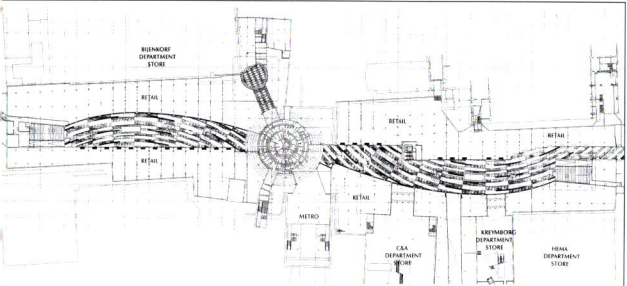

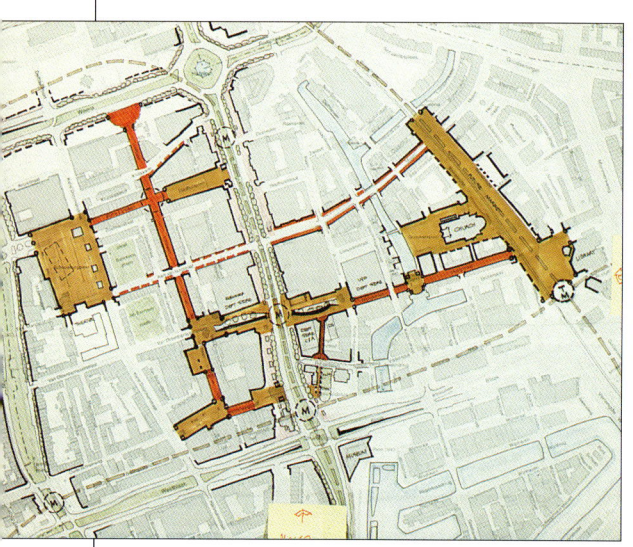

Top: *Promenade plan, with underpass and metro station at center.*
Above: *District plan, with Promenade passing under Coolsingel Boulevard at center.*
Right: *Steel framed glass canopies line the Promenade.*
Photography: *Christian Richters.*

below-grade and street levels and provide symbols of revitalization that glow appealingly after dark.

Right: Coolsingel Boulevard crosses over Promenade.
Below Right: Easy stairs leading to Promenade, landmark Bijenkorf department store, designed by Marcel Breuer, at left.

The Jerde Partnership International, Inc.

Fremont Street Experience
Las Vegas, Nevada

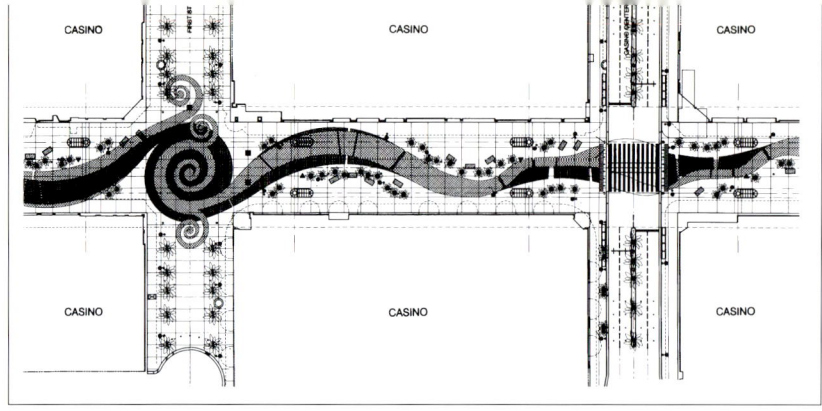

Above right: One-block-plus portion of street plan.
Right: Vault in context of reviving downtown.
Below: Minimal steel struts support space frame.
Facing Page: Vault with after-dark light show.
Photography: Aerial view, Charles LeNoir; all others, Timothy Hursley.

In the 1940s Fremont Street, then the heart of the Las Vegas gaming industry, was dubbed Glitter Gulch for its density of neon signs, powered by nearby Boulder Dam. But in recent decades, the street declined as ever more ambitious mega-resorts opened on the Strip, outside the city limits. In 1992, downtown casino owners joined with the city to develop an ambitious plan to upgrade the image and the customer base of Fremont Street. Challenged to complement the individual properties active along the street, with their still dazzling density of competing signs, the architects proposed a four-block-long curved space-frame canopy to form a "celestial vault" of light, sound, and motion, 100 feet wide and 100 feet high. During the day, the vault's "lighting trellis" blocks 50 percent of the city's intense sunlight, and by night it comes alive with 2.1 million lights and a 540,000-watt sound system, operated by computers to generate light shows with symphonic-quality sound. The resulting huge outdoor room serves as a grand lobby for the compact precinct of hotels and casinos along it.

Completed in 1995, the project has revived businesses along the street, attracted substantial new investment to nearby downtown blocks, and encouraged proposals for a performing arts center and an arena downtown. By introducing kinetic illumination of the plane above observers, synchronized with an urban-scaled sound system, the Fremont Street Experience has made a quantum leap in the exhilarating lighting effects for which Las Vegas has long been famous. There is no longer any question as to whether visitors to Las Vegas must spend some time downtown, and many are now finding it an appealing place to stay.

Above: Vault seen from entrance canopy of hotel.
Right: Night activity seen from upper floor of same hotel.
Photography: Timothy Hursley.

JJR Incorporated
A SmithGroup Company

30 West Monroe Street
Suite 1010
Chicago
Illinois 60603
312.641.0770
312.641.6728 (Fax)

One North Pinckney Street
Madison
Wisconsin 53703
608.251.1177
608.251.6147 (Fax)

500 Griswold Avenue
Suite 200
Detroit
Michigan 48226
313.983.3866
313.983.3990 (Fax)

110 Miller Avenue
Ann Arbor
Michigan 48104
734.662.4457
734.662.7520 (Fax)

225 Bush Street
11th Floor
San Francisco
California 94104
415.227.0100
415.495.3223 (Fax)

JJR Incorporated

The University of Michigan
Ann Arbor, Michigan

Right: Monument at stadium entry displays university's fight song on entablature.
Below: Fountain at the Engineering Center.
Photography: JJR.

JJR's Master Plan improvements to the University of Michigan campus have included gates and a monument at the stadium, the Wave Field; a fountain at the Engineering Center, and a redesign of the Ingalls Mall at the campus core. For the stadium, new gates were designed to accommodate 100,000 or more spectators per game and to honor all UM athletes. A monument listing all teams and championships won is crowned by the school's fight song inscribed on the circular lintel. Stadium improvements were funded completely through brick paver sales. For the privately funded Wave Field, an earth sculpture measuring 100 feet square by Maya Lin, JJR had to work out ways to get grass to grow evenly on peaks and valleys, using custom topsoil mix, selected grasses, special mowers, and irrigation. The Engineering Center fountain, donated by alumni, comprises 20 jets in a pyramidal configuration, rising from a 250-

Above: Monument columns commemorate teams and championships.
Right: Paved portion of Ingalls Mall.
Below: Grass of Wave Field, designed in collaboration with Maya Lin, had to be made sustainable and durable.

foot-long pool as part of a JJR-designed plaza. The tree-lined axis of the Ingalls Mall is the setting for a sequence of distinct spaces, fountains, and other elements designed in relation to buildings sited along it.

JJR Incorporated

Sears Merchandise Group Headquarters
Hoffman Estates, Illinois

Below: Lakeside dining outside Sears offices.
Above right: Native plantings predominate in landscape.
Right: Formal allée in area close to Sears building.
Below right: Enhanced natural landscape.
Photography: JJR.

In the planning of this 780-acre business park, 200 acres have been set aside as public open space, including enhanced examples of the area's wetlands, prairie and other native landscapes. Five miles of walkways and nature trails link the development to the Spring Creek and Poplar Creek Forest Preserves to the north and south respectively. In the office developments to date, a 120-acre site accommodates a two-million-square-foot home office for the Sears Merchandise Group, and 57 acres is occupied by the Park Center, which includes a Northern Illinois University satellite building and three speculative low-rise office buildings. Major considerations in JJR's planning and landscape architectural design were: innovative management of on-site storm water; intro-

Right: Pedestrian-friendly terrace and landscaping in immediate vicinity of Sears offices.
Below right: Dining terrace outside Sears offices can be used for company events.

duction of native plantings to enhance habitat and reduce maintenance; reduction in landscape maintenance through the use of native plantings; reduction of required parking spaces at Sears by incorporating a secondary transit-oriented entry; creation of a generous landscaped "island" around buildings to screen view of parking lots. Sears' desire for an exterior "celebration space" was met with a dining terrace on the edge of a newly created lake.

JJR Incorporated

Crosswinds Marsh
Wetland Preserve
Sumpter Township, Michigan

Right: Marsh with distant view of screenhouse, a wood structure that shelters individuals or school groups from inclement weather and mosquitoes.
Below: Boardwalk bridges waterway.
Photography: JJR.

A 1,050-acre tract has been transformed into mitigated wetlands, required as a condition for permission to expand Detroit Metropolitan Wayne County Airport. It was the county's decision to make acres of this tract accessible to the public as an interpretive park/preserve. The project involved creating hundreds of acres of new wetland habitats on land previously used for farming. The effort required detailed hydrological/hydraulic, soils, and vegetation analyses, extensive earth-moving, construction of water-control structures, and introduction of native plants, including aquatic species. Provisions for visitors include hiking trails and boardwalks, canoe trails, and interpretive signage. Lighting is strictly minimized to enhance the appeal for wildlife. The $12-million project was opened in 1997 and has become a popular destination for school groups as well as casual visitors to Southeast Michigan.

Top: Trails are interspersed with boardwalks.
Above: Canoe trail passes under bridge.
Right: Boardwalk passes over water and wet meadows.

JJR Incorporated

Houston Street San Antonio, Texas

Below: Widened sidewalks and reduced traffic lanes add appeal for shoppers and tourists.
Right: Seating groups and traditional light standards.
Bottom photos: Details of telephone kiosk, streetcar stop shelter, planters, and light standards.

Houston Street is part of a 70-block downtown area being improved under the aegis of the TriParty Improvement District, established by the city, the local transit authority (VIA) and the Downtown Owners Association. JJR was selected to redesign Houston Street, traditionally the main shopping street, which is becoming the tourist link between the Hispanic market, El Mercado, and the Alamo. A unique VIA streetcar route between these two destinations was installed, vehicular lanes were reduced to two, and sidewalks were widened. The city's diversity is reflected in streetscape elements such as Hispanic tile patterns and rough-cut limestone in the tradition of Canary Islanders.

Kohn Pedersen Fox
Associates PC

111 West 57th Street
New York
New York 10019
212.977.6500
212.956.2526 (Fax)

Kohn Pedersen Fox
Associates PC

**The World Bank
Washington, DC**

Right: Filling its city block, the complex has alternating vertically and horizontally striated façades.
Below: Tower of stacked conference rooms punctuates 150-foot-square atrium; glass cones on floor are skylights for dining areas below.
Photography: Timothy Hursley.

Right: Evening event in atrium.
Far right: Main façade, facing public square, is angled slightly off vertical.
Below right: Bold planes subdivide atrium; concrete columns topped with steel struts support roof.
Bottom right: Linear pool drops to form a small waterfall outside below-grade staff dining area.
Photography: Scott Suchman, right; Michael Dersin, far right; Timothy Hursley, others.

KPF won the commission for World Bank through an international design competition, submitting the only scheme that retained the bank's two earlier buildings on the full-block site. By integrating these two 1960s structures into their complex, they were able to reduce construction time and allow the bank to remain open as the work advanced in phases to its 1996 completion. Taking the existing buildings as starting points, the architects continued office structures around the perimeter of the block, enclosing an atrium 150 feet square, which admits sunlight to offices facing it. In order to accommodate the required two million square feet of offices around the atrium within the city's 130-foot height limit, the architects found a way to fit in 13 stories rather than the customary 12. Using post-tensioned floor slabs, with vertical distribution of mechanical services to shorten horizontal runs, they achieved nine-foot ceilings within only a 10-foot floor-to-floor height. There are also three below-grade levels, including staff dining areas below the atrium that overlook a sunlit sunken pool. On the street fronts, the challenge was to develop a single identity integrating the new and old portions of the complex. This was accomplished through an interplay of vertical patterns, found in the old portions and repeated in some new parts, with strong horizontal banding that characterizes the main façade. The project won a 1999 AIA Honor Award.

Kohn Pedersen Fox Associates PC

Dallas Federal Reserve Bank
Dallas, Texas

Below: Panorama of Dallas from elevated main entry.
Right: Functional blocks of bank are composed informally, with office slab at right.
Photography: Richard Payne.

Monumentality representing the federal banking system is tempered in this building by an informal composition expressing a humane mode of operation. A series of distinct volumes, organized irregularly on the six-acre site, accommodate 800,000 square feet of working spaces plus parking for 775 cars. As in all regional Federal Reserve Banks, a large volume of general office space is linked to highly secure, specially designed areas for processing vast quantities of checks, securities, and other highly sensitive items. The main employee entrance here is located on the second floor, which is organized around a central courtyard that provides natural light to surrounding spaces. On this floor, around the court, are public facilities including the cafeteria, lounge, auditorium, exercise and day care areas, a training/conference facility, and a currency museum. The plan anticipates requirements of a 50-year expansion program. Originally estimated to cost $171 million and require 48 months for design and construction, the facility was completed $30 million under budget and 14 months ahead of schedule.

Top left: Main entry at base of office block.
Top right: Lobby in evening.
Bottom: Structure is clad in limestone, granite, and aluminum-framed curtain wall.

Kohn Pedersen Fox
Associates PC

Mark O. Hatfield
United States Courthouse
Portland, Oregon

Top: Entrance is through loggia at base of park façade.
Left: Courthouse comprises 16-story courtroom tower and eight-story "sidecar" administrative block, with roof garden at its top.
Above: At entrance, limestone cladding on columns and first-floor walls expresses civic dignity.
Photography: Timothy Hursley.

The complex functional components of this 566,000-square-foot building are expressed in its cluster of asymmetrical building volumes. The 39,000-square-foot site faces a downtown park that is surrounded by the city hall and other major civic buildings. A 300-foot height limit severely restricted the possibilities for organizing the building. Functions have been separated into a 16-story tower, comprising two courtrooms per floor, with their ancillary rooms, and circulation for judges, prisoners, and the public. The vertical circulation tower at one corner has a distinctive metal canopy that identifies the building on the skyline. The curved metal roof of the Special Proceedings courtroom at the top extends to form a trellis over the 16th-floor terrace, which provides spectacular views east toward Mt. Hood. The lower "sidecar" portion, hugging the base of the tower, houses administrative functions, its mass providing a park façade in scale with other buildings around the park. The architects for the Courthouse were Broome, Oringdulph, O'Toole, Rudolf, Boles & Associates (BOORA), and KPF were design architects.

Above right: Curved top-floor roof extends over 16th-floor terrace.
Right: Courtrooms at heart of building require complex circulation provisions.

Kohn Pedersen Fox Associates PC

Atlanta Federal Center
Atlanta, Georgia

Located in the center of Atlanta, adjacent to the Richard B. Russell Federal Building, this 1.8-million-square-foot complex houses offices, a conference center, a day care center, a cafeteria, and health and fitness facilities. A major design consideration is the incorporation into the complex of the Rich's Department Store building, dating from 1924. All special functions are located on the first two floors. The cafeteria includes a landscaped outdoor eating area. The campus organization of the buildings encloses a large green area at its center that serves as a downtown park.

Top: Remodeled department store is integrated into project.
Above: Center's varied components spread over two blocks, with multi-story bridge spanning street.
Right: Landscaped court at center of complex.
Photography: Top of the page and right, Thorney Lieberman. Above, Wes Thompson.

MBT Architecture

185 Berry Street
Suite 5700
San Francisco
California 94107
415.896.0800
415.495.5237 (Fax)

MBT Architecture

MBT Architecture

University of California, Berkeley
Silver Space Sciences Laboratory Expansion
Berkeley, California

Below left: Building presents a striking profile against its hilltop site.
Right: Circulation spaces are sunny and playful.
Right below: Metal detailing distinguishes entries.
Photography: David Wakely.

MBT provided complete design services, including site selection analysis, for this 42,000-square-foot expansion of the university's space research facilities. Established in 1959, the Space Sciences Laboratory has long been an important center for space research and technology. The expansion adjoins the older laboratory high in the Berkeley Hills, above the main campus. The heart of the complex is a group of communal rooms – lounge, library, and conference room – centrally located for access from both buildings. These rooms, along with the building's stairs and lobbies, take maximum advantage of sweeping views of the city. Working spaces include computer labs, multipurpose wet labs, a clean room lab, offices, and a 1,500-square-foot high bay for payload assembly and maintenance of large instruments. In keeping with the building's purpose, the exterior strives for an appearance of lightness. Metal components are used selectively against scored stucco surfaces.

MBT Architecture

Genencor International Technology Center
Palo Alto, California

Above: End of laboratory wing opens to landscaped terraces.
Left: Main entrance to complex.
Below left: Dining room and terrace in evening.
Right: Skylit "street" connecting building's work areas and common spaces.
Photography: David Wakely.

The spine of this 128,000-square-foot facility is a skylit "street" that links its diverse functional areas. All interaction spaces in the building – dining room, auditorium, coffee bars, and conference rooms – are positioned on this street. Windows along the corridor allow staff and visitors to view most of the research and development activities, thus facilitating customer tours with minimum disruption of operations. In this first phase of a two-stage technology center development Genencor, the nation's sixth largest biotechnology company, employs some 270 people, with 105 more in administrative roles and 50 staffing a pilot plant facility. A special feature of the design is that all labs and most offices have access to landscaped open spaces, which are used for dining, recreation, and informal meetings. The complex received *R&D* magazine's 1997 Lab of the Year Award.

MBT Architecture

Vincent E. McKelvey Federal Building
Menlo Park, California

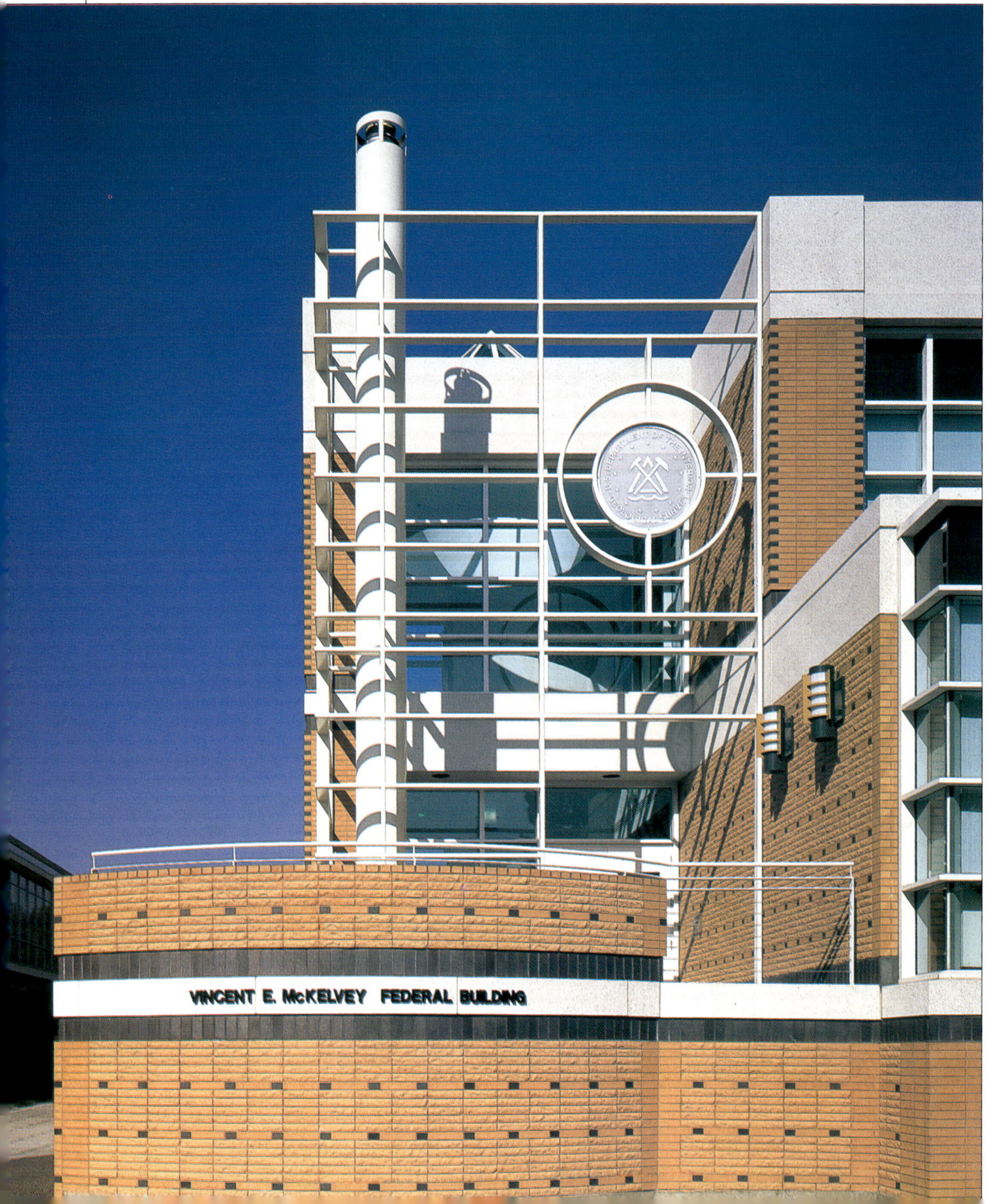

This 157,000-square-foot building, commissioned by the General Services Administration, consolidates laboratories and offices for the geological and hydrological research at the U.S. Geological Survey's Western Regional Center. The need to fit into an existing campus of USGS buildings and meet a local building height limitation in its predominately residential neighborhood led to a distinctive design solution. A 14-foot floor-to-floor height was necessary to facilitate horizontal routing of laboratory ducts, piping, and conduits. To reduce both the real and perceived building height, the lowest of the building's three floors was set approximately

eight feet below grade. Contouring of the site provides daylight and accessibility to this level. This interruption of the ground plane allowed the building to emerge as an almost abstract topographic feature. The stratification and erosive texture of its masonry walls – chosen for low embodied energy and high thermal mass – reinforce the suggestion of a landscape element as a component of an earth sciences research community. An extensive retaining walls system preserves existing mature trees and defines outdoor use areas near the building. Internally, each of the three floors is divided into three separate laboratory zones, each served by a central

Facing page, left: *Metal elements emerge from stratified masonry at library entrance.*
Left: *Lower landscaped plaza and raised walk at laboratory entrance.*
Above: *Geological laboratory.*
Photography: *David Wakely.*

Above: Library reading room.
Left: Characteristic exterior, with horizontal emphasis in masonry and curtainwall.

mechanical shaft, with related research offices located at the building perimeter. The distinct easternmost segment of the facility houses mechanical rooms, administrative offices, and a 300,000-volume library, which is open to the public. A separate 3,000-square-foot Paleomagnetics Laboratory is sited away from other campus buildings and constructed of wood to avoid interference of ferrous metals with its sensitive equipment. The complex is the recipient of a 1996 General Services Administration Design Citation.

The Planning Collaborative

Pier 33 North
San Francisco
California 94111
415.398.8197
415.398.8201 (Fax)

The Planning Collaborative

San Francisco Lands in the City of Pleasanton, California

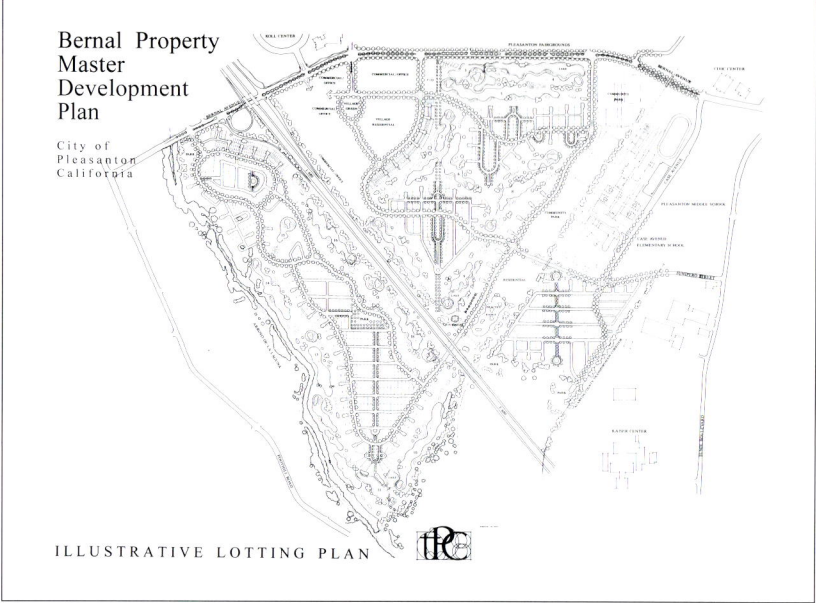

Top: Plan shows housing of various types surrounding central golf course, with commercial facilities concentrated at upper left.
Above: Golf course with pond along fairways.
Above right: Shaded promenade connecting mixed-use area to Village Center.
Illustrations: Jim Lerritz

In 1999, the Planning Collaborative celebrated the 25th year of its urban design, land planning, and landscape architecture practice with the completion of the Bernal Project Master Plan for surplus lands of the City of San Francisco. Since 1930, the City's Water Department has owned 550 acres of land, when it was acquired as a well field, near the center of Pleasanton. No longer used as a water resource, the land is now in a prime development location. The Planning Collaborative, working with several consultants, has drawn up a master plan for a primarily residential community on this tract. It would be centered around an 18-hole golf course and include 1,900 housing units, along with an elementary school and a Village Center with 777,000 square feet of retail, office, and public facilities. The plan envisions plazas and water features at the Village Center, with parks, trails, and bikeways throughout the site. Since the property is now an unincorporated area of Alameda County, and is proposed for incorporation in the City of Pleasanton, the plan must be approved by both jurisdictions, as well as San Francisco officials, and must be attractive to potential developers and land buyers. Pleasanton has already acquired 30 acres at one edge of the tract for a junior high school, and its General Plan has long called for a golf course available to local residents on this site.

Above right: Typical Village Center streetscape.
Right: Village Center central plaza.
Below right: Golf course.

The Planning Collaborative

Vallejo Waterfront Plan
Vallejo, California

Top: Aerial view, with Vallejo on far shore.
Above: Waterfront green and hotel.
Left: Main downtown street with multiplex cinema.
Below left: Waterfront hotel.
Illustrations: Peter Hasselman.

The plan's objective is to revitalize a depressed downtown and urban waterfront by increasing opportunities for public and private uses. Among the major proposals is a realignment of the waterfront road, curving it back from the water's edge to create significant park areas, plus sites for a hotel/conference center, an athletic club, and a new terminal for the town's expanding ferry service. The new alignment would reduce and slow through traffic and provide a new gateway to the existing downtown. Ferry parking, now occupying much waterfront land,

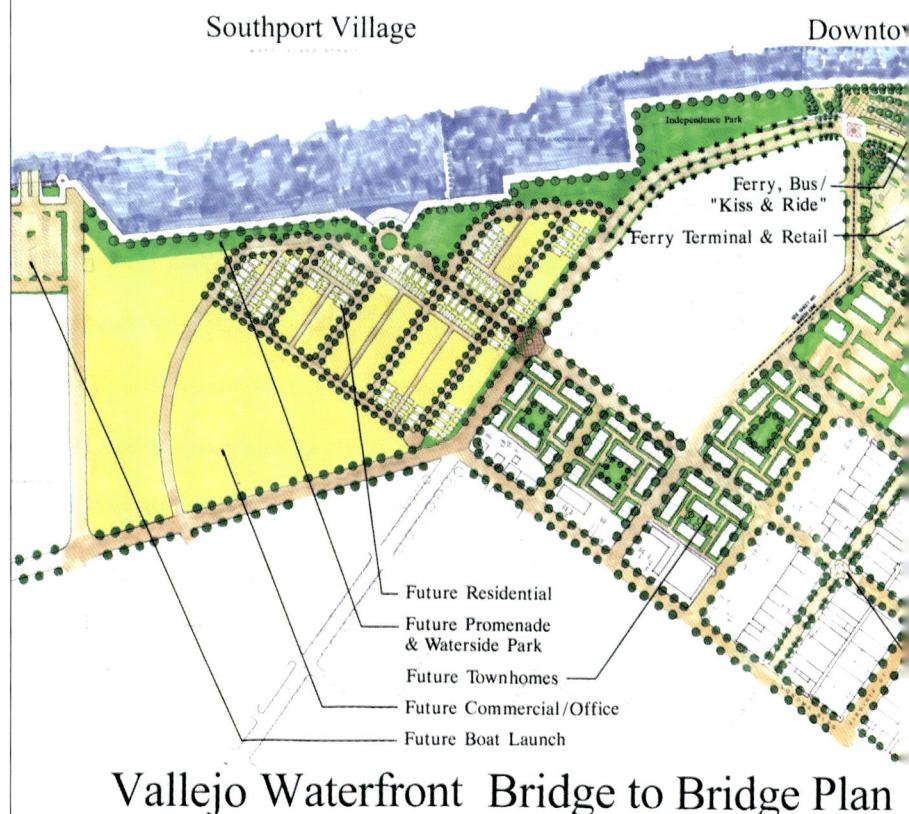

Right: Circle where new waterfront road intersects downtown spine.
Below: Central portion of waterfront plan.

would be concentrated in a new parking structure. A new town square, along with a multiplex cinema and a performing arts center, would extend the downtown to the realigned road, reconnecting it to the waterfront. A marina and landings for water taxis and excursion boats would further encourage water activities. New waterfront residential areas, a downtown artists' loft, studio, and gallery area, and new strategically placed retail facilities would generate further activity in what is expected to be a pedestrian-friendly downtown/waterfront district.

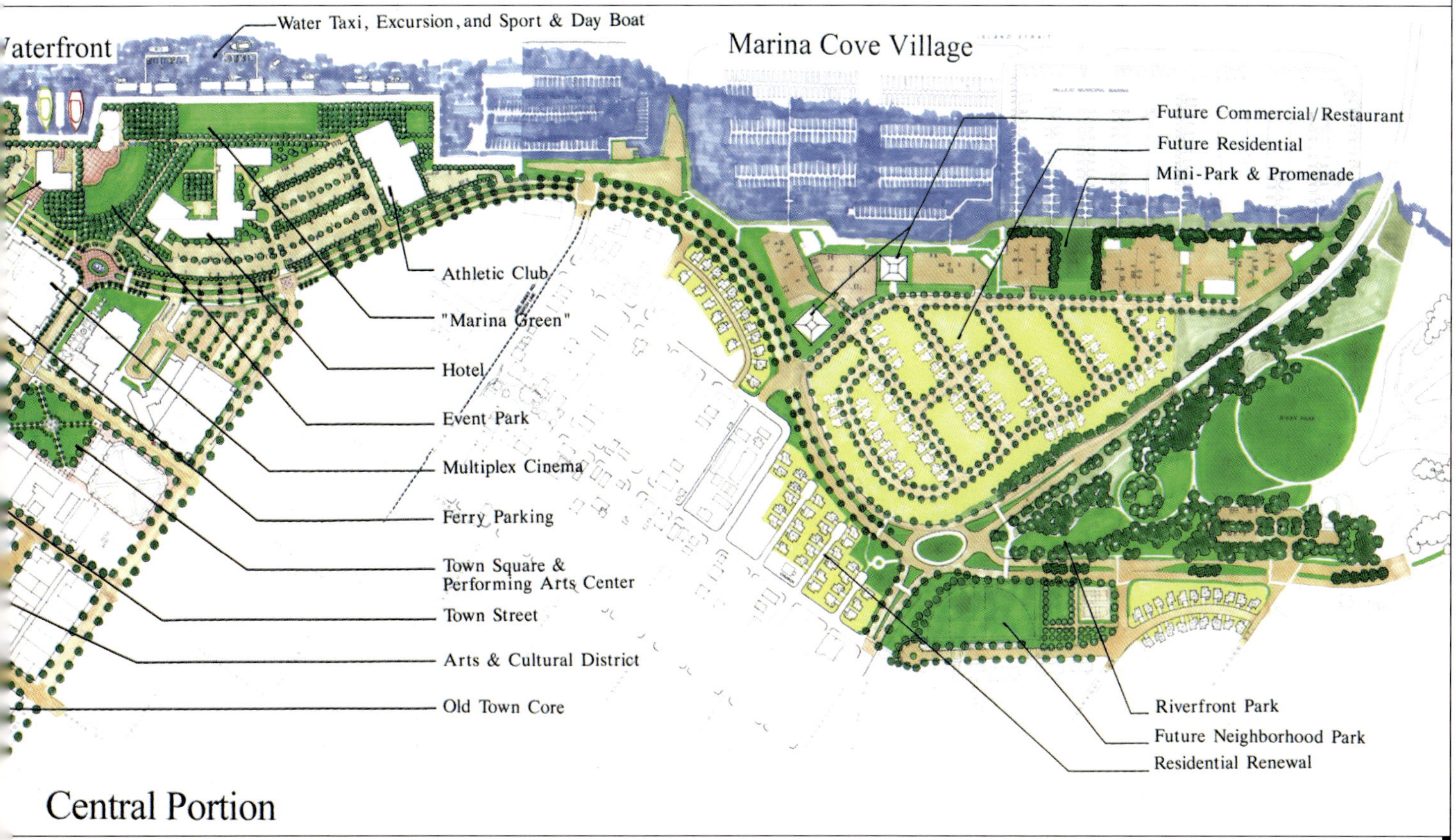

Central Portion

The Planning Collaborative

Downtown Livermore Urban Design Plan
Livermore, California

Above: Historic view of main street.
Right: Wrought iron arbor over pedestrian way.
Below: Restored main street with bluestone paving and traditional light standards.

The old downtown, dating from 1860, is the gateway to the Livermore Valley wine region. As a former agricultural service center, downtown was a focus of commercial, social, and cultural activities. In developing a revitalization plan, historic building preservation and the wine country theme were important values expressed by citizens who collaborated in the design process. So too was the imagery of gateways and portals. The design included proposals for reuse of long-dormant railroad-oriented industrial sites and for new high-density downtown housing. In the existing downtown commercial area, storefront restoration, stone paving, historic lighting, and shade trees enhance the wine country atmosphere.

Right: Spanish Colonial building restored.
Below right: Plan of main street, showing parking, tree planting, open space design.
Below: Bollards, potted plantings, and awnings reinforce historical feeling.
Bottom: Benches and shaded storefronts.
Bottom left: Signage with agrarian theme.

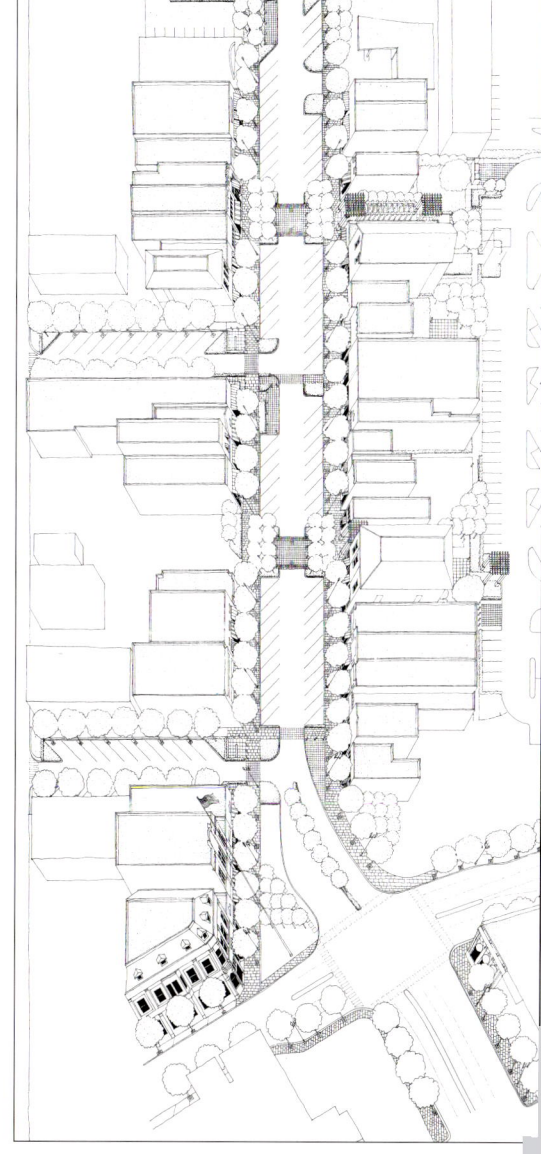

The Planning Collaborative

Downtown Fairfield Urban Design Plan
Fairfield, California

Above: Plan for a portion of Texas Street.
Left: Traditional arbor with street fair.
Below left: Planters and benches.
Bottom left: Street-corner planter/seating with traditional lighting.
Below right: Seating in use at street fair.
Photography: Jeffrey A. Grote.

The Planning Collaborative undertook two phases of work for the City of Fairfield: a downtown urban design plan covering 385 acres and a streetscape master plan for 59 acres along the Texas Street corridor, which was continued through design and construction phases. Proposals for the downtown as a whole included a community theater, a "paseo" retail project, a heritage building conservation office park, the coordination of county center expansion, and streetscape improvements. Improvements carried out along Texas Street include broadened sidewalks with benches, corner planters, historical lighting, brick and precast paving, new signage, and arbor structures for open-air retail and special events. Parking courts are strategically placed to serve a weekend farmer's market and other events.

ROMA Design Group

1527 Stockton Street
San Francisco
California 94133
415.616.9900
415.788.8728 (Fax)

ROMA Design Group

Mid-Embarcadero Roadway and Open Space Design
San Francisco, California

Below: *Plaza in front of Ferry Building is centerpiece of project.*

"The once and perhaps future focal point of the city" is how Landscape Architecture magazine (May 1998) describes this site, where Market Street meets the Embarcadero at the landmark Ferry Building. After 30 years in the shadow of an elevated freeway, this one-time transportation crossroads is now being developed as a significant civic open space. In 1990, ROMA was commissioned to redesign about 20 acres along this central reach of the Embarcadero with parks, plazas, and a new alignment for historic trolleys.

With improvements planned to ferry terminals and landside transit, the area will again become a true cross-roads for the city and region. Working with a large interdisciplinary team of consultants, City Staff and an Advisory Committee, ROMA participated in an extensive public outreach process that guided the direction of the final design. The focus of the public space improvements is a major urban plaza that will re-unite the city and the bay and create a place for staging large-scale civic events, parades and celebrations. This space will be framed by monumental palm trees; the inland edge will be terraced to accommodate seating and viewing as well as an elevated promenade. The plaza will be paved with large-scale granite blocks in a broad weave pattern reflecting the cadence of columns along the Ferry Building arcade. The nighttime experience of this space will be enhanced by two light "cannons," which will provide a place for people to gather and sit, and on special occasions will shoot beams of light 600 feet into the night sky.

Left: The Music Concourse is planned as a flexible open space that will enhance the recreational and cultural opportunities within the area and feature a new home for the historic Exposition Organ, which was built for grand performances during the 1915 Pan Pacific Exposition.

Right: The Embarcadero Plaza is part of an assembly of parks, open spaces and promenades that will transform the character of the urban waterfront and provide for a wide range of recreational opportunities.

Below: Two ferry basins to accommodate expanded ferry travel will be created, with new public access areas in, around and through the historic Ferry Building. The project includes a new breakwater and public access pier, berths, floats, dolphins and mooring areas.

ROMA Design Group

Pier 7
San Francisco, California

On a waterfront from which shipping and commercial fishing have largely withdrawn, this is the first new pier constructed since 1940, and the longest measuring 825 feet. Only the second San Francisco pier ever constructed for public recreation, this pier is designed to accommodate fishing, jogging, promenading, sitting and viewing. It overlooks relatively open water from which earlier commercial piers have been removed. With a typical width of 25 feet, the pier widens into three "plazas," at the land end, at the midpoint, and at the end. Fish cleaning tables and water fountains are included at the end plaza to accommodate fishing uses. Construction is straightforward with concrete structural elements and wood decking. Originally planned in the late 1970s by ROMA, the project was not completed until 1989. Design had to be coordinated with two city departments acting as clients — the Port of San Francisco and the Parks and Recreation Department — and other funding agencies — the Coastal Conservancy and the State Wildlife Conservation Fund — plus such review agencies as the Bay Conservation and Development Commission. Pier 7 is adjacent to one of the most intensely developed portions of the city. For many, it creates the closest thing to being out over water on a ship, creating at the same time a sense of detachment and immediacy with the surrounding city. The pier is actively used throughout the day and at night by people of all ages, and provides a dramatic setting for feature films, nightly news, and special interviews with visitors to the Bay Area. The New York Times named Pier 7 second only to the cable cars as a memorable San Francisco experience.

Top and Left: The pier provides a unique perspective of the city and the adjacent downtown, and is on axis with the Transamerica Pyramid building.
Above: Balconies surround traditional light fixtures at each structural bay, creating intimate places for viewing.
Right: "Plazas" extend from pier at midpoint and end.

Right: The pier offers expansive views of the bay, Bay Bridge and offshore islands (Yerba Buena and Treasure Island), as well as occasional close-up views to passing vessels and ships.
Below Right: The pier is actively used by strollers for viewing and fishing.
Photography: San Francisco Chronicle.

ROMA Design Group

Third Street Promenade
Santa Monica, California

Above: The Promenade has become a stage for lively street performances and entertainment.
Top right facing page: The use of banners, pavilion buildings, landscaping, bollards, street curbs and fountains has helped to rescale the street and structure activities along it.

ROMA Design Group prepared a full-scale redesign of Santa Monica's outmoded pedestrian mall, located in the heart of the vital beachfront community. The redesign of the street was instrumental in creating a more attractive pedestrian environment and more viable retail district. Completed in 1990, the Third Street Promenade is a dynamic, pedestrian-dominated open space which recognizes the critical relationship between the scale of the street and the activities within it. The redesign restructured the scale and character of the street by reintroducing a curb adjacent to a narrow "street" with widened sidewalks for walking and sitting as well as designated zones for the extension of outdoor cafés and restaurants from adjacent buildings. The Promenade is a mixed use street that combines the spontaneity and exuberance of a successful downtown district with the dynamism of a public gathering space. Today, it is recognized as one of the most attractive public spaces in Los Angeles and a regional urban entertainment destination. In order to extend the success of the Third Street Promenade into the surrounding downtown, the City of Santa Monica together with ROMA Design Group has established a plan for improvement to cross-streets emphasizing transit, pedestrian, and bicycle movement. This plan includes the creation of a new Transit Mall on two downtown streets as well as the removal of one-way streets and the reinstatement of two-way auto traffic throughout the downtown.

Above: Outdoor dining is facilitated in café zones along the Promenade.
Right: Third Street Promenade extends three blocks (or about 2,000 feet) from Wilshire Boulevard to Broadway.
Photography: Jane Lidz

ROMA Design Group

Pacific Avenue Streetscape
Santa Cruz, California

Top: A flower kiosk at a major intersection.
Left: Programmed activities draw crowds.
Below left: Planters on the extra wide east sidewalk face across narrow traffic lanes to cinema.
Below right: Wide sidewalks allow extensive outdoor dining.
Bottom right: Stone planter walls double as public seating.
Photography: Left and below right, Pat Carney. Others: Bob Swanson.

The Pacific Avenue commission grew out of ROMA's 1991 Downtown Recovery Plan for Santa Cruz and the extensive damage caused by the Loma Prieta earthquake. Many unreinforced masonry buildings along Pacific Avenue, the town's main commercial street, had either collapsed or had to be demolished, and a subsequent frost destroyed many of the street's trees. The new plan took into account changes in retailing and the goal of making the street the principal community gathering space with outdoor cafés, festivals, and other draws. In the central area, the design concept is an asymmetrical layout with 22- to 30-foot sidewalks on the east side of the street allowing for outdoor dining and large planters. A narrow roadway, with parking on both sides, assures a slow traffic flow.

RTKL Associates Inc.

One South Street	140 South Dearborn Street
Baltimore	Suite 200
Maryland 21202	Chicago
410.528.8600	Illinois 60603
410.385.2455 (Fax)	312.704.9900
http://www.rtkl.com	312.704.9910 (Fax)

2828 Routh Street
Dallas
Texas 75201
214.871.8877
214.871.7023 (Fax)

22 Torrington Place
London WC1E 7HP
United Kingdom
0171.306.0404
0171.306.0405 (Fax)

1250 Connecticut Avenue NW
Washington
District of Columbia 20036
202.833.4400
202.887.5168 (Fax)

5-17-6 Roppongi, Minato-ku
Tokyo 106-0032
Japan
03.3583.3401
03.3583.3402 (Fax)

333 South Hope Street
Los Angeles
California 90071
213.627.7373
213.627.9815 (Fax)

32-36 Hollywood Road
Suite 1304, Kinwick Centre
Central, Hong Kong
852.2905.8500
852.2905.8505 (Fax)

RTKL Associates Inc.

Addison Urban Center
Addison, Texas

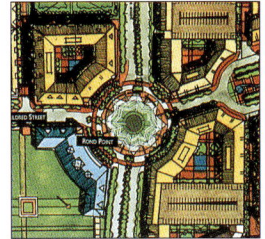

Top: Overall aerial.
Top center: Plan of Addison Circle.
Top right: Building at Addison Circle
Above: Texas Trellis is proposed as centerpiece of Addison Circle at main intersection.
Middle and bottom right: Street scenes in Addison Urban Center.
Photography: C. Blackmon.

RTKL was commissioned by Post Properties to develop a master plan and development guidelines for a special residential district in the Dallas suburb of Addison. RTKL's comprehensive plan provides a pattern of streets and alleys intended to accommodate a wide range of integrated land uses at a scale that is conducive to pedestrian activity. In essence, this framework is the rediscovery of the small-town grid of simple city blocks. The development guidelines are flexible enough to permit a full range of uses, and they encourage: 1) the integration rather than the compartmentalization of residential land uses; 2) pedestrian activity; 3) reduced dependence on private automobiles; and 4) an urban fabric with a sense of neighborhood. RTKL has been responsible for the architectural design for the first two phases of the development, which includes a total of 900 residential units, 125,000 square feet of retail, and a 300,000-square-foot office building. The firm is now designing the Phase 3, which includes another 300 units of housing.

RTKL Associates Inc.

Courtyard Shops of Encino
Encino, California

Right: Street frontage, with upper-level dining terrace.
Below: Three-level courtyard.
Photography: Jay Venezia.

Designed for Security Pacific Corporation, the Courtyard Shops of Encino offer the affluent residents of this California city a dramatic open-air environment for shopping, dining, and services. The 100,000-square-foot center efficiently arranges courtyard shops on three levels to provide customers with easy access to a wide variety of high-quality merchandise from around the world. A courtyard makes it possible to view shops on the ground level and the upper level from the street; a lower courtyard provides access to lower-level shops. The ground and lower levels are directly accessible from parking levels for more than 490 cars at the rear of the site. Features include a full-service gourmet grocery market, three restaurants with indoor and outdoor dining, a fitness center, and over 30 specialty shops.

RTKL Associates Inc.

Reston Town Center
Reston, Virginia

RTKL's competition-winning architecture for Phase One of Reston Town Center meets the community's growing demand for commercial development while evoking a contemporary "Main Street" character. The 15-acre, four-block Phase One encompasses two 250,000-square-foot office buildings, a 510-room Hyatt Regency hotel, 150,000 square feet of retail and cinemas, and an open-air pavilion. The mirror-image, 11-story office buildings, One and Two Fountain Square, form an appropriate gateway to the development and the beginnings of a recognizable skyline for Reston Town Center. The profile of the towers and the individualized façades of the street-level shops recall the picturesqueness of the original Reston. A variety of materials, an irregular massing scheme, and a full palette of texture and color give the Phase One components a common identity, yet a stimulating variation in appearance. RTKL's architecture establishes a civic scale and sense of importance that set the stage for subsequent phases of the 85-acre town center development. In 1992, the Reston Town Center won a national AIA Urban Design Award of Excellence.

Top of page: Portion of Town Center plan, with 4-block Phase One highlighted.
Top left: Fountain Square and open pavilion, with hotel in background.
Above: Retail street looking toward Fountain Square.
Right: Fountain Square, with flanking office buildings.
Photography: Max MacKenzie.

RTKL Associates Inc.   Santa Lucia Riverwalk Monterrey, Mexico

Commissioned by the governor's planning and economic development task force, RTKL prepared a redevelopment plan to revitalize downtown Monterrey. A primary goal of the planning process was to determine the feasibility of developing the existing underground Santa Lucia River as a riverwalk entertainment district in the style of San Antonio's Paseo del Rio. Key planning strategies included identifying reinvestment opportunities to draw activity back into the plan area. Among those identified were the construction of Class A office space and the sale of government property to fund new public-sector developments. Other tactics include protection of residential zones from traffic and commercial "infill" development and improvement of traffic conditions by instituting off-street parking, realigning intersections, and installing modern traffic signals. The first phase of the plan included restaurants, a central plaza for public events, and the initial leg of the waterway system, with a museum of Mexican history as a focal element. RTKL worked with the museum architect in developing its site plan and massing.

Top right: Aerial perspective representing RTKL's master plan and urban design guidelines. **Above right:** History museum seen across initial portion of riverwalk. **Right:** Riverwalk seen from History Museum. **Photographer:** David Whitcomb.

RTKL Associates Inc.

Camden Yards Sports Complex
Baltimore, Maryland

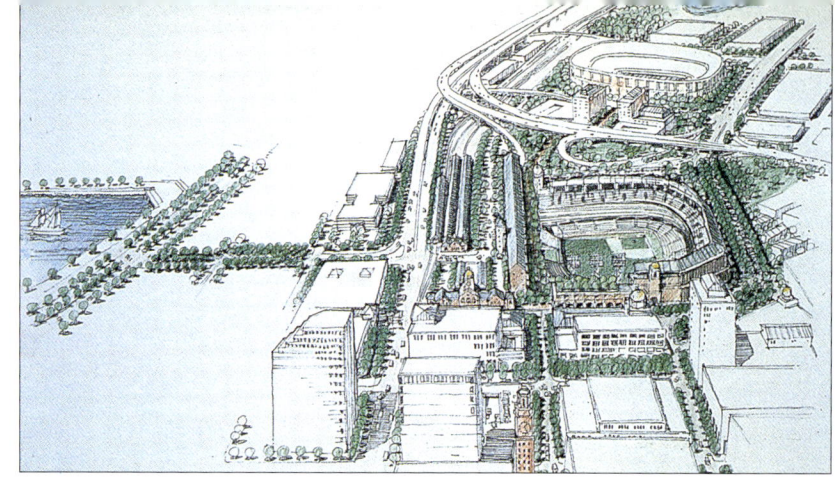

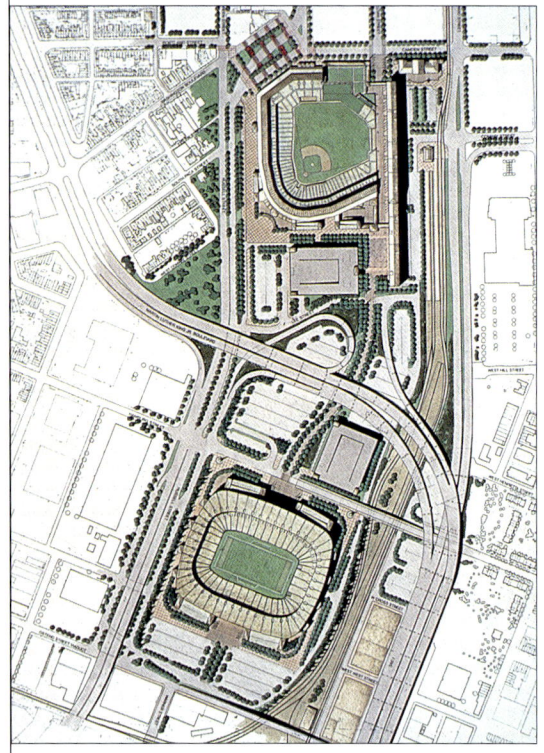

Above: Aerial perspective looking south shows baseball park in middle distance, football stadium beyond.
Left: Plan shows two stadiums, highway connection, downtown area at north end (top).
Below left: Baseball park, pedestrian street, and rehabbed B&O warehouse.
Photography: Janice Rettaliata.

Working as master planning coordinator and urban design consultant, RTKL led a team of consultants in creating a comprehensive development plan and urban design recommendations for the area of the two-stadium Camden Yards Sports Complex. Located in downtown Baltimore near the Inner Harbor, the 85-acre site was planned to make strong connections to the existing city fabric. The plan included Phase One construction of the new baseball park for the Baltimore Orioles and a Phase Two football stadium with structured parking. The character of the site makes a transition from the urban character of Camden Street and downtown at the north end to the natural environment of Middle Branch Park at the south. The master plan recommended that the baseball facility have the qualities of a traditional urban ball park, with building edges parallel to existing streets and with exterior materials and details that blend the building into its context. Completed in 1992, this baseball park has set the pattern for a whole generation of subsequent U.S. ball parks. The plan also proposed that the existing 1,100-foot-long B&O warehouse be renovated for Orioles office space and to serve as a dramatic signature backdrop for the outfield. The football stadium was completed in 1998. Other important plan components included integrating light rail transit and commuter rail service with both stadium sites, new public spaces to serve as gateways to the city, and the Eutaw Street pedestrian spine, which physically and visually connects the stadium to the city. The plan addressed a wide range of complex access, parking, and circulation issues, as well as potential locations for future development.

RTKL Associates Inc.

Centro Oberhausen
Oberhausen, Germany

Top of page: Aerial view of The Promenade.
Middle of page and right: Entry to retail center.
Above: Busy day on The Promenade.
Photography: David Whitcomb.

RTKL's design transformed Centro Oberhausen's 250-acre site from a former Thyssen steel mill into one of Europe's favorite day-trip destinations, auspiciously fulfilling the client's high expectations. Located in the Ruhr Valley, one of the continent's most populous regions, this multi-use retail and leisure center comprises: shops; Oasis food court; The Promenade, a European-style streetscape of restaurants and other amenities; the Centropark leisure park; multi-level parking for about 8,500 cars. The retail center is anchored by three premier department stores and showcases some 15 mid-sized stores and 200 small shops. Architecturally reminiscent of botanical gardens, this component is designed with animated urban passages and landscaped garden courts. Recalling the European high street tradition, Centro Promenade features a Planet Hollywood restaurant, a microbrewery, a Warner Brothers multiplex cinema, and an anchoring 11,000-seat arena. Centropark is a 20-acre child-oriented adventure island well integrated into the overall development, offering restaurants, theaters, and other attractions.

RTKL Associates Inc.
The Entertainment Center
Irvine Spectrum
Irvine, California

Above: Intimately scaled parts of the center have passages at scale of Moroccan medinas.
Right: Public space opens up around fountain pool.
Below right: Night lighting enhances subdued patterns and colors.
Photography: Bryan Mar.

Located at the confluence of two major freeways, the new Entertainment Center, Irvine Spectrum, draws visitors from the entire metropolitan area to its 255,000 square feet of dining and entertainment options. As Southern California's first center of this nature, it is designed to blend indoor and outdoor experiences. It integrates four retail units for a total of 67,000 square feet, the Oasis food court with seating for 400, and two restaurant pads with a 21-screen Edwards cineplex. The Moroccan-inspired design concept was derived from the area's Spanish Colonial tradition. While still maintaining a Mediterranean atmosphere, Moroccan design speaks to simpler issues of mass, light, shadow, and color. This bolder and stronger character helps to balance the intimate, human-scale environment of the Entertainment Center with the 105,000-square-foot cineplex portion of the complex. Public spaces are kept large and open at the cinema end of the project and narrow gradually into medina-style passageways. A softer wayfinding system developed by RTKL's environmental graphic designers contributes to humanizing the project. In particular, subdued patterns and clustered elements are used to outline gathering areas and to draw people through the project.

Sasaki Associates, Inc.

64 Pleasant Street	900 North Point Street
Watertown	Suite B300
Massachusetts 02472	San Francisco
617.926.3300	California 94109
617.924.2748 (Fax)	415.776.7272
e-mail info@sasaki.com	415.202.8970 (Fax)
www.sasaki.com	e-mail sanfrancisco@sasaki.com

Sasaki Associates, Inc.

Pusan Harbor Urban Design Plan
Pusan, Korea

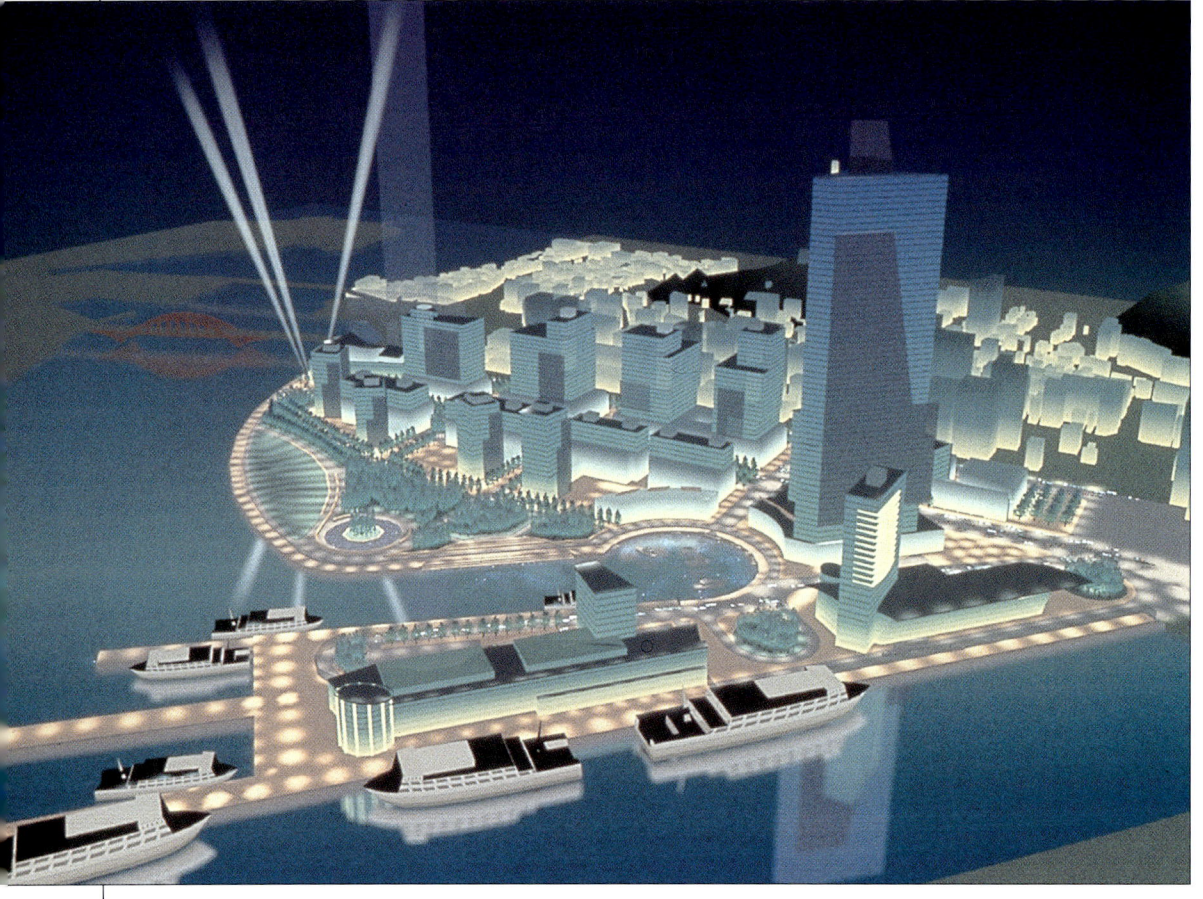

The Pusan Inner Harbor presents an extraordinary opportunity for waterfront redevelopment adjacent to an urban core. As the city's maritime activities relocate to a new state-of-the-art port, the mountain-rimmed city can expand onto a 29-hectare (71-acre) harborfront tract. Plans call for a mix of public parks, entertainment facilities, offices, retail, housing, and hotels. A new ferry terminal and customs facility will be welcoming landmarks on historic Pier One (the thumb of the mitten-shaped site). Other notable buildings will include a Landmark Tower at one end of the site, near the existing downtown, and a Public Performance Building at the opposite end, to be the home of the Pusan Film Festival, among other events. The total projected construction is 850,000 square meters (9,200,000 square feet). The plan will be implemented in phases over a 15-year period, with the initial phase to be in place by 2002, when Korea will host the World Cup games.

Top left: Aerial view with ferry terminal in foreground; performance hall marked by searchlights.
Bottom left: Hotel, retail, and residential development will face harbor-front park.
Right: Performance hall will open onto waterfront plaza.
Below right: Plan, with ferry terminal at bottom.
Photography: Sasaki Associates, Inc.

Sasaki Associates, Inc.

Capital City Landing
Indianapolis, Indiana

Below: Canal walkway joins downtown to river.
Bottom: Canopied seating along the canal.
Photography: Sasaki Associates, Inc., Landslides.

Capital City Landing is one crucial component of a master plan, also by Sasaki, for a nine-mile stretch of the White River and the associated Central Canal. The intention of the entire river corridor scheme, developed for the White River State Park Board, the City of Indianapolis, and the Corps of Engineers, is to make the river accessible to the public by providing gateways in the massive levees and flood walls erected in the past. Located at the point where the river passes the downtown core, Capital City Landing ties together the city and the river. In addition, riverfront and canal promenades connect recreational corridors to the north and south. The historical relation of the city to the river has been recognized by integrating remnants of its urban past – industrial and commercial buildings, roads,

Above: Canal basins cascade toward river, and lawn extends across bridge.
Right: Amphitheater steps down to river.
Above right: Park and city.

bridges, canals, and levees – as elements of the Landing's design. Following a historic right-of-way, the National Road Promenade provides the main pedestrian route to the river from downtown. The promenade terminates at McCormick Terrace, site of the first settler's cabin and the first bridge across the river. To one side of the promenade, Celebration Plaza takes the form of a grass-and-stone amphitheater oriented toward the river, breaking through the existing flood wall. The renovated Old Washington Street Bridge connects this plaza with the new entrance to the Indianapolis Zoo, across the river.

Sasaki Associates, Inc.

Cleveland Gateway
Cleveland, Ohio

Below: *Plaza between ballpark and arena, with light towers by artist R.M. Fischer.*
Photography: *Roger Mastroianni, Alan Ward, Susan Duca.*

Right: Master plan, with downtown core at top, arena and ballpark at center.
Below right: Sports facilities are a short walk from office towers, but close to highways.

The challenge of Sasaki's master plan was to fit two major sports facilities, customarily built on expansive suburban sites, onto a 28-acre tract at the edge of a dense downtown. The non-profit corporation that commissioned this plan wanted to show that a 42,000-seat baseball park and a 20,000-seat indoor arena could complement the urban core and promote downtown economic growth. The striking success of the $425-million development has made it a model for other cities. Sasaki provided the framework that made the project work, then worked with architects of the specific structures to ensure they supported the plan's goals. One important strategy was

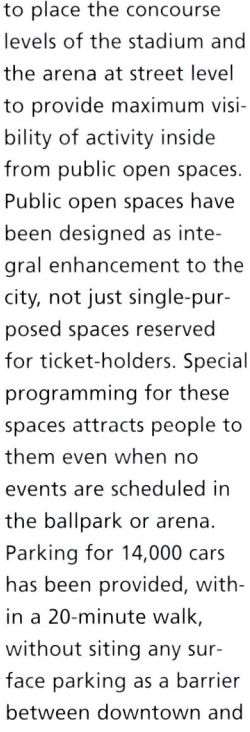

to place the concourse levels of the stadium and the arena at street level to provide maximum visibility of activity inside from public open spaces. Public open spaces have been designed as integral enhancement to the city, not just single-purposed spaces reserved for ticket-holders. Special programming for these spaces attracts people to them even when no events are scheduled in the ballpark or arena. Parking for 14,000 cars has been provided, within a 20-minute walk, without siting any surface parking as a barrier between downtown and Cleveland Gateway. A 2,100-car garage is included in the project. Full advantage is taken of existing streets and parking facilities, as well as Cleveland's well-used transit system.

Above, left: Gateway graphics underscore logic of plan.
Above: Plaza area between arena and garage blends into city street pattern.

SITE

25 Maiden Lane
New York
New York 10038
212.285.0120
212.285.0125 (Fax)
sitejw@interport.net
www.siteenvirodesign.com

SITE

Museum of Islamic Arts
Doha, Qatar

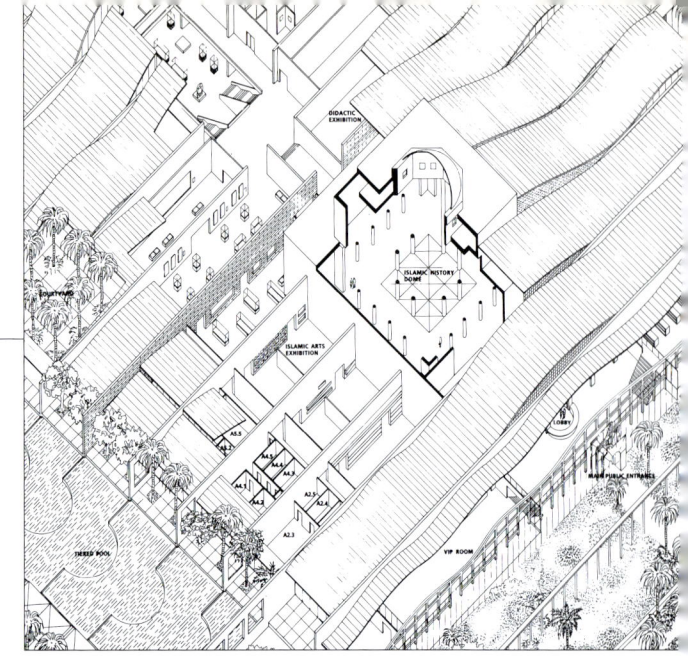

Right: Drawing shows parallel walls and bands of roof, with domed space for display of religious objects at center; mosque in garden at left.
Below: Model, with waterwall entrance in foreground.

Above: Undulating dunes of Qatar region.

Below, top to bottom: Model showing parallel museum walls extending outward, with linear bands becoming irregular toward edges of site; photo of site, the Gulf in distance; drawings of two interior walls incorporating architectural fragments.

Designed so that "the building is the garden and the garden is the building," this museum stresses the continuity of indoor and outdoor space. A series of parallel walls 12 meters apart extends through the galleries and out into the landscape. The sequence of walls includes a long glass water wall that filters light and cools the lobby (a grid structure showcasing fragments of Islamic architecture), and other walls with varying degrees of opacity, transparency, and perforation. Undulating roof planes create interiors with varied ceiling heights. The imagery of these roofs recalls several elements intrinsic to Doha: the rolling desert, the sea, nautical commerce, and the Islamic heritage. Technologically, the museum had to provide for the preservation of fragile objects without wasting energy. The design proposes radiant and passive solar cooling, planting to shade walls and courtyards, thermal storage using cool night air, and exhaust of daytime heat build-up. Exhibition showcases are built into walls, along with electronic display and communications systems, demonstrating a commitment to integration of architecture, cultural heritage, and information technology.

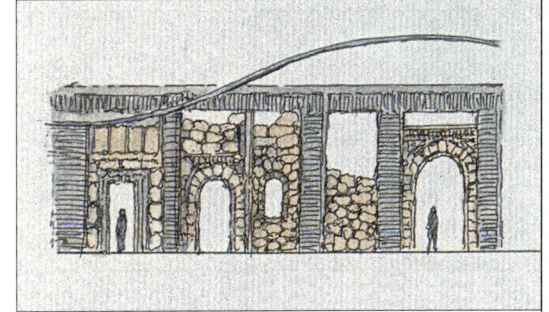

SITE

Ross's Landing Park and Plaza
Chattanooga, Tennessee

The public space and gardens at Ross's Landing are treated as a microcosm of the entire city and its region, encompassing both urban grid and flowing landscape. Part of a mixed-use revitalization program, the park area is the site of the Tennessee Aquarium, designed by Cambridge Seven Architects as the world's only aquarium dedicated to fresh-water aquatic life. One objective of the park and plaza design is to integrate the aquarium mass into riverfront public space. To create a readable equivalent for the regional terrain and cityscape, the site has been divided into 35 ribbons of paving, vegetation, and water, each 20 feet wide. Each band is assigned a period of years, progressing through the area's history, using artifacts, art, and quotations embedded in the paving to represent events such as the original settlement, the Civil War, and the Civil Rights Movement. Landscape elements trace the sequence from the mountains to the narrow valleys to the broad, fertile Tennessee Valley. Completed in 1992, the project is designed for future extensions to include playing fields, an amphitheater, and full access to the river edge via underpasses beneath a redesigned River Front Parkway.

Top: Watercourse disguising basement wall.
Above: Stonework with archeological and historical references.
Right: Ribbons of paving crossed by small stream.
Far right: Fountain at park entry with bridge-like "lifted landscape" and aquarium beyond.
Photography: SITE.

Above: Stream with small bridge and "lifted landscape" recalling mountain silhouette.
Right: Terraced water area offers variety of play options.

SITE

Horoscope Ring
Toyama, Japan

Top: Model of the ring.
Left: Horoscope designs on paving and planted landscape dividers.
Below left: Restaurant kiosk between dividers.
Bottom left: Ring at night.
Photography: SITE.

This project was designed to provide a small commercial complex surrounding a children's park in the mountain town of Toyama. At the request of community leaders to make this space a celebration of the horoscope, the project has been realized as a 62-meter-diameter circular plaza symbolically representing the constellations and the orbits of the planets. The paved surface is painted deep blue, with dividers that correspond to the intervals on a clock face. A six-meter wide ring enclosing the park shelters restaurants, food markets, and gift shops. The fin-shaped elements enclosing these shops suggest a ritual sundial. Regional vegetation planted on these raised elements echoes the forested mountains surrounding Toyama. Between these raised structures are rock gardens laid out in the pattern of star constellations. Toward the middle of the circle, concentric terraces accommodate changing displays of children's entertainment and play equipment.

SITE

Four Continents Bridge
Hiroshima, Japan

This commemorative footbridge is intended to celebrate the links between people and the natural environment. The form of the structure is derived from traditional arched Japanese bridges, but this project integrates that concept with contemporary technology and vegetation. Glass walls defining the ends and spine of the bridge are pierced by portals that offer pedestrians a variety of routes across the bridge. On one side of the central glass wall is a series of four terraria containing vegetation typical of four main geological and climatic quadrants of the earth. On the opposite side of the wall, visitors are able to see the layers of the earth through the glass. This glass wall's surface is washed by a continuous flow of water that forms a series of streams, then cascades over the edge of the bridge in an arc-shaped waterfall.

Top: Waterfall at edge of bridge.
Above: Overall view showing geographically varied plant life in terraria.
Right: Glass portal, with layers of earth visible to either side.
Photography: Natori (above), SITE (others).

223

SITE

USA Pavilion
Expo 2000
Hannover, Germany

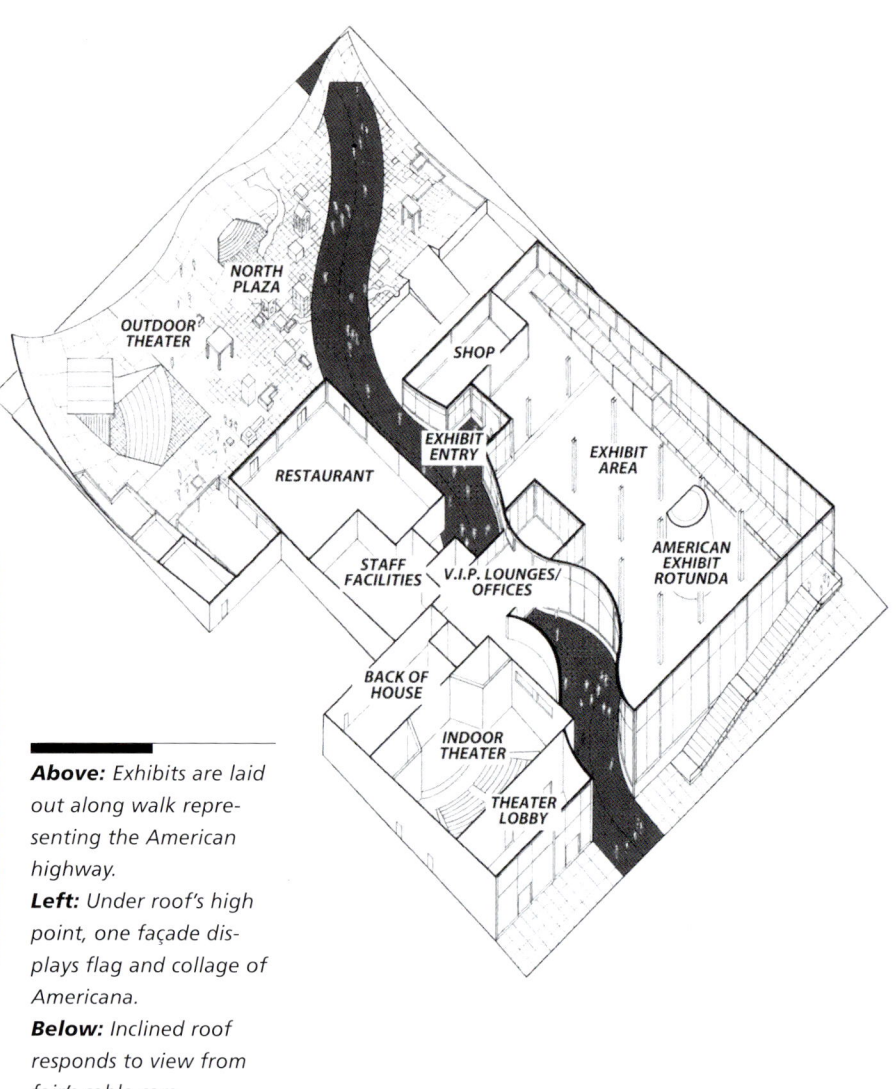

Above: Exhibits are laid out along walk representing the American highway.
Left: Under roof's high point, one façade displays flag and collage of Americana.
Below: Inclined roof responds to view from fair's cable cars.
Photography: SITE.

Embodying the theme of America's Diversity and Opportunity, this unbuilt proposal was designed as a microcosm of the country. The plaza and the roof levels are fused into a patchwork representing the American landscape. This design recognizes the site's aerial visibility from the fair's cable cars, which will carry 4,500 passengers per hour overhead. The planes of the plaza and roof form spaces for outdoor music and dance. A meandering walkway, inspired by the famous Route 66, carves out a processional route through the pavilion. Following the fair's environmental policies, the pavilion was to be composed of recyclable components and include demonstrations of devices such as photovoltaic panels and rammed-earth construction.

Skidmore, Owings & Merrill LLP

14 Wall Street	224 South Michigan Ave.
New York	Chicago
New York 10005	Illinois 60604
212.298.9300	312.554.9090
212.298.9500 (Fax)	312.360.4545 (Fax)
One Front Street	46 Berkeley Street
San Francisco	London, W1X 6NT
California 94104	United Kingdom
415.981.1555	011.44.171.930.9711
415.398.3214 (Fax)	011.44.171.930.9108 (Fax)

Skidmore, Owings & Merrill LLP

State Street Renovation Project
Chicago, Illinois

Left: Iron-fenced planting areas.
Above: Two-tiered lamp posts and subway entrance.
Facing page: Lighting and signage integrated in a corner lamp post.
Photography: Steincamp/Ballogg.

Only occasionally do cities recognize streets as urban spaces demanding architectural treatment. In the case of Chicago's State Street, the current objective was to undo damage inflicted by a 1979 conversion of the right-of-way through The Loop into a transit mall. Traditionally Chicago's center of shopping and entertainment, State Street had been flagging, despite such major projects as the new Central Public Library, the renovation of the great Marshall Field store, and the conversion of a former department store into the DePaul University Music Center. The $23-million renovation project, begun in 1996, called for narrowing the 50-foot sidewalks to their original width, with planting beds along the curb, new street lights replicating those that stood here from 1926 to 1958, and new subway entrances in harmony with the historic buildings. A self-guided culture walk, with enameled signs, celebrates the street's architecture.

Skidmore, Owings & Merrill LLP   Riverside South
New York, New York

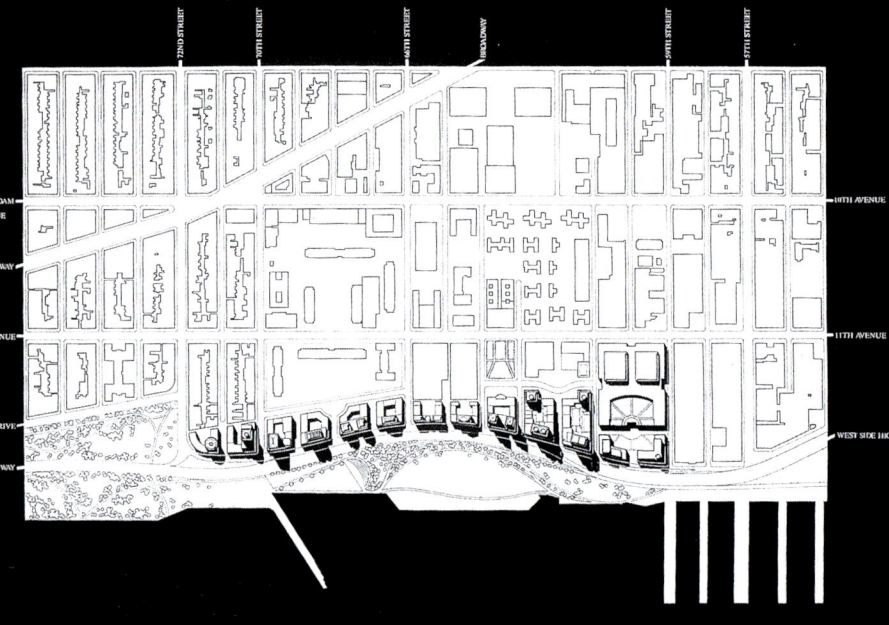

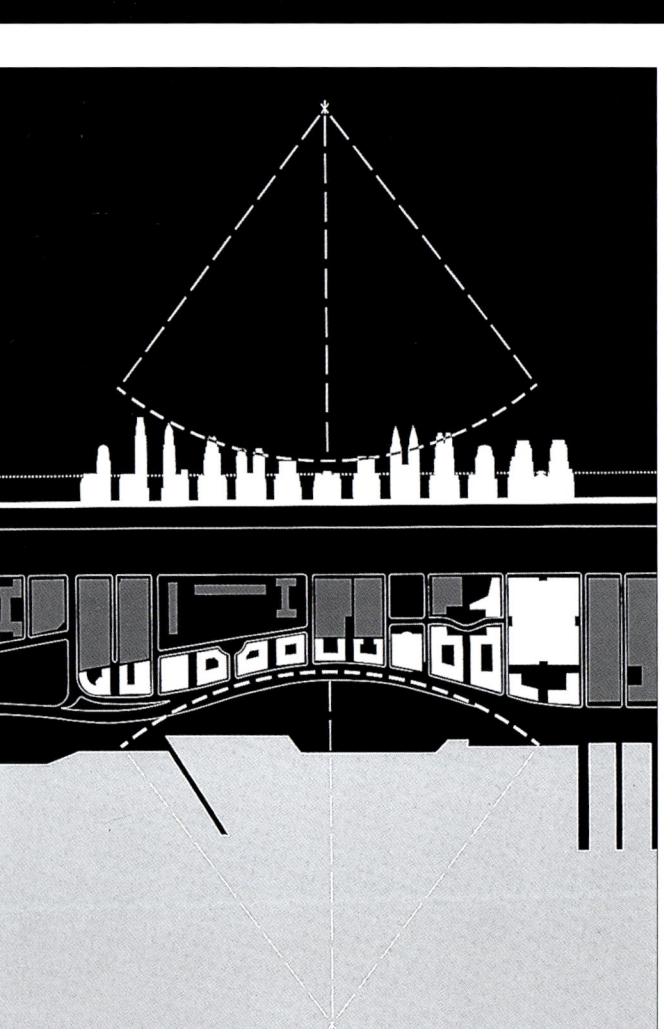

Left: Plan respects city's grid.
Below, left: Towers are tallest at ends of arc plan.
Model Photo: Skidmore, Owings & Merrill LLP.

The 55-acre tract along New York's Hudson Riverfront, between 59th and 72nd Streets, had already been the subject of several development plans that succumbed to community objections before a team led by SOM and architect Paul Willen produced this one in 1992. Formerly the site of a rail yard – and still crossed by an active Amtrak line – the property is separated from the river by the elevated West Side Highway and dilapidated piers. The plan calls for reconnecting the city to the river by continuing the street grid westward, extending Riverside Drive southward, and creating a 23-acre park along the waterfront. A key part of the proposal is the relocation of the West Side Highway inland and at grade, partially covered by the park. The proposed 8.3 million square feet of development includes 5,700 residential units, retail, offices, cultural and community facilities, and film studios. Guidelines for building massing maintain the traditional Manhattan pattern of streetwall townhouses and apartment blocks, with narrow towers taking advantage of the extraordinary views. Developed in intensive consultation with community and civic groups, the plan won city approval for extensive zoning revision and numerous special permits. Residential towers at the north end of the site are now under construction, and the relocation of the West Side Highway is still a subject of political debate.

Left: *Proposed building masses and park, looking south.*

Skidmore, Owings & Merrill LLP

Shanghai Waterfront Redevelopment Master Plan
Shanghai, China

Left: The Crescent presents its bold, consistent band of public space and mid-rise buildings.
Below left: The Panorama: A city the size of Shanghai needs generous and varied public open spaces. The Panorama provides such a space at the water's edge, allowing for passive and active recreation.
Artist: Christopher Grubbs.

Right: Historic Pier 16 will become festival marketplace, served by water-borne transit.
Below: Fingers of public green space will extend through residential developments to the river's edge.

The objective of this plan is to extend the most memorable image of Shanghai, the riverfront boulevard and esplanade of its historic Bund, along the entire waterfront. The plan conveived for Koos Real Estate Development Group outlines the strategy for redeveloping port properties along the Huangpo River. An opportunity is presented to create new vitality by reintegrating the city with its waterfront, providing generous public space, all within a climate of development and profit maximization. Along The Crescent, a consistent band of roadway, esplanade, and mid-rise residential buildings will reinforce the city's distinction and identity. Fingers of public green space will extend back from the river, deep into the urban fabric, providing view corridors and recreational amenities, along with enhanced property values.

Skidmore, Owings & Merrill LLP

G-MEX District Master Plan
Manchester, United Kingdom

Below left: Tree-lined link to G-MEX.
Bottom left: New square in front of renovated warehouse, office building site to left, retail units incorporating historic wall to right.

Below: Square incorporates hard and soft landscaping, and allows for easy pedestrian flow around amphitheater.
Photography: Andrew Putler.

The 50-acre site surrounding Manchester's G-MEX exhibition hall and its new concert hall had been the subject of numerous redevelopment proposals that failed to reconcile various public and private concerns. Undertaken with Leslie Jones Architects of Manchester, this scheme involves £5 million in public works and is now well into construction. Within an overall master plan that includes new residential, office, retail, hotel, and leisure uses, particular attention was given to the 12-acre site around the landmark Great Northern Warehouse. A new public space, Great Northern Square, in front of the warehouse, serves as a destination for a tree-lined thoroughfare leading to the G-MEX and the concert hall. Centering on a terraced amphitheater, the new square will be the forecourt for a mix of retail and leisure activities in the refurbished warehouse and new retail, restaurant, and commercial office structures on surrounding sites.

Smallwood, Reynolds, Stewart, Stewart & Associates, Inc.

One Piedmont Center
3565 Piedmont Road
Suite 303
Atlanta
Georgia 30305
404.233.5453
404.264.0929 (Fax)

Smallwood, Reynolds, Stewart, Stewart & Associates, Inc.

Residential

Right: Townhouses define garden at base of circular tower.
Photography: Gabriel Benzur.

The Oaks
Atlanta, Georgia

Opened in 1991, the Oaks has maintained its reputation as a prestigious address in the Buckhead section of Atlanta. A 30-story circular tower makes a strong statement on the skyline, and three-story townhouses are arranged to enclose a garden courtyard. A parking deck is situated behind the residences. Individual units vary from 1,012 square feet to 2,410-square-foot penthouse suites. The complex provides high-level security via card access and closed-circuit security monitoring.

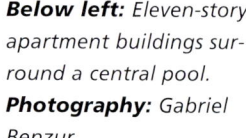

Below left: Eleven-story apartment buildings surround a central pool.
Photography: Gabriel Benzur.

Melville Park
Singapore

Situated on an 18.6-acre site, this project includes seven apartment buildings, with a total of 1,232 units. Each building is 11 stories high, with brick and plaster exterior walls designed to suggest a Mediterranean setting. Large-scale cornices, balcony projections and pediments give the complex unity and dignity. The largest private condominium project in Singapore, the development includes tennis courts, squash courts, a clubhouse, a swimming pool and below-grade parking for 1,200 cars.

Right: High-rise unit opens to formal gardens.
Below right: Paved entry court is between project's two buildings.
Photography: Gabriel Benzur.

The Mayfair
Atlanta, Georgia

For a site in Midtown Atlanta, the architects designed an apartment development with 675 units in two buildings. A high-rise tower and a medium-rise structure flank a paved entry court, sharing formal gardens and a croquet lawn. The design of the buildings follows 18th-Century British precedent, with distinctive iron railings on balconies. The wide variety of unit types range from studio apartments to two-bedroom suites. Amenities in the complex include a club room with a pub, a fitness center and a classically designed library. A 460-space parking deck is located behind and beneath the buildings. When the property was recently converted from a rental property to condominiums, two-thirds of the original renters purchased their units.

Smallwood, Reynolds, Stewart, Stewart & Associates, Inc.

Hotels

**J.W. Marriott
Atlanta, Georgia**
Rising above the upscale Lenox Square Mall, the 24-story Marriott Hotel and Conference Center is a highly visible destination. Its polished exterior of green glass and black granite, accented with stainless steel bands, is intended to add "sparkle" to its location. The 310,000-square-foot complex includes a penthouse level with a corporate lounge and presidential suite, high-tech meeting rooms, a ballroom, a 139-seat restaurant, a club and lobby lounge, an indoor swimming pool and health club, and a 400-space parking deck. The hotel is connected to both the Lenox Square Mall and the nearby MARTA transit station.

Left: New wing of Georgian Terrace at left defers to the original structure.
Photography: Gabriel Benzur.

Above: J.W. Marriott atrium between offices and lobby.
Photography: Gabriel Benzur.

**The Georgian Terrace
Atlanta, Georgia**
Built in 1912, the original Georgian Terrace (right in photo) is an Atlanta landmark. Just across the street from the historic Fox Theater, the hotel has welcomed many performers, including the stars of "Gone With the Wind" at its 1939 premier. By 1990, when the architects were commissioned to remodel and expand it, the building had been vacant and derelict for a decade. In addition to extensive renovation efforts to the original building, a new L-shaped, 19-story extension with similar brick, limestone and terra cotta details was sited to preserve the landmark's identity in the streetscape. The steel-and-glass link between the two structures is designed in the spirit of a turn-of-the-century conservatory.

Smallwood, Reynolds, Stewart, Stewart & Associates, Inc.

Federal Home Loan Bank
Atlanta, Georgia

Right: Symmetrical frontispiece distinguishes main facade.
Below right: Three-story segmental arch and fountain mark the main entrance.
Photography: Gabriel Benzur.

Reflecting the stability of its occupant, the 11-story structure housing the Federal Home Loan Bank has been designed as robust and composed, with a symmetrical facade suggesting its civic role. Cladding of sunset red granite, with bronze reflective glass, helps the structure to harmonize with surrounding buildings in its Peachtree Street location, including a landmark church. A three-story vaulted entrance arcade leads into the lobby, which features gray-pink Tennessee marble, mahogany veneer and railings, accented with stainless steel. A 415-space parking deck is situated behind the structure.

Smallwood, Reynolds, Stewart, Stewart & Associates, Inc.

Eleven Hundred Peachtree Street
Atlanta, Georgia

Left: Dining terrace at the tower's base.
Below left: Symmetrical tower with signature stepped pyramid crown.
Below right: Granite, marble and bronze-toned metal details at street level.
Photography: Gary Knight & Associates.

Readily identifiable on the Atlanta skyline is the stepped pyramid roof of this 28-story tower, whose prime tenant is Bell South Enterprises, Inc. The 618,000-square-foot structure features the symmetry and order of Neo-Classical precedents in the city. Its square shaft gives rise to an octagonal crown; its pyramid clad in nickel-colored metal recalls historic lead roofs. The base relates sensitively to smaller-scaled neighbors in the Midtown district. Polished granite and green marble lend distinction to the lower floors, where a landscaped plaza and dining terraces give the complex an appealing pedestrian scale.

Smallwood, Reynolds, Stewart, Stewart & Associates, Inc.

IJL Financial Center
Charlotte, North Carolina

Standing 30 stories tall, the IJL Center is a major component in the transformation of Charlotte's "Central City" district into a lively business, arts, retail, and entertainment area. The architects provided design services for the 750,000-square-foot structure, as well as master planning for the entire city block surrounding it. The office tower is notable for the oblong element with curved walls that appears to rise on the diagonal out of a rectangular lower block. The two parts are distinguished by varied cladding, using blue-gray tinted glass, precast concrete verticals, aluminum grillwork and polished metal finials. At the base of the structure is a plaza with shade trees, water features, outdoor seating and sculptural elements that connect it visually with the neighboring NationsBank Plaza to form a coherent "outdoor room." Street-level businesses in the building's low-rise extensions encourage pedestrian activity. The connected parking deck accommodates 1,000 vehicles on 10 levels.

Above left: Low-rise retail wings open from the plaza.
Above right: The tower appears to be composed of interlocking forms.
Right: Consistent canopies and facade details lend dignity to street-level businesses.
Photography: Gabriel Benzur.

Smallwood, Reynolds, Stewart, Stewart & Associates, Inc.

Capital Commons Public Plaza
Tallahassee, Florida

Above: The domed kiosk is the entrance to parking beneath the plaza.
Left: Formal plantings lend urban character to platform over underground garage.
Photography: Brian Robbins.

The City of Tallahassee faced a familiar challenge: balancing the practical need for downtown parking with the aesthetic need for public space. One solution is the development of Capital Commons, a landscaped two-acre plaza atop a five-level underground garage accommodating more than 1,000 vehicles. The highlight of the public space is a central steel and glass kiosk, which provides access to the parking below. Smallwood, Reynolds, Stewart, Stewart & Associates, Inc. provided master planning for the landscaped public space and architectural design for the garage below.

The Stubbins Associates, Inc.

1033 Massachusetts Avenue
Cambridge
Massachusetts 02138-5387
617.491.6450
617.491.7104 (Fax)
www.tsa-arch.com

The Stubbins Associates, Inc.

Citicorp Center
New York, New York

Left: With its 45-degree roof and smooth aluminum-and-glass envelope, Citicorp Center rises 914 feet above Midtown Manhattan streets.
Above: Retail court in the project's commercial atrium.
Photography: Norman McGrath.

Completed in 1977, Citicorp Center revealed new possibilities for the development of public open space and mixed-use facilities related to a high-rise office tower. By elevating the office block on 114-foot pylons, the design opened up ample space and light for a two-level plaza and a new St. Peter's Lutheran Church, built under an agreement to replace the 1905 church previously at the same location. Centering the pylons on the four faces of the square tower reduced their impact on the areas below and made the structure appear to almost levitate. The innovative 400-ton concrete inertia block at the top of the tower minimizes sway under wind loads. The 45-degree slope at the top of the tower, giving it a signature silhouette, is repeated in the roof of the church, which rises up through the street-level portion of the plaza like a polygonal outcropping. The church is clad in the same granite used in the plaza paving and stairs, which contrasts effectively with the sleek aluminum cladding of the tower. The complex's public open spaces begin one story below the street, where a sunken plaza offers access to two subway lines that cross at this point, to the

Above left: Sunken plaza at southwest corner of site leads to subways, church, and retail atrium.
Above right: Three levels of shops and restaurants facing atrium are topped by four floors of offices.
Right: Street-level plan of entire city block.
Below: Church (bottom left in photo) is self-contained landmark integrated into design. From sidewalk, passersby can look into 67-foot-high sanctuary.

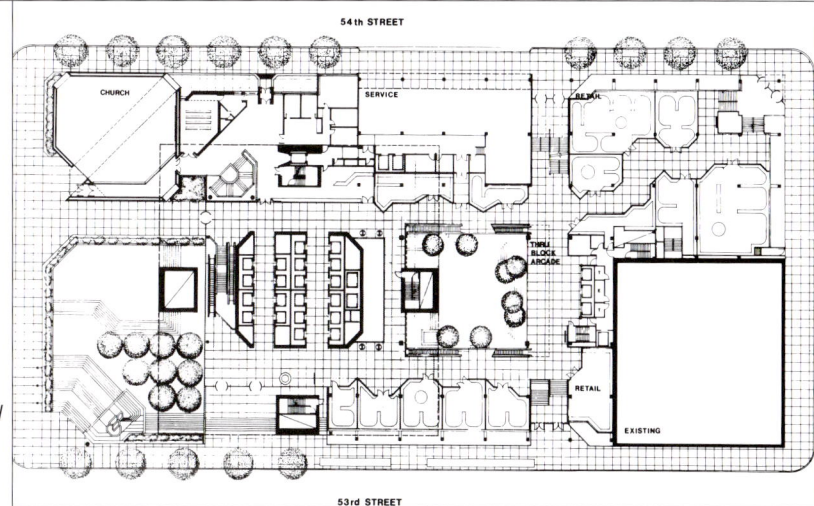

main level of the church, and to a low-rise commercial structure that covers most of the city block. The skylighted atrium at the center of this area is surrounded by three levels of retail and four floors of low-rise offices. Recent remodeling of Citicorp's public spaces confirms the long-term validity of its original concept.

The Stubbins Associates, Inc.

Treasury Building
Singapore

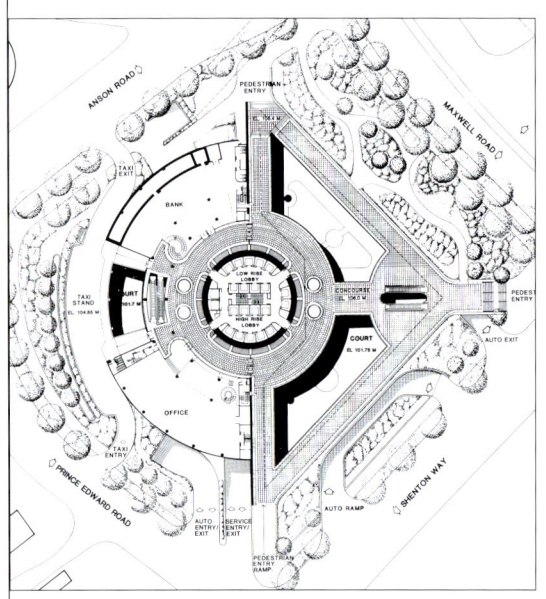

When completed in 1986, the 774-foot-high cylindrical shaft of this government and investment office building was the tallest building in Asia. The tower's composite structure, free of interior columns, responds to the client's request for a memorable landmark with a progressive, high-tech image, incorporating energy conservation strategies. The circular floor plan minimizes exterior surface in this hot, sunny climate, while two vertical notches integrate the tower with the site development and provide visual reference points to the city. Bronze-tinted glazing and painted aluminum spandrels minimize heat gain through the curtain wall. The site is bisected diagonally to provide pedestrian access from three corners. The east half of the tower is elevated to accommodate a space-frame canopy for weather protection at both street-level and lower-level entries. From the lower level courtyard, pedestrians can reach underground connections to neighboring buildings and to a planned transit station.

Left: Broad space-frame entrance canopy extends from the cylindrical tower.
Far left: Plan shows pedestrian entry from three corners of site, bridging lower-level courtyard.
Bottom photos: Space-frame canopy, partially exposed, shelters broad areas at street and lower courtyard levels.
Photography: This page, Peter Aaron; facing page, Kouo Shang-Wei.

Right: Continuous notches at two points on the tower's cylindrical envelope emphasize its verticality.

Also at the base of the complex are retail shops and an underground garage for 715 cars. The 1,431,000-square-foot project includes lobbies and banking facilities on the lower two floors, typical office floors on floors 7 through 48, except for dining, lounge, and meeting rooms on the 30th and 31st floors, and executive offices on the 50th floor.

The Stubbins Associates, Inc.

Venetian Casino Resort
Las Vegas, Nevada

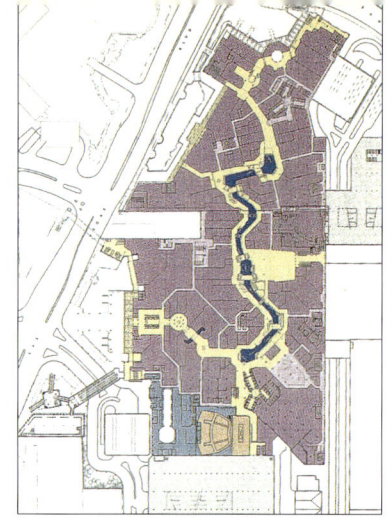

Top of page: Plan of the retail level, centered on an indoor canal environment.
Above: Two vignettes of Venetian-themed settings.
Above right: Phase I development, with the "Strip" in the foreground, guest room tower rising above casino and retail areas.

Currently under construction, the new Venetian Casino Resort and Convention Center will become the largest such facility in the world when completed in the year 2002. The master plan by The Stubbins Associates calls for two linked hotels, each with 3,300 suites. Each hotel will support its own casino and restaurants, and an enclosed retail mall will connect them to America's largest privately owned convention center and to Las Vegas Boulevard, the legendary "Strip." With a total of over 12 million square feet, the complex will be unified by The Stubbins Associates and collaborating architects WAT&G with one "fantasy architecture" theme. Lagoons and canals, with gondolas, along with architectural elements derived from the storied city of Venice, will surround visitors with an atmosphere of luxury and romance. Phase 1, shown here, will include casino and retail facilities at the base of the 37-story Venetian hotel tower and is to be completed in 1999. The adjoining Phase 2, currently in design, will include a second high-rise hotel, additional retail, ballroom/meeting rooms and parking.

The Stubbins Associates, Inc.

Shenzhen Cultural Plaza
Shenzhen, China

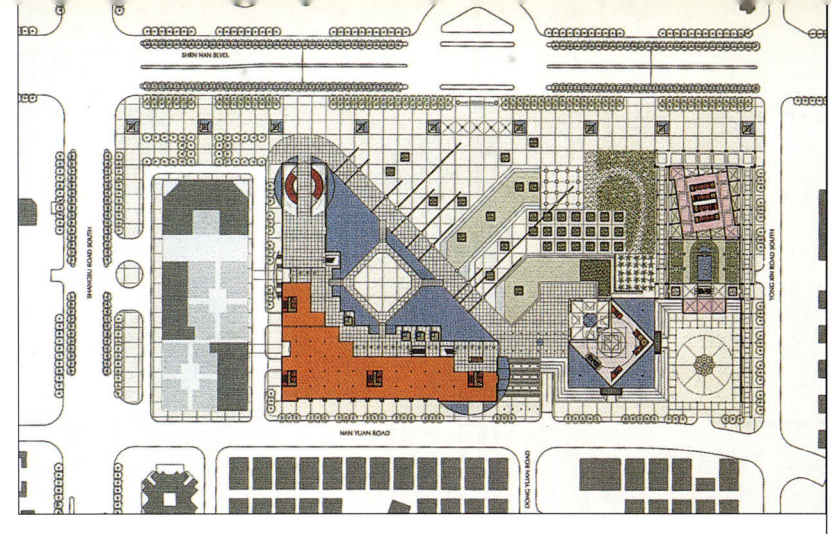

Top of page: Plan of site, main artery to north, residential area to south.
Above: Plaza with outdoor performance.
Right: Computer rendering of plaza with night lighting.
Below right: Plaza with evening events.

Twenty years ago, Shenzhen was a fishing village located across the border from Hong Kong. As a result of its designation as China's first Special Economic Zone, it has grown into a strikingly modern city of 3.3 million people. The Stubbins Associates has been commissioned to design a five-hectare (almost 13-acre) Culture Plaza complex in the heart of the city, on its central artery at the site of a proposed subway station. Uses of the complex will include retail, food service, exhibition, office, and communication. The plan will feature a diagonal pedestrian connector between the station and the existing residential neighborhood to the south. Activities will be most intense on the plaza during the evening hours, after the heat of the day, and lighting design will be critical. Emerging technologies will be incorporated in fountains, sound systems, and projection, using both conventional and laser devices. Traditional Feng Shui considerations have been applied to the design, seeking to capture the energy of both natural and human forces affecting the site.

The Stubbins Associates, Inc.

The Landmark Tower
Yokohama, Japan

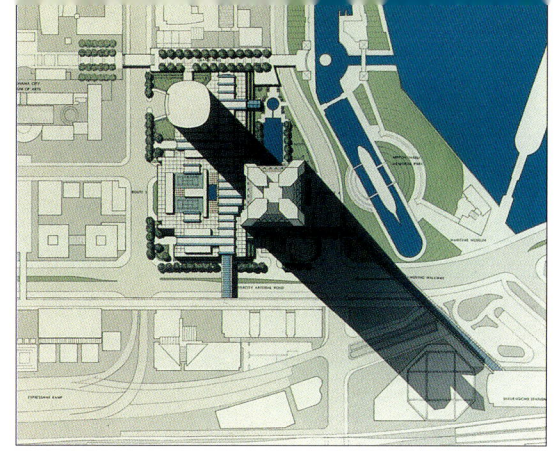

The 1,000-foot Landmark Tower, the tallest in Japan, is the focal point and first phase of a 4.5-million-square-foot megastructure known as Minato Mirai 21, on the Yokohama harborfront. Combined in one tapering tower are 1,750,000 square feet of office space on 52 floors and a 600-room Nikko Hotel on the top 15 floors. Above the guest room floors, which have X-shaped plans to yield desired exterior wall area, the topmost floors expand to accommodate restaurants and an observation deck. Hotel swimming, health, meeting, and banquet facilities are in a low-rise wing.

Top of page: Plan of built-out development.
Above and above right: Tower in waterfront context, with Mount Fuji in distance.
Right: Atrium in lower floors of complex.
Photography: Above, courtesy of Nikko Hotels; above right, courtesy of Mitsubishi Estate Co.; right, Kokyu Miwa.

SWA Group

2200 Bridgeway
PO Box 5904
Sausalito
California 94966.5904
415.332.5100
415.332.0719 (Fax)

Laguna Beach
714.497.5471
714.494.7861 (Fax)
Houston
713.868.1676
713.868.7409 (Fax)
Dallas
214.954.0016
214.954.1720 (Fax)

SWA Group

Capitol Commons
Indianapolis, Indiana

Below: Park picks up axis of capitol, although site is asymmetrical to it.
Bottom: Focal point of park is fountain of clashing jets.
Photography: Tom Fox.

A four-acre, full-city-block site has been developed as a park setting off Indiana's boldly sculptural 19th-Century capitol building. Developed in conjunction with an underground garage, the $6-million project provides a key connection between the capitol, the convention center, two major hotels, and the nearby Hoosier Dome. Brick walls and piers, wood trellises, and straightforward plantings make the park an orderly, relatively low-keyed foil for surrounding structures, while providing a variety of settings for quiet outdoor activities. The single dramatic element is the large fountain to one side of the central axis, in which jets of water converge in a dome-like mass of white foam, then fall into a shallow pool. Two smaller water jets rise from side pools in a composition that abstractly recalls the capitol's central and flanking domes.

Above right: Brick and wood details lend intimacy to parts of park.
Right: Distinctive fountain draws visitors.
Below: Trellises along site boundary screen unwanted views.
Bottom right: Space is well suited for social and civic gatherings.

251

SWA Group   Dallas West End Historic District
Dallas, Texas

To revive this near-downtown neighborhood, SWA was commissioned to draw up a land-use plan and an open-space policy, along with designs for public spaces and signage. The intention was to use public investment in open spaces to spur private investment in the area's existing loft structures and in compatible new structures. About $1 million in public funds was expended for brick walls, brick and concrete paving, outdoor seating, and live oak street trees. Historically authentic street lighting, compatible with pedestrian use, was installed. The area has attracted tenants and generated street life.

Right: Opening celebration for a renovated building.
Bottom left: Carriage rides and outdoor dining enliven area.
Bottom right. Bold night lighting, close by and in distance.
Photography: Tom Fox.

Top right: A nationally recognized tenant.
Middle right: Encouragement for street life.
Bottom right: Plan capitalizes on disruptions in street grid.

SWA Group

Arizona Center
Phoenix, Arizona

Left: Water cascades from curved food court terrace.
Below: Garden as seen from flanking office buildings, fan-shaped food court at upper right.
Photography: This page, Dixi Carrillo.

Right, top: Street entertainment in a paved peripheral area.
Right, middle: Canopies with vines and indirect uplighting.
Right, bottom: Date palms on circular pads along stream lined with river cobbles.
Photography: Dixi Carrillo, except bottom, Tom Fox.

A three-acre park is the centerpiece of a six-city-block redevelopment project, carried out by the Rouse Company. Walkways lead from the park to adjoining downtown destinations, including the convention center and the sports arena. The central focus is a modern-day oasis, with paving and plantings laid out in bold, modern geometrics. Ponds meander in a suggestion of natural streams, but between clearly artificial edges. Special efforts have been made to mitigate the city's severe low-desert heat. Water is present in still pools, running streams, and in fine temperature-reducing mists in some planted areas. A slight depression below grade at the center

tends to contain cooled air, as in a natural oasis. The most prominent plantings are the mature date palms, which survive in desert conditions while symbolizing oasis comfort. They were obtained by purchasing an entire California palm grove. While there are some ficus and other leafy trees, most shading is provided by canopies, designed to carry vines, over public spaces, and by denser louvers over the two-level food court structure. By night, indirect lighting set into railings and canopy supports generates a soft glow. The presence of lighted office building lobbies, restaurants, and nightclubs around the perimeter provides night safety without bright outdoor lighting.

Left, top: Gardens as a ceremonial setting.
Left, middle: Meandering walks through complex.
Left, bottom and above: Soft lighting integrated into railings.
Photography: Left, top: Tom Lamb; left, bottom: Gerry Campbell; others: Dixi Carrillo.

Torti Gallas and Partners • CHK

1300 Spring Street
4th Floor
Silver Spring
Maryland 20910
301.588.4800
301.650.2255 (Fax)

1528 Walnut Street
Suite 1225
Philadelphia
Pennsylvania 19102
215.546.3803
215.546.3805 (Fax)

Torti Gallas and Partners • CHK

The Garden in the Town and the City

The public realm has been shaped to give identity and coherence to a new town and a new city outside Istanbul. The steep topography of the sites interacts with local landscape traditions to inspire the design of distinctive gardens, piazzas, streets, stairs, terraces, esplanades, and other public spaces.

Left: Rendering shows main square at base of slope, overlooking playing fields.
Left, below: Core of development plan, main square at bottom.
Below: Spine of public spaces.
Rendering: Dariush (overall view).

Bahcesehir Phase 2 Istanbul, Turkey
The developer of Bahcesehir, Emlak Bankasi, has created a number of satellite towns around Turkish cities, responding to the nation's rapid urbanization and providing housing options for the growing middle class. For Bahcesehir, plans include 2,320 dwelling units ranging from apartments to freestanding villas, all within a walkable area, linked to Istanbul by rapid transit. There will be 10,000 square meters of office and retail space, including a six-theater cineplex, plus parking for 220 cars under the square. Public buildings, schools, mosques, and a number of parks will complete the community.

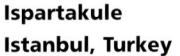

Left: Overall view, downtown in foreground.
Below left: Downtown scene.
Bottom left: Promenade high in a residential area.
Top right: High-rise apartments near downtown.
Right: Overall plan, downtown at top left.
Renderings: Risden McElroy.

Ispartakule
Istanbul, Turkey

At Ispartakule, a satellite city will be carefully fitted into 1,150 acres of demanding topography, bordered in part by existing squatter settlements. The downtown will be at one end of the site, along a rail line and the Trans-European Motorway. The completed development will include some 14,000 housing units, ranging from villas to high-rise apartments, plus about 550,000 square meters of retail, office, and entertainment facilities. The downtown includes a modern version of a Turkish bazaar, fronting on the main public spaces. Features elsewhere on the site include a Winter Plaza, sheltered from cold winds, and a Summer Plaza, placed at a high point to capture summer breezes.

259

Torti Gallas and Partners • CHK

Urban Plazas and Town Greens

The identity of any place, urban or rural, is shaped in large part by its public spaces and buildings. In a series of projects, the firm creates appropriate settings for new civic institutions by placing them on prominent open spaces. The specifics of the places and buildings rely on the character of the larger contexts in which they are set.

Left: New town is represented by 8,000-square-foot Community Building on first of its neighborhood greens.
Photography: Ali Etili

Neighborhood Green and Community Building, South Riding, Loudoun County, Virginia

The first public building for the new town of South Riding rises along a green in one of the five planned residential neighborhoods. The building includes offices, a meeting hall, and exhibits explaining the neo-traditional planning of the privately developed community. Planned to have over 6,000 housing units, plus extensive office, retail, industrial and public facilities, the town will have a larger-scaled town green with public and commercial buildings fronting onto it.

Left: Canopy for new metro stop stands in front of old market structure reused as Children's Museum.
Photography: Alain Jaramillo

Shot Tower West Entrance Plaza, Baltimore, Maryland

The Shot Tower stop on the Maryland Mass Transit new underground extension is the closest to Baltimore's thriving Inner Harbor culture/entertainment/retail area. The diagonal orientation of the stop to the city grid inspired the layout of the entrance shelter. Sailcloth stretched between double-curved trusses suggests the festive waterfront nearby. Areas of grass in the gridded brick paving provide picnic areas near the adjoining Children's Museum.

Left: Village Center symbolizes the mixed uses and planning principles of the new town.
Rendering: Dariush

Village Center, The King Farm, Montgomery County, Maryland

Adjacent to the last stop on a Washington Metro line, the Village Center represents the New Urbanist philosophy of the 440-acre King Farm new town. Retail, office, residential, and senior living buildings, convenient to transit, ensure activity for the historically evocative space. A larger town center and a light rail line to other points in Montgomery County (seen in rendering) are included in the town's long-range plans.

Old Town Commons, Alexandria, Virginia
Adjacent to Alexandria's historic district, Old Town Commons is a five-acre residential and commercial project around a 1.5-acre public space. Its principal street, leading to the Eisenhower Metro stop, is designed to provide the animated building fronts and outdoor seating found in the nearby old town. The one-million-square-foot project includes 1,860 parking spaces, about half underground and half in above-ground "podiums."

Right: Retail street and plaza.
Rendering: Dariush

Arlington Courthouse Plaza, Arlington, Virginia
A privately developed $150-million mixed-use development around the Arlington County Courthouse has become, since its 1991 completion, the downtown center for this Washington suburb. Its more than two million square feet of construction includes 395 residential units, 530,000 square feet of offices, 80,000 square feet of retail and an eight-plex cinema. The classical layout and detail of the public space reflects its civic role.

Left: Banner-decked canopy animates space.
Right: Traditional plantings set off stone facades.
Below: Fountains in traditional spirit.
Photography: Torti Gallas and Partners • CHK

Artery Plaza, Bethesda, Maryland
This 277,500-square-foot urban office building, completed in 1986, had to reconcile conflicting street grids in a congested area. A 1,500-square-foot plaza with a generous pedestrian loggia facilitates pedestrian movement between office lobbies, retail, and underground parking. Public art includes a cast glass fountain by Howard Ben Tre, seen in foreground of photo, and a building column by Jim Sanborn, located at the end of the loggia.

Right: Art in project includes cast glass fountain, foreground.
Photography: Torti Gallas and Partners • CHK

Torti Gallas and Partners • CHK

The Residential Street

The primary public space of cities and towns—the residential street—relies on building walls to define it. In developing street facades for new and infill streets across the Eastern United States, the firm reflects local traditions, whether shuttered windows in Old Town Alexandria, Virginia, bay fronts in Bethesda, Maryland, or the severely flat planes of Baltimore houses.

Left: Brick-and-wood house fronts echo historic houses of Old Town Alexandria.
Photography: *Torti Gallas and Partners • CHK*

Hearthstone Mews, Alexandria, Virginia
This 29-unit project had to fit into the historical context of Old Town Alexandria and win neighborhood association support. In order to retain the traditional relationship of house front to street, a mid-block alley was introduced for easy access to rear-load garages. Fenced private courtyards and trees planted on rear lot lines ensure an attractive environment in these alleys.

Left: Some of the nine houses in this private development.
Photography: *Torti Gallas and Partners • CHK*

Courts of Foxhall, Washington, D.C.
Nine townhouses of 3,000 square feet each maintain the architectural character of their existing residential neighborhood, as they were required to do. It was essential to respect the high degree of architectural detail on surrounding blocks, in this case by the use of custom precast elements in the house fronts and forecourt walls, and the design of unique front stairs. Garages are separate from the houses.

Left: Regular house fronts frame corner of new square.
Right: Rendering of fronts stresses vertical proportions and bold cornices.
Photography: *Alain Jaramillo*
Rendering: *Torti Gallas and Partners • CHK*

Lafayette Courts Baltimore, Maryland
In the imaginative conversion of a 1950s' public housing project to a sector of the city with real streets and squares (see page after next), the design of the house fronts was crucial. There was little question that the buildings should have the flat fronts typical of Baltimore rows, with low stoops and vertically proportioned openings. Arched street-level openings between houses are patterned after traditional shared passages to back yards.

Kemer Country, Istanbul, Turkey
In an unusually beautiful rural area outside Istanbul, adjacent to a 15th-century aqueduct, Kemer Country is a 180-unit resort community with the dual attractions of a golf course and a waterfront. Design of the buildings, comprising flats and duplex townhouses, reflects Turkish traditions, with walled courts forming the street edge and terraces overlooking the water to the rear. Waterside walkways encourage interaction among residents. The developer was delighted that all units sold from the architects' drawings within three months.

Right: Houses along typical street.
Below: Backs of houses and public walkway overlook water.
Renderings: Dariush

Montgomery Lane, Bethesda, Maryland
In this enclave in the heart of downtown Bethesda, 17 townhouses are laid out in short rows, facing a common street-scaled garden. A variety of projections and detail enliven the brick and precast concrete fronts. High parlor floors and fine detailing of cornices, gutters, and downspouts underscore the luxurious ambiance. Double garages for each unit are entered from rear alleys.

Right: Houses seen across common court.
Below: Distinctive details of bays, gables, and dormers.
Photography: Torti Gallas and Partners • CHK

Torti Gallas and Partners • CHK

The Urban Room

While the street remains the primary spatial volume of the American city, the residential square has persisted in our older cities, including Baltimore. In a new neighborhood that replaces a failed high-rise public housing project, the architects have organized streets of rowhouses around a central square.

Left: Community Building at the head of a boulevarded street.
Below: Formal residential square at opposite end of boulevarded street.
Below left: Plan, central portion of neighborhood.
Bottom row: Figure-ground plans of 1950, 1960, and 1997.
Photography: Alain Jaramillo

Lafayette Courts, Baltimore, Maryland
This neighborhood transformation replaced the no-man's-land layout of 1950s' public housing with a street pattern that rejoins it to the rest of the city. A major open space, designed as a formal square, gives the area a distinctive identity while providing opportunities for casual interaction and more formal community rituals. On axis with this main square is a Community Building created by remodeling an existing building on the site.

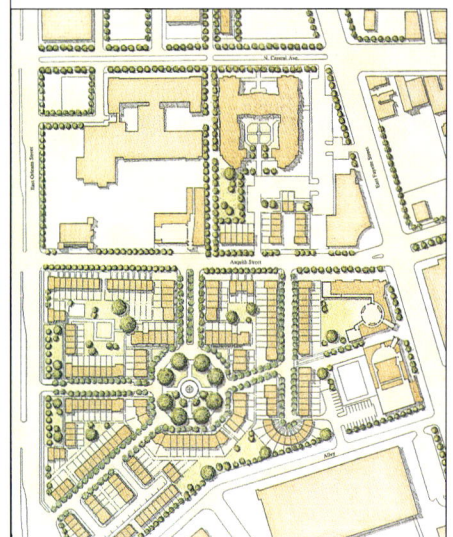

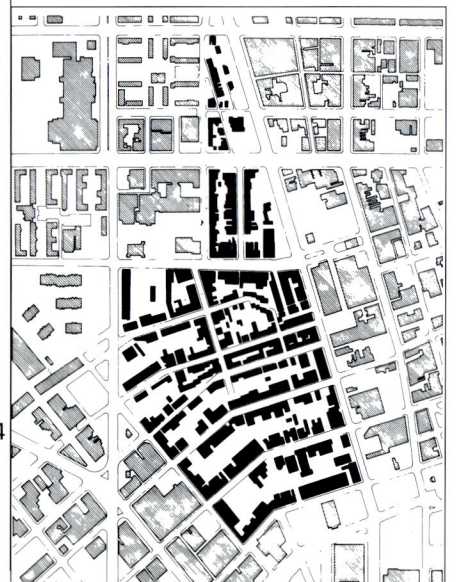
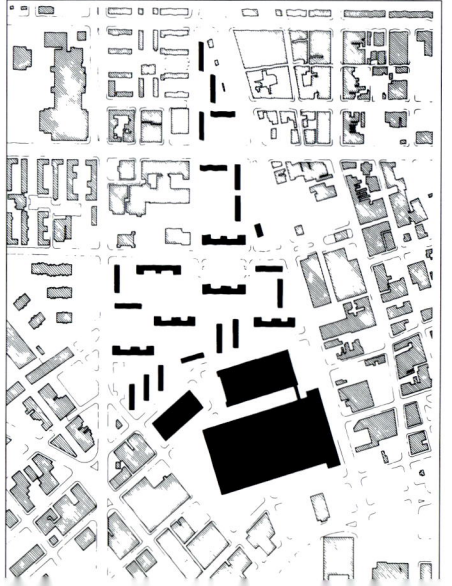
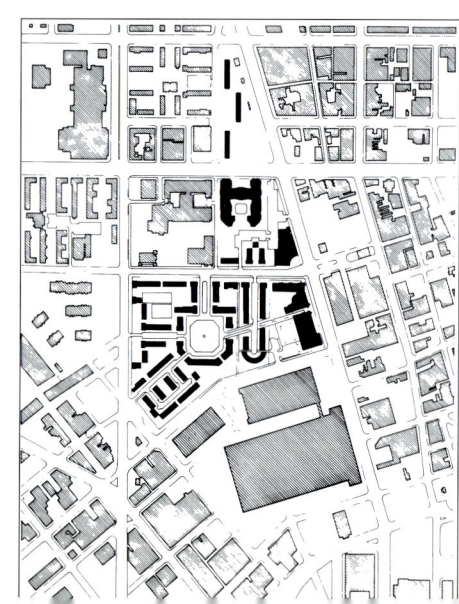

TVS/Thompson, Ventulett, Stainback & Associates, Inc.

2700 Promenade Two
1230 Peachtree Street NE
Atlanta
Georgia 30309.3591
404.888.6600
404.888.6700 (Fax)

TVS/Thompson, Ventulett,
Stainback & Associates, Inc.

McCormick Place
Chicago, Illinois

Left: *Concourse bridging Lake Shore Drive; Loop towers in distance.*
Below: *West entrance square.*
Right: *West entrance lobby.*
Far right: *Fountains at East Crescent.*
Far right, below: *Grand Concourse looking east.*
Photography: *Brian Gassel/Thompson, Ventulett, Stainback & Associates.*

TVS's 1997 addition to McCormick Place, the nation's largest convention center, brings its total floor area to over six million square feet. In designing this latest phase of a complex that had been growing incrementally for decades, TVS as design architects with A. Epstein and Sons International as architect of record were challenged to tie all of its parts together coherently and to give it a distinct public face. Their addition includes a quarter-mile-long Grand Concourse spanning Lake Shore Drive to link all the parts of the complex and make their relationships clear. In one bold stroke, it provides a linear reference point, offering orienting views toward the Loop. A new entrance to the whole center, by way of this concourse, takes the form of a public square, with appropriate urban landscaping around fountains. Also fronting on the square is an 800-room Hyatt Regency Hotel. The architects have emphasized daylight and views in the concourse and other interior public spaces. For durability and a sense of stability, the public interiors feature precast concrete columns and terrazzo floors. Sculptural walls, painted yellow, signal major transition points along the concourse.

TVS/Thompson, Ventulett, Stainback & Associates, Inc.

Georgia International Plaza
Atlanta, Georgia

Above: *70-foot towers light plaza and give it strong identity.*
Top: *Sculpture, "The Flair," by Richard MacDonald.*
Photography: *Brian Gassel/Thompson, Ventulett, Stainback & Associates.*

The new seven-acre plaza, completed for the 1996 Olympics, gives Atlanta a vital new public space between three structures that generate vast crowds: the Georgia World Congress Center, the Georgia Dome, and a future Atlanta Hawks arena. It extends the urban fabric by matching the elevation of the city's viaduct system, while concealing beneath it garages with 1,000 existing plus 1,000 new parking spaces. Precast concrete structural members carry the plaza over the garages, as well as a railroad track far below. On the plaza surface, fields of grass and tree-shaded groves are crossed by paths linking the flanking public assembly buildings, the adjacent transit station, and the city beyond. A large opening carved into the surface provides a light well and a monumental staircase leading down to the parking decks. Sixteen 70-foot-high light towers on a 110-foot grid define the central plaza, giving it a festive yet dignified image while providing virtually all the lighting for the entire space. By establishing a convincing public ground level far above actual grade, the project serves as a valuable precedent for future air-rights developments.

Top: Crowds on the plaza.
Above: Light towers with lower lighting pylons.
Left: Spacious lightwell/stairwell leading down to parking levels.

TVS/Thompson, Ventulett, Stainback & Associates, Inc.

Pennsylvania Convention Center
Philadelphia, Pennsylvania

Locating a major convention center in the heart of Philadelphia's business district was not easy, but the benefits to convention-goers and the center-city economy justified the effort. Fortunately, TVS with associated architect Vitetta Group and consulting architect Kelley/Maiello were able to reuse the vast landmark train shed of the Reading Terminal to provide a major part of the 1.3 million square feet required. In adapting the 90-foot-high, 260-foot-wide structure, dating from 1893, it was essential to leave its rare three-hinged wrought iron frame exposed to view. Half the shed's volume was left undivided as the Grand Hall, the major entry point for the center. In the other half, levels of meeting rooms were inserted below a 33,000-square-foot ballroom, in which the original frame is also

revealed. An extensive glass wall preserves the view of the continuous roof canopy from both the ballroom and the Grand Hall. Complementing the reused Reading Terminal to form the center is a new exhibition building, with a street front that recalls the rhythm and materials of surrounding streets. Projecting bay and bow windows reinforce the interrelationship of the lobby space with the street outside. The client's request for "hotel quality" finish materials has been met with the use of granite and limestone, patterned brick walkways, and ornate handrails. Vast areas of custom carpeting have been woven in patterns derived from 6 architectural elements of the old terminal. Over 100 artworks and craft pieces by six area artists enrich the complex.

Far left: Reading Terminal train shed, reused as component of convention center, with famous public market still operating on ground floor.
Left: Ballroom under old terminal roof, with unobstructed Grand Hall beyond glass wall.
Above and bottom left: Lobby of new exhibition hall portion interacts with lively street.
Photography: Brian Gassel/Thompson, Ventulett, Stainback & Associates.

TVS/Thompson, Ventulett, Stainback & Associates, Inc.

Plaza at King of Prussia
King of Prussia, Pennsylvania

Left: The Café Court recalls historic shopping arcades.
Below: Ornamental metal and traditional moldings combine to give the Café Court historical ambiance.
Bottom left: Multi-colored glass is combined into an elaborate and memorable pattern over the Café Court.
Photography: Brian Gassel/Thompson, Ventulett, Stainback & Associates.

The master plan by TVS for the redevelopment of the Plaza at King of Prussia provided the 2.7-million-square-foot shopping center with a strong organizing concept. A "figure 8" plan, with large courts at each anchor department store converges on a central Café Court, which serves as a meeting point at the heart of the complex. Restaurants on the upper level overlook a classical fountain at the center of the pedestrian street below. Architectural elements, combining exposed steel framing with classical moldings and ornate balustrades, recall the rich architectural heritage of the Philadelphia region. Domed skylights with individualized colored glass patterns create a unique identity for each department store court. Curved two-level retail arcades between the courts, with glass chandeliers and coffered ceilings provide a rhythm of warm light and elegant detailing.

Urban Design Associates

Gulf Tower
31st Floor
707 Grant Street
Pittsburgh
Pennsylvania 15219
412.263.5200
412.263.5202 (Fax)

Urban Design Associates

Tidewater Community College
Norfolk, Virginia

The college is a key element in the Downtown Norfolk 2000 plan to revitalize a commercial district that had died. It creates an urban campus in which college activities reactivate the streets. Campus quads were opened through selective demolition of old structures, and a sense of security established by linking these open spaces visually to the interiors of college buildings that flank them. The principle is illustrated in the relationship between the newly constructed science center, the central campus plaza, and the library, which is adapted from an old department store. Designed with architects Williams Tazewell & Associates, the new building has its main entrance facing the plaza, at the corner closest to the library, and generously glazed circulation spaces running along its plaza front. The longer-term intention is to revitalize Granby Street, which links these campus features and a third building – an old structure remodeled for classroom use. The college project is encouraging the street's transformation into a mixed residential, cultural, and retail corridor.

Above: Glazed circulation area in the science center faces plaza and library.
Top right: Science center and library adapted from old store define two sides of new plaza.
Right: Lighted corridors on every floor of science center maintain visual contact with plaza.
Photography: Paul Rocheleau.

Urban Design Associates

High Street Landing
Portsmouth, Virginia

Right: Section through inlet.
Middle right: Seaboard Building, a memorable landmark, includes waterside restaurant.
Bottom right: Aerial sketch of project.
Photography: Urban Design Associates.

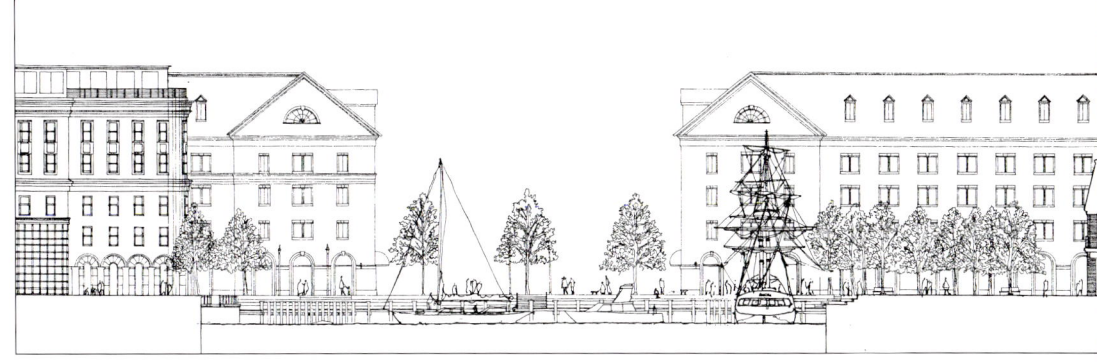

The first project of many improvements proposed in Urban Design Associates' Portsmouth Vision 2005 report, High Street Landing connects this city to the water at a key point. A new inlet was created at the foot of High Street, a commercial corridor threatened with decline, as a landing for the Portsmouth-Norfolk ferry. New landscape treatment around this water gateway continues the brick paving, historic lighting, and tree canopies specified for High Street. Park redevelopment along the seawall to either side of the inlet links several components of an urban museum, including the Naval Shipyard Museum facing the inlet, a light ship, a railroad caboose (representing Portsmouth's growth as a water-rail hub), and an outdoor display of historical maritime cannons. New lighting and landscaping will stress the continuity of the waterfront public space and make it a visible attraction as seen from the water. At the center of the inlet development, on the axis of High Street, is the existing Veteran's Memorial with its tall flagpole, a focal point for naval ceremonies. The Vision 2005 proposals, based on extensive community discussions, are widely supported as components of the city's economic development program.

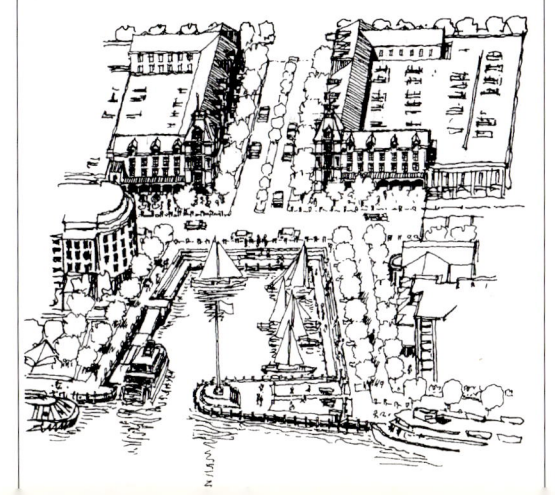

Urban Design Associates

Diggs Town
Norfolk, Virginia

Left and bottom left: Before and after drawings indicate measures taken.
Right and bottom right: Before and after photos show physical transformation.
Photography: Paul Rocheleau.

The barren open spaces of Diggs Town Public Housing have been transformed into livable neighborhoods with individual front yards, porches, and street addresses. Built in the 1950s, the low-rise structures suffered from anonymous façades and no-man's-land open spaces. Six months of local meetings contributed to the rehabilitation plan. Such elements as traditional streets and fences give residents a feeling of control and pride. Simultaneous community efforts addressed problems of drugs, unemployment, and education. As a result, police calls to Diggs Town have dropped from about 200 a week to two or three. The project has won several awards including a Presidential Design Award and an AIA Honor Award for Urban Design.

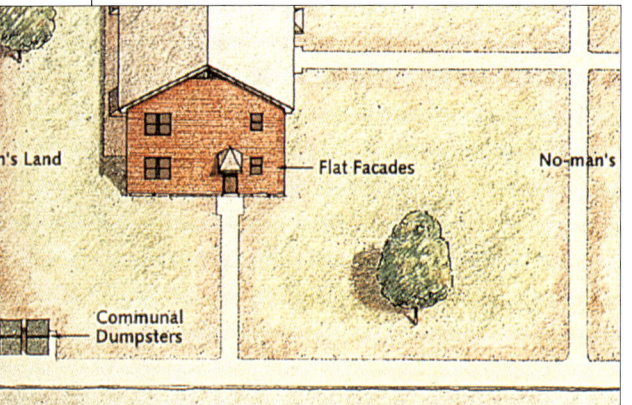

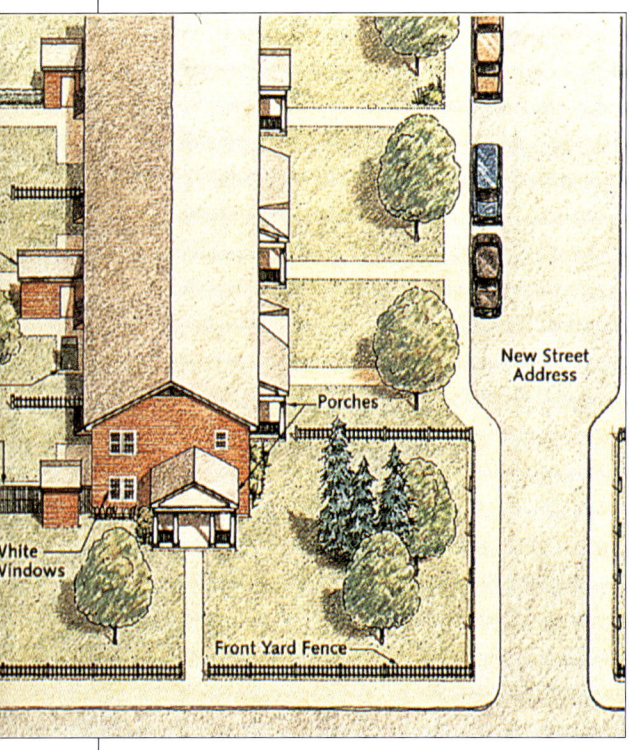

Urban Design Associates

Randolph Neighborhood
Richmond, Virginia

Above and Right: Porches survey street.
Below and bottom: Pattern book guided façades.
Photography: Tom Bernard.

The master plan for this 76-acre tract, cleared for urban development more than a decade earlier, called for some 600 dwelling units, including public housing, subsidized rentals, and affordable units for sale. The street plan replicates Richmond's traditional small blocks, with rear service alleys, and includes three parks. A UDA Pattern Book™ specified allowable building volumes, roof pitches, façade projections, and porches, among other features required of the builders.

277

Urban Design Associates

Pattern Book
Celebration, Florida

Above: Townhouses facing school grounds are limited to Classical style.
Left: Freestanding houses illustrate consistency of setbacks from street, variety of styles.
Photography: Sylvia Martin, © 1997 Southern Living, Inc.

For the new town of Celebration, Florida, Urban Design Associates drew up a pattern book for residential design to accompany the master plan by Cooper Robertson Associates and Robert A.M. Stern Architects. Established by the Disney Development Company, Celebration is meant to demonstrate how Neo-Traditional planning can revive a sense of community, with residents at various income levels living in close proximity, within walking distance of stores, schools, and other community facilities.

House design is governed by the pattern book, which specifies six styles appropriate to the region – Classical, Victorian, Colonial Revival, Coastal, Mediterranean, and French – spelling out each design's allowable dimensions, eaves projections, window and door details, etc. To give distinct character to certain streets and squares, tighter limitations are set on permitted styles or other design options.

Above right: Core of Celebration built out according to pattern book. Houses front distinctive streets and squares, with downtown on lake at upper left, town golf course at right.
Right and bottom right: Colonial Revival, one of six permitted styles, is illustrated with sketches and text that specify elements such as simple roofs ("ridge usually parallel to street") and multipaned ("6 over 6" or "8 over 8") windows.

Urban Design Associates

SMS Engineering Building
Pittsburgh, Pennsylvania

Reestablishing an urban street space was a prime objective of Urban Design Associates' new building for the SMS Engineering Company. Redevelopment demolition had left big gaps in this former industrial area, just across the bridge from Pittsburgh's downtown. Sited across a major street from two renovated warehouses, one adapted for offices and one as the Andy Warhol Museum, the five-story, 80,000-square-foot structure does not quite meet the warehouses' height, but reaches toward their cornice lines with a prominent steel canopy above the entry. The city's tradition of practical industrial architecture is recalled in the building's red brick walls and piers and horizontal window bands in aluminum-clad bays.

Top: Section of SMS, with facing warehouse structures and bridge towers beyond.
Above: Canopy marks entry on a facade that acknowledges area's industrial past.
Photography: Paul Rocheleau.

Van Tilburg, Banvard & Soderbergh, Architects, AIA

225 Arizona Avenue
Penthouse
Santa Monica
California 90401
310.394.0273
310.394.2424 (Fax)

1860 Blake Street
Suite 170
Denver
Colorado 80202
303.675.0041
303.675.0052 (Fax)

Van Tilburg, Banvard & Soderbergh, Architects, AIA

Janss Court
Santa Monica, California

This mixed-use complex not only meets the provisions of the specific plan for revitalizing Santa Monica's Third Street Promenade, but interprets them creatively to further the city's goals. The Promenade is a late 1980s' rehab of a failed 1960s' pedestrian mall. The first new project built along the Promenade, Janss Court benefited from density bonuses by providing a 20-foot-wide passage to a city garage behind the site, and for including housing within the downtown area. The result is a 131,041-square-foot structure with restaurants at street level, four cinemas at and below street level, three floors of rental office space, and 32 apartments at the top. Although on-site parking was not required, there are 203 spaces below grade, assigned to the office and residential tenants. The cinemas, entered through an Art Deco movie house façade already on the site, support evening activity. Although market-rate apartments on a commercial street were previously untried in Santa Monica, the location and amenities of these units have supported 100 percent occupancy.

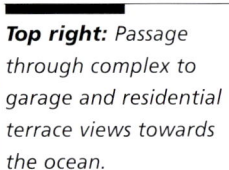

Top right: Passage through complex to garage and residential terrace views towards the ocean.
Above: View from Promenade.
Right: Urban plaza with sculpture in front of Janns Court.
Photography: Michael Arden.

Van Tilburg, Banvard & Soderbergh, Architects, AIA

225 Arizona Avenue
Santa Monica, California

Located, like Janss Court, on the newly revived Third Street Promenade, this building houses the architects' own offices, along with other tenants. With its long elevation on Arizona Avenue, the structure terraces back from the promenade to a vaulted peak above the main entrance and lobby. The extensive metal-framed windows and the shallow vaulted roofs recall elements prevalent in Santa Monica's old warehouses and workshops, transposed into a very different scale and setting. Another design source evident in the composition and details of the façades is the Wiener Werkstätte, the pioneering Modern Movement of Vienna circa 1900. The 26,500-square-foot structure contains restaurants on the ground floor, with offices on the upper stories.

Top right: Building's tiered volume marks a key intersection.
Center right: Entry leads into gardened lobby.
Right: Wall details recall spare ornamentation of turn-of-the-century Vienna.
Photography: Michael Arden.

Van Tilburg, Banvard & Soderbergh, Architects, AIA

Holly Street Village Pasadena, California

Above right: Paseo through complex from park to City Hall.
Left: Main entry plaza.
Below left: Former Hall of Justice, adapted for artist lofts, forms one side of the pool court.
Bottom: Aerial view shows village in relation to civic center, dominated by Baroque Revival City Hall and of churches.
Photography: Michael Arden and Slone Photography.

An "urban village" comprising 384 rental apartments plus community facilities constitutes, say the architects, "a paradigm for mixed-use development in Southern California." New three-, four- and five-story structures, arranged around courtyards of various sizes and shapes, share the site with the city's former Hall of Justice, adapted for spacious but spartan "artist loft" units. The project also includes the adaptive reuse of the historically significant adjacent YMCA building, into a 120 single-room-occupancy residential facility. Neighborhood needs are served by 11,000 square feet of retail and restaurants, with sidewalk cafés along the principal street frontages. Twenty percent of apartments are reserved for lower-income families. The whole village is constructed above two levels of parking, plus an active railroad right-of-way. Within the garage is a "shell" for a future MetroRail Blue Line station, linking downtown Pasadena to downtown Los Angeles.

Van Tilburg, Banvard & Soderbergh, Architects, AIA

Venice Renaissance
Venice, California

Top right: *Historical Venice from Venice of America.*
Above: *Retail arcade.*
Right: *"Ballerina Clown" at one corner by Jonathon Borofsky.*
Center right: *Senior units along street have small balconies.*
Bottom right: *Condos at rear overlook pool.*
Photography: *Michael Arden, except above, by architects.*

Built in a beach community with strong anti-growth sentiment, this project responded in part to a survey on community attitudes. Originally conceived as a residential development, the project includes 26,000 square feet of retail to support the rejuvenation of Main Street, 66 market-rate condominiums, and 23 low-cost rental units for seniors, some designed for wheelchair accessibility. Parking at and below grade goes beyond the 368 spaces needed for tenants to include 26 spaces for neighbors and 79 for weekend beach visitors. The three chevron shaped condominium buildings provide ocean views for the residents and define the active and passive landscaped courtyards with generous pool and lawn areas with walks and benches. Street-level arcades, balconies, and red tile roofs capture the Mediterranean look envisioned by Venice's visionary developers back in 1911. The ornate column capitals are duplicates of a surviving capital from that period.

Van Tilburg, Banvard & Soderbergh, Architects, AIA

Wilshire Borgata
West Los Angeles, California

Above left: Pool and garden between residential wings.
Above center and right: Interior views of top floor loft unit.
Left: Fountain at residential motor entry.
Far left: Commercial frontage with two-story retail windows.
Bottom left: Plan of third floor, with apartments around pool.
Photography: Michael Arden, except far left, by architects.

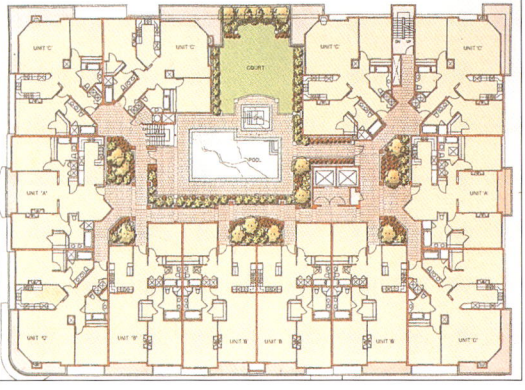

The mixed-use "boulevard" buildings of 19th- and early 20th-Century European cities are models for this six-story, 88,000-square-foot structure. It was built under an ordinance that permits the floor-area ratio to double (from 1.5 to 3.0 in this case) for residential projects that include retail and reserve 20 percent of the residential units for low-to-moderate-income tenants. The ground floor includes 10,000 square feet of retail, along with commercial tenant parking, the residential motorcourt and entry lobby, and access to two below-grade parking levels. On the second floor, 12 affordable condominiums surround a core of offices, fitness facilities, and meeting and community rooms. From the third to the sixth floors, 48 market-rate condominiums surround a court with a pool and garden shared by homeowners and their guests.

Van Tilburg, Banvard & Soderbergh, Architects, AIA

Villas of Renaissance
La Jolla, California

Right: Pedestrian paseo leads to courtyards and recreation areas.
Below: Clubhouse is distinguished by arcades and Renaissance-inspired dome.
Photography: John R. Bare.

This 922-unit apartment development occupies 15.5 acres of a master-planned community for which an Italian Hill Town theme had been established. Design guidelines call for elements such as tile roofs, pale washed walls, arches and columns, and buildings set at varied angles. Courtyards with pergolas and fountains underscore the theme. For construction economy, two standard building footprints were established and situated either singly or in pairs, as site characteristics determined. Selectively eliminating fourth-floor units and strategically locating loft units allowed for three-, four-, or five-story elements of various street elevations, for the desired variety of massing. Residents share the use of heated pools and spas and a 15,000-square-foot clubhouse, with a fitness center, an entertainment center, lounges, and meeting rooms.

Van Tilburg, Banvard & Soderbergh, Architects, AIA

Oxnard Factory Outlet
Oxnard, California

This 284,500-square-foot outlet was inspired by Oxnard's agrarian history interpreted through the use of vibrant colors, roof material and shapes, structural farm building framing, and fruit crate label signage. Enlarged reproductions of fruit labels appear on tilt-up concrete walls; sheet metal ventilators cap roofs of the corrugated metal; a windmill and a water tank form the skyline. Building materials were selected with economy and scheduling among the main considerations. The landscape concept was to treat the entry drive as a shaded allée and the parking lots as traditional orchards.

Top right: Windmill, exposed framing, and industrial lights establish farmland image.
Above: Corrugated sheet metal awnings and attic ventilators recall the area's agrarian history.
Right: No-nonsense construction includes exposed steel members and tilt-up concrete walls.
Photography: Mark Lohman.

"I told my architect we wanted a place where ideas can't help but collide. A space that gives us an edge on the competition. Where the techi and the artist both feel at home. And work is what you escape to, not from." When you want an architect to build on your vision, call a member of The American Institute of Architects.

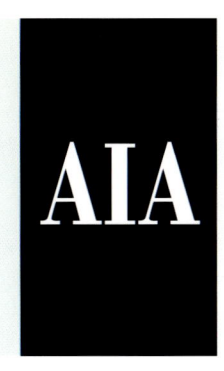

AIA

Building on Your Vision.

THE AMERICAN INSTITUTE OF ARCHITECTS

aiaonline.com

Buildings that engage.

Client: Samitaur Constructs • Tenant: Pittard Sullivan, Culver City, California • Architect: Eric Owen Moss Architects

Ten Easy Lessons on Urban Redevelopment

Daniel A. Biederman

For 20 years, Daniel A. Biederman has been working to turn around commercial districts in Midtown Manhattan at the invitation of property owners and three New York City mayors. He has created three highly successful Business Improvement Districts, two of which he leads today. BIDs, called by various names in different states, are financial vehicles that allow the private sector to supplement—and in some cases replace—public services in areas where the private sector feels it has been underserved. Biederman's experiences offer plenty of lessons for those interested in replicating his success.

Private property owners and their tenants have been the real heroes of our efforts in Midtown Manhattan. They have spent hundreds of hours working with us and have generously supported our programs to reclaim these districts, so that today the Midtown BIDs constitute a $20-million "business" devoted to improving the quality of life for the area's office workers, shoppers, tourists, and residents.

By any standard, our BIDs have been successful. Bryant Park, our first project and showpiece, has been transformed from a park with 150 robberies a year (and an occasional murder), ugly drug markets, and graffiti into a world-renowned park with beautiful gardens, exciting entertainment, attractive and successful concessions, and total crime of only four felonies in the past seven years. Drugs in Bryant Park are just a bad memory.

The Grand Central Partnership is the most ambitious in the United States, setting an example for others in the comprehensiveness of its programs, the sophistication of its financing techniques, and its attention to minute details. Crime is down more than 70 percent in the Grand Central area, street litter is nonexistent, more than 800 homeless people who used to occupy the streets and the terminal are now in temporary or permanent housing, and a beautiful new streetscape greets office workers and other travelers on their way through this vital urban district.

The latest of these efforts, the 34th Street Partnership, succeeded—in just five years—in cutting crime more than 50 percent, eliminating what used to be ankle-deep litter on every corner, removing graffiti from the area, and lighting up streets so that visitors to Madison Square Garden, the Empire State Building, Macy's flagship Herald Square store, and Pennsylvania Station no longer feel intimidated and enjoy walking the streets. We have just opened a smaller version of our success with Bryant Park, fixing up the legendary Herald and Greeley Square parks.

Every week, I am asked by representatives of other neighborhoods, cities, and nations how to replicate this success. I have boiled down most of what I have learned in this business into the following 10 easy lessons for reviving commercial neighborhoods:

1. **Top quality people are essential.** Private consulting firms and Silicon Valley companies take this for granted, but sometimes the public organizations that usually run neighborhoods don't seem to get it. The workers who police, clean, and rebuild the capital plants of commercial districts must be chosen strictly on merit. They must be led by someone with vision and allowed to make mistakes in pursuit of top quality. When managers and staff members clearly cannot get the job done, they must be replaced by those who can. And a sizable portion of the organization's work week must be consumed in teaching all employees how to serve their clients better.

2. **Choose great models to emulate.** Most of the great ideas and accomplishments in our projects were copied from other places, many of them far from Midtown Manhattan. Much of our work is not invention but synthesis of the best ideas of others. In place-making, some groups we've admired are the Rouse Company, the Disney Company, Rockefeller Center, the city of Paris, and even the U.S. National Park Service. One can also learn a lot by wandering around Union Station in Washington, D.C., any city or town run by a top city manager, or many of America's small towns.

3. **High standards are essential.** Although it is often a disagreeable role, leaders of any renovation effort must be absolutely insatiable in their quest for the best possible performance from all of their people. In the security area, for example, we aim for no crime. We learned early on in our quest to fix Bryant Park that Rockefeller Center had less than one armed robbery per year, and we decided that we'd get there, too! Zero tolerance of graffiti also turned out to be an achievable goal, as did the placement (against all conventional wisdom) of beautiful trees, flowers, and vines throughout the formerly gray pavement of Midtown.

4. **Begin with the basics.** It has become a bit of a downtown management cliché, but "clean and safe" are two standards that must be achieved before people feel comfortable in an area. Once these are achieved, other existing problems seem to be more glaring: the absence of vegetation; the functioning of urban amenities like taxis (we put in staffed taxi stands); the ugliness of many public and private signs. Once you have achieved clean and safe, you have the credibility and support to attack dozens of smaller problems.

5. **Learn to look at the street differently.** I once sat in a car on K Street in Washington, D.C., with a famous marketing executive and asked if he'd like to hear the 50 things I could see wrong with the street from where we sat. After 17 years of obsessing about these details, it wasn't hard to name them. The executive told me that he'd "never look at a street in the same way again." I've learned to look at streets differently from dozens of mentors: William H. Whyte, Jr., Ben Thompson, Ed Bacon, Peter Malkin, Hugh Hardy, Laurie Olin, Fred Papert, Frank Stanton, Marshall Rose and many of the property owners, asset managers, and building managers who have supported our efforts over the years. Any effort to fix up a deteriorated commercial district needs people with trained eyes to lead it.

6. **Avoid peripheral issues.** Many cities and developers have come to me for help only to describe an apparently insurmountable, unrelated problem that they believe will make progress very difficult. The problems cited almost always seem to me to be completely beside the point: racial politics, conflicts between residential neighborhoods and commercial/retail areas over city funds, loyalties to longstanding but unsuccessful civic organizations, and many more. To succeed, you simply must ignore these kinds of distractions, pressing forward with tunnel vision toward your objective. It is not always a recipe for popularity in the public forum, but it works!

7. **Avoid political views of the world.** Politics is the art of the possible, and compromise is admired and valued. But compromising your vision of a great commercial district is almost fatal to the success of your effort. In turning around Bryant Park, we said "no" to countless groups that wanted to chip away at the pristine nature of our vision. Many of those who originally demanded that we compromise now enjoy, admire, and reward the final results. But without the backing of people like the Rockefeller brothers and the leaders of the New York Public Library, we might not have been able to keep our vision intact.

8. **Think of your district as the center of the world.** Once your district is on its way to a turnaround, arguing its centrality helps in marketing the results to outsiders. Almost every city or commercial district had an original reason for being, and efforts like ours often rediscover that reason. Urban redevelopment is not a game for the modest.

9. **Create multiple revenue sources to finance capital and operating needs.** Bryant Park, in particular, has benefited from the diversity of its several revenue sources, allowing us to avoid service reductions and to surprise the public with continual improvements in park services. Arranging dedicated revenue streams that survive the coming and going of city administrations is crucial. While I question whether the BID movement is the right long-term vehicle for urban rehabilitation, I'm quite interested in the future of dedicated, segregated revenue sources of other kinds.

10. **Have patience!** Having worked for more than five frustrating years on a single project, one day on the subway I met one of New York's savviest environmental lawyers. I poured out my frustration to him, questioning whether the project would ever be successful. I often tell my staff members what he told me that day. "The public forum," he said, "is ultimately a rational place. Any sensible proposal to create a public good, backed by intelligent and reasonably powerful people of good will, will ultimately be accepted." He was right. Your project *will* succeed.

Daniel A. Biederman is an urban redevelopment consultant whose projects have included Midtown Manhattan's Bryant Park, Grand Central Partnership and 34th Street Partnership.

Now you can know who's who, how-to, what's news—anytime, anywhere.

It's Independence Day. Now, ULI members have even greater access to the resources of the Institute, and each other, at www.uli.org. The ULI Web site has been redesigned for easier navigation, and better yet, there will be more to find once you're there, such as:

Land Use Digest Europe
Joining ULI's popular Land Use Digest will be a new online newsletter for Europe. Every other month, ULI will publish a dozen abstracts of articles and research published in Europe.

E-News
A new e-mail newsletter on Smart Growth launches this summer, delivering 25-30 abstracts of articles weekly.

Inside Capital Markets
ULI Fellow Steve Blank is hosting a section of the Web site on capital markets, filled with practical information and insights on what's happening and what it means for real estate.

District Councils
For fast access, ULI's 40 District Councils have their own pages on ULI's site.

Need work?
Every month, *Urban Land* features Requests for Qualifications (RFQs) and Requests for Proposals (RFPs), but readers needed more time to craft their response and advertisers are looking for fast action. Now, *Urban Land* has its own section on the Web site for "Business Opportunities" which will be updated with the most recent advertisements as they come in.

Easier to use
Now you can search ULI's entire Web site using a keyword search. You'll find every reference in abstracts, bookstore descriptions, *Urban Land* text and research reports published at www.uli.org. You can narrow your search to keep it targeted or look at every reference. Search engines for the Bookstore have been overhauled so you don't have to have exact titles, just your topic.

Members-only
In addition to the directory of ULI's 15,000 members, you can also find some new services behind the member log on screen: Ask Joan; *Urban Land*; referral and prospect directories.

Ask Joan is ULI's new web bibliographic service. Keyword searches will generate bibliographies of everything we have on hand, freeing you to work when and where you want.

Text archives of *Urban Land* magazine articles published since 1992 will be online for easy keyword searches and downloadable text.

New additions to the Web directory are listings for prospective members and personal access to referrals. Find out how to cash in points earned in the Talent Search Sweepstakes, update your own record or make additional referrals, all online.

Join ULI and connect wtih more than 15,000 members worldwide. Call 800-321-5011 to join today and get your password I.D.

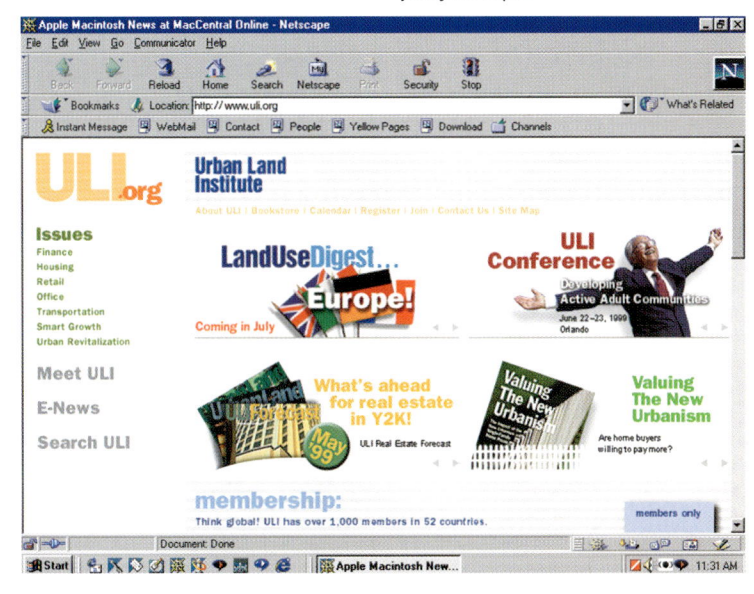

Join ULI. Get connected.

PROJECT CREDITS

ALTOON + PORTER ARCHITECTS

Fashion Valley Center
Client: The Equitable Life Assurance Society of the United States
Developer: Lend Lease Real Estate Investments
Principal Consultants:
Altoon + Porter Architects, site master plan, architectural design
Robert E. Bayley Construction, general contractor
Robert Englekirk, Inc., structural engineer
Store, Matakovich & Wolfberg, plumbing engineer
Nikolakopulos & Associates, electrical engineer
Francis Krahe & Associates, Inc., lighting designer
Rolf Jensen & Associates, fire protection/building code consultants
Ralph Mellman & Associates, specifications
Woodward-Clyde Consultants, soils engineer
Wimmer Yamada Associates, landscape architect

Kaahumanu Center
Client: Maui Land and Pineapple, Inc.
Principal Consultants:
Altoon + Porter Architects, master planning, architectural design
Robert Englekirk, Inc., structural engineer
Critchfield Mechanical, Inc., mechanical engineers/subcontractor
Toft Moss Farrow Associates, electrical engineer
Rolf Jensen & Associates, code consultant
Wheel Gersztoff Friedman Shankar, Inc., lighting designers
Keller Construction USPB, general contractor
Birdair, Inc., fabric roof
Ronald M. Fukumoto Engineering, Inc., civil engineer
Tongg, Clarke & McCelvey Landscape Architects, landscape architect

Tower Place
Client: Faison Associates
Principal Consultants:
Altoon + Porter Architects, architectural design
The FWA Group, Inc., associated architects
Turner Construction, contractor
Benner & Fields, mechanical engineer
Engineers, Inc., electrical engineer
King/Guinn Associates, structural engineer
Rolf Jensen & Associates, fire safety/building code
Francis Krahe & Associates, Inc., lighting designer

ARAI / JACKSON ARCHITECTS AND PLANNERS

Seattle Central Community College Student Activities Center
Client: Seattle Central Community College
Principal Consultants:
Arai/Jackson Architects & Planners, architect of record/urban design
Streeter & Associates Architects, associate architect
KPFF Engineers, civil and structural engineer
Abacus Engineers, mechanical and electrical engineers
Swift & Company, landscape architect
Cecelia Alvarez, Frank Video, artists

Tacoma Dome Transportation Station
Client: Pierce Transit
Principal Consultants:
Arai/Jackson Architects & Planners, architect/urban design
Berger/ABAM Engineers, Inc., engineer of record
BCE Engineers, lighting design
Hornall Anderson Design Works and Pierce Transit, graphic design, graphics
Don Shimono Associates, landscape architect

Southwest Harbor Project, Terminal 5 Expansion Public Access
Client: Port of Seattle
Principal Consultants:
Arai/Jackson Architects & Planners, architects of record
KPFF Engineers, engineer of record
Hough Beck and Baird, landscape architect
Path Engineers, mechanical and electrical engineers

Angle Lake Park Improvements, Phase 1
Client: City of SeaTac
Principal Consultants:
Arai/Jackson Architects & Planners, architect of record
MacLeod Reckord, landscape architect
Pai Lin Engineering, structural engineer
Path Engineers, mechanical and electrical engineers

Meadowbrook Community Center
Client: City of Seattle, Department of Parks and Recreation
Principal Consultants:
Arai/Jackson Architects & Planners, architect of record
Kobayashi & Associates, landscape architect
Abacus Engineered Systems, mechanical and electrical engineers
Symonds Consulting Engineers, structural and civil engineers

BRENNAN BEER GORMAN / ARCHITECTS

Sudirman Central Business District, Gateway Precinct
Principal Consultants:
Brennan Beer Gorman / Architects, master planners, Gateway Precinct
Nippon Koei Co., Ltd. and CMPS & F Pty., Ltd., joint master plan consultants, entire district
Philip Cox Richardson Taylor and Partners Pty, Ltd., town planning consultant, entire district

Conrad International Center
Client: P.T. Arthayasa Grahatama
Owner/Developer: Conrad International Hotels
Principal Consultants:
Brennan Beer Gorman / Architects, design architects
P.T. Airmas Asri, local architect
Thornton-Tomasetti Engineers with Wiratman & Associates, structural engineers
Lehr Associates Consulting Engineers with P.T. Arnan Pratama Consultants, mep engineering

Jakarta Financial Tower
Client: P.T. Artasanga Utama (Intama)
Principal Consultant:
Brennan Beer Gorman/Architects, design architect

Jakarta Stock Exchange Building
Client: P.T. Danareksa Jakarta International
Principal Consultants:
Brennan Beer Gorman/Architects, design architect
JSEB Local Design Consortium, local architect
Encona Construction Management, construction manager
P.T. Arnan Pratama Consultants, mep engineering
Becca, Carter, Hollings & Ferner, Ltd., with JSEB Local Design Consortium, structural engineers
P.T. Arkonin, local architect and structural engineer
P.T. Encona Engineering, Ltd., local architect
Atelier Six, local architect

The Colgate Center
Client: The Colgate Palmolive Company
Principal Consultants:
Brennan Beer Gorman/Architects, master plan architects
Cushman Realty Corporation, development consultants
Sasaki Associates, landscape consultants
Atlee, King, Rosen & Fleming, environmental consultants
Langan Engineering, civil engineers
Gorove/Slade, traffic engineers
Woodward-Clyde Engineers, environmental engineers

101 Hudson
Client: LCOR Incorporated, developer
Principal Consultants:
Brennan Beer Gorman/Architects, architects
Morse Diesel, general contractor
Jaros, Baum & Bolles, mep engineers
Severud Associates, structural engineers

CALLISON ARCHITECTURE, INC.

U.S. Bank Centre

Harbor Steps — Phase I
Arthur Erickson, plaza design

Carillon Point

Wells Fargo + Starbucks

Fashion Show Mall

COOPER CARRY, INC.

SunTrust Financial Centre
Clients: Joint venture of The Landmarks Group, Collier Enterprises, and The Teachers' Insurance Annuity Association
Principal Consultants:
Cooper Carry, Inc., architectural design, landscape architecture, master planning, interior design of public spaces

Post, Buckley, Schuh, Jernigan, Inc., traffic
Walter P. Moore & Associates, Inc., civil and structural engineer
B&A Consulting Engineers, mechanical and electrical engineer
Walker Parking Consultants, parking
Newmont Elevator Analysts, Inc., elevator
Shen, Milson & Wilke Associates, Inc., acoustical engineer
Gordon H. Smith Corporation, curtainwall
Fisher Marantz Renfro Stone, Inc., lighting design

Bethesda Retail District
Client: Federal Realty Investment Trust
Principal Consultants:
Cooper Carry, Inc. master planning, architectural design
Structural Design Group, Limited, structural engineer
Macris, Hendricks and Glascock, P.A., civil engineer
Allen & Shariff Corporations, mep engineer
Core Group, Inc., associate architect
Mobius Design, associate architect

Mizner Park
Clients: Crocker & Co./TIAA and Boca Raton Community Redevelopment Agency
Principal Consultants:
Cooper Carry, Inc., master planning, architectural design, interior design
Fisher-Marantz, lighting design
Tracy Turner Design, environmental graphics
Gorove-Slade, transportation design
Haynes Whaley and Burton Braswell Middlebrooks & Associates, structural engineers
Caulfield & Wheeler, Inc., civil engineers
Warren E. McCormick, landscape architects
R.A. Kamm & Associates, mep engineers
Centex Rooney and HCB Contractors, contractors

DUANY PLATER-ZYBERK & COMPANY

Kentlands
Founders: Joseph Alfandre & Co.
Great Seneca Development Corporation
Many contributors

Town of Seaside
Founder: Robert Davis
Many contributors

Village of Windsor
Founders: Galen and Hilary Weston
Many contributors

Riverside by Post
Founder: Post Properties
Principal Consultants:
Niles Bolton Associates
Smallwood, Reynolds, Stewart, Stewart & Associates, Inc.
Planners and Engineers Collaborative

EDAW

Centennial Olympic Park
Client: Georgia World Congress Center Authority
Principal Consultants:
EDAW, Inc., master planning, urban design, landscape architecture, project management, prime consultant
Turner Associates, project architect
The SWA Group, associated landscape architect
Thompson Ventulett Stainback & Associates, associated urban designer
Project for Public Spaces, Inc., public art program
Law Engineering & Environmental Services, environmental analysis
Delon Hampton & Associates, civil/site engineering
Thompson Company, Inc., water feature engineering
Cecil Chan & Associates, structural/MEP engineering
Lighting Design Alliance, lighting design, phase 1
Ramon Luminance Design, lighting design, phase 2
Street Smarts, traffic/parking analysis
Wm. Hobbs, Ltd., fountain design

Washington Harbour
Client: Western Development Corporation
Principal Consultants:
Arthur Cotton Moore, architect, prime consultant
EDAW, Inc., preliminary site planning, landscape architecture and urban design for all open space, including plaza, rooftop, and adjacent parking

Canal City Hakata
Client: Fukuoka Jisho Urban Development
Principal Consultant:
The Jerde Partnership International, Inc., architects; prime consultant
EDAW, Inc., landscape/hardscape design; overall coordination of all site components

Selbert Perkins Design, environmental graphics
WET, water features
Joe Kaplan Architectural Lighting, lighting

Coors Field
Client: Denver Metropolitan Major League Baseball Stadium
Principal Consultants:
HOK Sport, architects; prime consultants
EDAW, Inc., site planning, landscape architecture
M.A. Mortenson/Barton Malow, general contractors

EDSA, EDWARD D. STONE, JR. AND ASSOCIATES

Fort Lauderdale Beach Revitalization
Client: City of Fort Lauderdale
Principal Consultants:
EDSA, planners, landscape architects
Williams, Hatfield and Stoner, engineering
Resource Management International (RMI), electrical/lighting

Broward County Library
Client: Broward County
Principal Consultants:
Marcel Breuer Associates and Miller & Meier and Associates, architects
EDSA, landscape architect
H.J. Ross, engineer
George Hyman Construction, builder/contractor

Riverwalk
Client: City of Fort Lauderdale
Principal Consultants:
EDSA, planning, landscape architecture, graphic design
DeRose and Slopey, electrical and structural engineer
ATF, architectural
EDSA, civil engineering

Barnett Plaza
Client: Paragon Group
Principal Consultants:
EDSA, planners, landscape architects
Howard Branston Lighting, lighting
Rudolf de Harak, graphics

ELKUS / MANFREDI ARCHITECTS LTD

28 State Street
Client: Equity Office Properties
Principal Consultants:
Congress Group Ventures, development manager
Elkus/Manfredi Architects Ltd, architect/interior designer
Suffolk Construction Company, general contractor
Hughes, Good, O'Leary & Ryan, landscape architect
Cosentini Associates, m/e/p consulting engineer
Weidlinger Associates, structural engineer
Heitmann and Associates, curtain wall
Lerch/Bates, vertical transportation
John Prosser, code consultant

Sansom Common
Client: University of Pennsylvania
Principal Consultants:
Elkus/Manfredi Architects Ltd, base building architect (hotel and bookstore)
Jones Lang LaSalle, development manager/client rep
William Jackson Ewing, Inc., leasing agent
Brennan Beer Gorman Monk, hotel interior architect
Antunovich Associates, bookstore interior architect
Pennell & Wiltberger, Inc., m/e/p engineer
O'Donnell & Naccarato, structural engineer
Andropogon Associates Ltd., landscape architect
Barton & Martin Engineers, civil engineer
Grenald Waldron Associates, lighting design

730 North Michigan Avenue
Client: Joint venture of Thomas J. Klutznick Company, McDonald's Corporation, and Himmel and Company, Inc.
Principal Consultants:
Elkus/Manfredi Architects Ltd, master planner/base building architect
Design Consultants:
Backen Aragoni & Ross, Inc., Pottery Barn
Polo/Ralph Lauren Store Design, Peter Marino Architect, Naomi Leff and Associates, Inc., Polo Ralph Lauren (Mansion)
James Harb Architects, Polo/Ralph Lauren (Townhouse)
Tiffany & Co. in-house design team
Banana Republic in-house design team
Kim, Casey & Harase, Inc., m/e/p engineer
John A. Martin & Associates, structural engineer
W.E. O'Neil Construction Company, general contractor

CityPlace
Client: CityPlace Partners (a partnership of Himmel and Company, Inc., The O'Connor Group, The Related Group of Florida, The Related Companies, LP)
Principal Consultants:
Elkus/Manfredi Architects Ltd, master plan and design architect
Roger Fry, residential architect
REG Architects, Inc., performance hall architect
Wolfberg Alvarez & Partners, architect of record and engineering
E&S Construction Engineers, Inc., mechanical engineer
Craven Thompson & Associates, civil engineer
Sasaki Associates, landscape design architect
Bradshaw Gill, landscape architect of record
Fisher Marantz Renfro Stone, lighting design.
Wet Design, fountain design

ELS / ELBASANI & LOGAN ARCHITECTS

The Shops at Arizona Center
Client: Rouse-Arizona Center, Inc.
Client Architect: Laurin B. Askew, Jr., FAIA
Principal Consultants:
ELS/Elbasani & Logan Architects
Plummer Hasan & Associates, structural engineers
The SWA Group, landscape architect
Communication Arts Inc., graphics consultant
Jules Fisher & Paul Marantz, Inc., lighting consultant

Pioneer Place
Client: Rouse-Portland, Inc.
Client Architect: Laurin B. Askew, Jr., FAIA
Principal Consultants:
ELS/Elbasani & Logan Architects
OLMM Structural Design, structural engineers
Sussman/Prejza & Co., Inc., graphics consultant
Jules Fisher & Paul Marantz, Inc., lighting consultant

Clarke Quay
Client: DBS Land/Raffles International Limited
Richard Helfer, executive director
Principal Consultants:
ELS/Elbasani & Logan Architects, design architect
RSP Architects Planners & Engineers, local architect & engineers
EDAW, Inc., landscape architect
Architectural Lighting Design, lighting consultant

A. EPSTEIN AND SONS INTERNATIONAL, INC.

Chicago Urban Entertainment District
Client: Name withheld upon request
Principal Consultants:
A. Epstein and Sons International, Inc., site analysis, development master plan, infrastructure design concept

Museum of Science and Industry New Parking Garage and Lobby
Client: Museum of Science and Industry
Principal Consultants:
A. Epstein and Sons International, Inc., architectural design, structural engineering, interior design
Jacobs/Ryan, landscape architects
E. Verner Johnson, museum planning
ESD, mep engineering

Midway Terminal Development Program
Client: Municipal and private clients
Principal Consultants:
A. Epstein and Sons International, Inc., HNTB, McDonough Associates Inc., architectural design, all engineering, signage, graphics, lighting
Dan Weinbach & Associates, landscape architects

"Four Elements," the Welcome to Chicago Midway Monument
Client: Municipal client
Principal Consultants:
A. Epstein and Sons International, Inc., programming, site selection, architectural design, construction documents

South Wells Self Park
Client: General Parking
Principal Consultants:
A. Epstein and Sons International, Inc., planning approval, architectural design
Jacobs/Ryan, landscape architects
Carl Walker, structural engineering
Don McLean, graphics

Midway Airport Exit Toll Plaza
Client: City of Chicago, Dept. of Aviation
Principal Consultants
A. Epstein and Sons International, Inc., architectural design and engineering
Rubinos & Mesia, structural engineering

Riga "Ratsnams" District
Client: Name withheld upon request
Principal Consultants:
A. Epstein and Sons International, Inc., design concept, development master plan

Quest International
Client: Quest International
Principal Consultants:
A. Epstein and Sons International, Inc., site selection, feasibility study, architectural design, engineering, construction documents
The Brickman Group, landscape architects

Moscow Botanical Garden
Clients: University of Moscow, plus private developer
Principal Consultants:
A. Epstein and Sons International, Inc., master planning
Kim Wilkie, landscape architect

GENSLER

Oracle Corporation Campus
Client: William Wilson & Associates
Principal Consultants:
Gensler, architects
Webcor Builders, Inc., general contractor
Dan Kiley / Peter Walker, master plan landscape architect
Peter Walker / Martha Schwartz, landscape design architect
Ron Herman, landscape design architect
Amphion, landscape architect of record

GLATTING JACKSON KERSCHER ANGLIN LOPEZ RINEHART, INC.

West Orange Trail
Client: Orange County Parks and Recreation Department
Principal Consultants:
Glatting Jackson Kerscher Anglin Lopez Rinehart, Inc., project management, landscape architecture
DAO Engineering Inc.
Lotspeich and Associates
Transportation Engineering, Inc.
GeoData Consultants
Donald W. McIntosh Associates, Inc.
Brindley Pieters and Associates, Inc.
Geotech Consultants, Inc.

Primera
Client: James E. Long, Commissioner of Insurance for the State of North Carolina
Principal Consultants:
Glenwood Properties, Inc., John (Sandy) Acton, client's representative
Glatting Jackson Kercher Anglin Lopez Rinehart, Inc., master planning, project management
Dyer Riddle Mills & Precourt, Inc., and Blount Sikes & Associates, engineers
Foster Conant & Associates, Inc., landscape architects
Shaughnessy Hart & Associates, Inc., signage

GOODY CLANCY & ASSOCIATES

Massachusetts Transportation Building
Client: Commonwealth of Massachusetts, Department of Public Works
Principal Consultants:
Goody Clancy & Associates, feasibility study, architectural design
Shooshanian, mep consultant
LeMessurier, structural consultant
Falk Associates, specifications and cost estimating

Harbor Point
Clients: Harbor Point Apartments Co. and Corcoran Jennison Co.
Principal Consultants:
Goody Clancy & Associates, urban planning, architectural design
Carol R. Johnson & Associates, landscape architects
David M. Berg, Inc., structural consultant
C.A. Crowley Engineering, Inc., mechanical consultant
Verne G. Norman Associates, Inc., electrical consultant

The Freedom Trail
Client: National Park Service
Principal Consultants:
Goody Clancy & Associates, master plan for entire Freedom Trail
Heritage Partners, Inc., management consultant
Candace Jenkins, historic preservation
CityDesign Collaborative, landscape design
Fay, Spofford & Thorndike, Inc., transportation
Office of Thomas J. Martin, economic feasibility
Shary Page Berg, cultural landscapes
Sherry Kafka Wagner, interpretation

Old State House and Faneuil Hall
Client: National Park Service
Principal Consultants:
Goody, Clancy & Associates, architectural design for renovation of Old State House and Faneuil Hall
LeMessurier, structural
R.G. Vanderweil Engineers, Inc., ME/E
Falk Associates, cost & construction
Carol R. Johnson & Associates, landscape
Preservation Technology, preservation
A.J. Martini, contractor

Tent City
Client: Tent City Corporation and Community Development Corporation
Principal Consultants:
Goody Clancy & Associates, feasibility, architectural design, site design
The Community Builders, development consultant
Zaldastani Associates, structural consultant
C.A. Crowley Engineering, mechanical engineer
Verne G. Norman Associates, electrical consultant
Halvorson/Moreice & Gary, landscape consultant
Falk Associates, specifications consultant
Turner Construction Co., contractor

Langham Court
Clients: Four Corners Development Corporation and Community Development Corporation
Principal Consultants:
Goody Clancy & Associates, architect
Lim Consultants, structural consultant
Verne G. Norman Associates, electrical consultant
C.A. Crowley Engineering, mechanical consultant
The Halverson Co., landscape consultant
Falk Associates, specifications consultant
Dimeo Construction Co., contractor

THE HARRIS GROUP / TBA² ARCHITECTS

Phillips Place
Developer: The Harris Group
Principal Consultants:
TBA² Architects, architect
LandDesign, Inc., site planning
LandDesign Engineering Services, Inc., civil engineering
Post Landscaping, landscape architect
SouthTrust, financing

HDR ARCHITECTURE, INC.

Centro Medico Integral Hospital Los Angeles
Client: ABA/Inmuebles S.A. de C.V.
Principal Consultants:
HDR Architecture, Inc., programming, architectural design
Fernando Sillier y Associates, associate architect

Centro Medico Integral Hospital Santa Engracia
Client: ABA/Inmuebles S.A. de C.V.
Principal Consultants:
HDR Architecture, Inc., architectural design
TenEyck, Merritt, Barnett, Pitt Consulting Engineers, Inc., structural engineer

Aire Plex
Client: Sound Trak, Inc.
Principal Consultants:
HDR Architecture, Inc., programming, master site planning, architectural design, engineering

Durham Western Heritage Museum:
Client: Durham Western Heritage Museum
Principal Consultants:
HDR Architecture, Inc., programming, architectural design, engineering
Kiewit Construction, general contractor/construction manager
Lee Skolnick, Architecture & Design Partnership, exhibit design

HELLMUTH, OBATA + KASSABAUM, INC.

Federal Reserve Bank of Minneapolis
Client: Federal Reserve Bank of Minneapolis
Principal Consultants:
Hellmuth, Obata + Kassabaum, Inc., site selection, site and landscape design, architectural and interior design
Walsh Bishop Associates, Inc., associate architect
McGough Construction Co., construction manager
Minnesota Valley Landscape, landscape contractor
Siebold, Sydow & Elfanbaum, structural engineering
Michaud Cooley Erickson, mechanical/electrical engineering

St. Louis Union Station
Client: St. Louis Station Associates
Principal Consultants:
The Rouse Company, development management
Hellmuth, Obata + Kassabaum, Inc., master planning, architectural design, civil engineering, landscape architecture, lighting design
Communication Arts, Inc., environmental graphics and design
Engineering Design Management, Inc., structural engineers

Apple Computer, Inc., Research and Development Campus
Client: ACI Real Properties, Inc. (a wholly owned subsidiary of Apple Computer, Inc.)
Principal Consultants:
Hellmuth, Obata + Kassabaum, Inc., master planning, architecture (shell and core), landscape architecture
Gensler and Associates, interior design, building 1
Studios Architecture, interior design, buildings 2 and 5
Holey Associates, interior design, building 3
Backen Arrigoni & Ross, interior design, buildings 4 and 6
Sussman Prejza & Company, graphic design

Kellogg Company Corporate Headquarters
Client: Kellogg Company
Principal Consultant:
Hellmuth, Obata + Kassabaum, Inc., master planning, architectural design, landscape architecture, interior design, programming, graphic design, artwork programs, lighting design
Miller-Davis Company, general contractor
GCE International, Inc. (now KKBNA), structural engineers

Hong Kong Stadium
Client: Hong Kong Jockey Club
Principal Consultants:
Hellmuth, Obata + Kassabaum Sports Facilities Group, Inc., master planning, architectural design, landscape architecture
Ove Arup & Partners Hong Kong, Ltd., civil/structural/mep engineers
Davis Langdon & Seah Hong Kong, Ltd., quantity surveyors
Wrightson, Johnson, Haddon & Williams, Inc., acoustical, audio-visual consultants
PHA Lighting Design, lighting
Rolf Jensen & Associates, fire protection/building code
Graf Consulting Group International, operations/food and beverage consultants

JAMBHEKAR STRAUSS ARCHITECTS PC

Buffalo Inner Harbor Project
Client: Empire State Development Corporation
Principal Consultants:
Jambhekar Strauss Architects PC, architects
Flynn Battaglia Architects PC, architects
Mathews Nielsen, landscape architects
Hayden Wegman Inc., civil engineering
Amman & Whitney, structural engineering
Lakhani & Jordan, mechanical, electrical and plumbing engineers

Hudson-Bergen Light Rail Transit System, SOS Phase
Client: New Jersey Transit
Principal Consultants:
Jambhekar Strauss Architects PC, architects
Parsons Brinckerhoff Quade & Douglas, Inc., project management/consulting engineers

Williamsburg Community Center
Client: New York City Housing Authority
Principal Consultants:
Jambhekar Strauss Architects PC, architects

Lehman College Communication Station
Client: The City University of New York/Dormitory Authority of the State of New York
Principal Consultants:
Jambhekar Strauss Architects PC, architects
Lakhani & Jordan, mechanical, electrical and plumbing engineers
Mathews Nielsen, landscape architects
Weidlinger Associates, structural engineers

Transit Hub Development
Client: The Arete Group
Principal Consultant:
Jambhekar Strauss Architects PC, architects

THE JERDE PARTNERSHIP INTARNATIONAL, INC.

Canal City Hakata
Clients: Fukuoka Jisho Co, Ltd.; Sumitomo Life Insurance Company; Fukuoka, Japan, Urban Design and Development Co.
Principal Consultants:
The Jerde Partnership International, urban planning, architectural design

Fukuoka Jisho, Urban Design Development Co., associate architects
The Zenitaka Corporation, Shimizu Corporation, Obayashi Corporation, Fujita Corporation, general contractors
EDAW, Inc., landscape architects
Selbert Perkins Design, environmental, merchandise designer
Wet Design, water features designer
Joe Kaplan Architectural Lighting, lighting designer
Fine Arts Services, Inc., art consultant

Beursplein
Client: Multi Vastgoed bv
Principal Consultants:
The Jerde Partnership International, Inc., T+T Design, De Architekten cie, Architectenbureau D & T van Manen, Van Moort & Partners Architectenbureau, Kraaijvanger Urbis Bureau voor Architectuur, project architects
Consortium Beursplein (Municipality of Rotterdam, Ing Vastgoed, Focas B.V.), C & A, Kreymborg, Hema, Vroom & Dreesmann, principals
Gallegos Lighting, lighting consultant
Environmental Image, environmental graphics designer

Fremont Street Experience
Client: Fremont Street Experience LLC
Principal Consultants:
The Jerde Partnership International, architectural design
Harry Campbell Architects, associate architects
Mary Kozlowski Architect, Inc., architect, parking structure
Marnell Corrao Associates, construction manager
Jeremy Railton & Associates, show designer

JJR INCORPORATED

The University of Michigan
Client: The University of Michigan
Principal Consultants:
Gary Steffey, lighting consultant
Jeff Lasko, fountain consultant
Neal Adams Inc., engineer

Sears Merchandise Group Headquarters
Client: Sears Roebuck & Co. with Homart Development
Principal Consultants:
Perkins & Will, architects
Rust Inc., civil engineers
Gary Steffey, lighting consultant
William Hobbs, Ltd., fountain consultant

Crosswinds Marsh Wetland Preserve
Client: County of Wayne, Michigan
Principal Consultants:
Tucker, Young, Jackson, Tull, civil engineering consultant
NTH Consultants, Ltd, geotechnical consultant

Houston Street
Client: Tri-Party
Principal Consultant:
Lawrence Speck Associates/Lake Flato Associates, architectural elements

KOHN PEDERSEN FOX ASSOCIATES, PC

The World Bank
Client: The World Bank
Principal Consultants:
Kohn Pedersen Fox Associates, PC, architects
KPF Interior Architects, PC, interior architects
Kresscox Associates, PC, associate architects
Weidlinger Associates, structural engineer
Flack & Kurtz, mechanical engineer, telecommunications
Heller & Metzger, specifications consultant
John A. Van Duesen & Associates, vertical transportation/materials handling consultants
Gorove, Slade & Associates, traffic consultants
V.J. Associates, cost estimating consultants
Loiederman Associates, Inc., civil engineering
Booz-Allen & Hamilton, security consultant
Jerry Kugler Associates, lighting consultant
Rolf Jensen & Associates, fire protection engineers
Rhodeside & Harwell, Inc. landscape
William Hobbs, Ltd., fountain consultant
Carbone Smolan Associates, graphic designer
Art Co., Limited, art consultant
The George Hyman Construction Co., general contractor

Dallas Federal Reserve Bank
Client: Federal Reserve Bank of Dallas
Principal Consultants:
Kohn Pedersen Fox Associates, Inc., design architects
Sikes Jennings Kelly & Brewer, associated architects
John S. Chase, AIA, Architect, Inc., associated architect
Kohn Pedersen Fox Conway Associates, Inc., interior design/interior architecture
Construction Manager/G.C., interior architects
Walter P. Moore & Associates, Inc., structural engineers
Datum Engineering, Inc., structural engineers
Charles Gojer and Associates, Inc., structural engineers
Blum Consulting Engineers, Inc., mep engineers
Carter & Burgess, Inc., civil engineer
Austin Commercial, Inc., general contractor
Douglas Harding Group, graphics consultants
Knight O'Connor and Associates, security consultants
Rolf Jensen & Associates, Inc., life safety consultants
The SWA Group, landscape architects
Blum Consulting Engineers, Inc., acoustical and energy conservation consultants
Walter P. Moore & Associates, traffic consultants
Jerry Kugler & Associates, lighting consultants

Mark O. Hatfield United States Courthouse
Client: General Services Administration
Principal Consultants:
Broome, Oringdulph, O'Toole, Rudolf, Boles & Associates, architects
Kohn Pedersen Fox Associates, PC, design architect
CRSS Constructors, construction manager
Hoffman Construction Company, general contractor
KPFF Engineering, structural engineer
Westlake Consultants, civil engineer
PAE Consulting Engineers, Inc., mechanical and electrical engineer
C.E. Marquardt Lighting Design, lighting consultant
Ackroyd, Inc., cost estimator/value engineering consultant
Murase Associates, landscape architect
Towne, Richards & Chaudiere, Inc., acoustical engineer
Kittelson & Associates, traffic consultant
Dames & Moore, environmental services consultant
Alta Consulting Services, security/communications consultant
Rolf Jensen & Associates, fire/life safety consultant
Lerch, Bates & Associates, vertical transportation consultants
Mayer/Reed, graphics consultant

Atlanta Federal Center
Clients: Prentiss Properties, Atlanta Economic Development Corp., General Services Administration
Principal Consultants:
Kohn Pedersen Fox Associates, PC, architect
Turner Associates Architects and Planners, Inc., associate architects
Stevens & Wilkinson, Inc., associate architects
Cheeks/Hornbein & Associates, associate architects
Federal Center Builders, construction manager
Walter P. Moore & Associates, Inc., structural engineers
Bennett & Pless, Inc., structural engineers
Newcomb & Boyd, mechanical/electrical engineers
Khafra Engineering, civil engineer
John A. Van Deusen & Associates, Inc., vertical transportation
Shen Milson & Wilke, accoustical

MBT ARCHITECTURE

University of California, Berkeley Silver Space Science Laboratory Expansion
Client: University of California, Berkeley
Principal Consultants:
MBT Architecture, architectural design, interior design
AGS Inc., civil engineer
Forell/Elsesser, structural engineer
Affiliated Engineers, Inc., mechanical engineer
F.W. Associates, electrical engineer
Patricia O'Brien, landscape architect
Adamson Associates, cost estimator
Infrastructure Design Associates, telecommunications

Genencor International Technology Center
Client: Genencor International
Principal Consultants:
MBT Architecture, programming, architectural design, interior design
Life Sciences International, process engineering
URS Greiner, structural engineer
Alfa Tech, mechanical engineer
MTH Engineers, electrical engineering
EDAW, landscape architect
MacKay & Somps, civil engineer
Charles M. Salter Associates, acoustical consultant

Vincent E. McKelvey Federal Building for the U.S. Geological Survey
Client: General Services Administration
Principal Consultants:
MBT Architecture, architectural design, interior design

Forell/Elsesser, structural engineer
Gayner Engineers, mechanical/electrical engineer
Kennedy Jenks, civil engineer
Geomatrix, soils engineer
Carter Tighe Leeming + Kajiwara, Ltd., landscape architect
Charles M. Salter Associates, acoustic consultant
Adamson Associates, cost estimator

THE PLANNING COLLABORATIVE

San Francisco Lands in the City of Pleasanton
Client: San Francisco Water Department, Public Utilities Commission
Principal Consultants:
The Planning Collaborative, prime consultant, land planning, golf course architecture, environmental specific plan and master plan documents
Team members: Economic Planning Systems, Inc.; Lamphier & Associates; Geo/Resource Consultants, Inc.; Baseline Environmental Consulting; Dowling Associates, traffic engineers, et al

Vallejo Waterfront Plan
Clients: The DeSilva Callahan, LLC Developers with the City of Vallejo Redevelopment Agency
Principal Consultants:
The Planning Collaborative, prime consultant, , urban design, land planning, landscape architecture, public workshops
A-N West, Inc., consulting engineers
Peter Hasselman, architect
Watry Design Group, parking garage consultants
Carlos Alonso, theater design consultant
Berloger Engineers and Geologists
TJKM, traffic engineers
Economic Planning Systems Inc., economic consultants

Downtown Livermore Urban Design Plan
Client: City of Livermore Redevelopment Agency
Principal Consultants:
The Planning Collaborative, prime consultant, urban design plan, streetscape master plan, and construction documents for public improvements
A-N West, Inc., consult engineer
The Engineering Enterprise, electrical/utilities
Russ Mitchell Associates, irrigation
DKS Associates, traffic
GFDS, structural engineers

Downtown Fairfield Urban Design Plan
Client: City of Fairfield, California
Principal Consultants:
The Planning Collaborative, prime consultant Urban Design Plan, streets, master plan, construction documents for Texas Street improvements.
Creegan & D'Angelo, civil engineers
Fairfield Public Works Dept., electrical
Blevens Associates, irrigation consultants

ROMA DESIGN GROUP

Mid-Embarcadero Roadway and Open Space Design
Client: City and County of San Francisco
Principal Consultants:
Peter Walker, Sasaki Associates, Heller Manus Architects, Mai Arbegast, Bill Maxwell, Buster Simpson, Vito Acconci, Barbara Stauffacher-Solomon, Stanley Saitowitz, Michael Manwaring, The Engineering Enterprise, Sierra Engineering Group, Treadwell & Rollo, and the community at large.

Pier 7
Clients: Port of San Francisco and the San Francisco Department of Recreation and Parks
Principal Consultants:
T.Y. Lin International, structural engineering
Y.E.I., electrical and mechanical engineering

Third Street Promenade
Client: City of Santa Monica
Principal Consultants:
Avacon Engineers (formerly Jaykim Engineers), civil engineering
Putterman/Davis, structural engineering
Russell D. Mitchell & Associates, irrigation
The Engineering Enterprise, lighting and electrical engineering
Weston Pringle & Associates, traffic signals
Claude and Francois LaLanne, sculptors

Pacific Avenue Streetscape
Client: City of Santa Cruz
Principal Consultants:
Adamson & Associates, Winzler & Kelly, H.M. Brandston & Partners, Inc., Mai Arbegast, Samson Hydrotechnical

RTKL ASSOCIATES INC.

Addison Urban Center
Client: Post Properties
Principal Consultants:
Brockette Davis Drake, Inc., structural engineer
Basharkhah Engineering, MEP engineer
Newman Jackson Bieberstein, Inc., landscaping
Theo Kondos Associates, lighting
M&M Lighting, lighting
Huitt-Zollars, civil engineer
Jenkins and Gilchrest, zoning consultant
De Shazo, Tang & Associates, Inc., traffic consultant

Courtyard Shops of Encino
Client: Security Pacific Corporation
Developer: Security Pacific Development Company
Principal Consultants:
Peck/Jones, contractor
Devcon, Inc., construction consultant
Jarvis & Associates, Inc., retail consultant
Harrison Teasley & Associates, civil engineer
Hillman, Biddison & Loevenguth, structural engineer
Rosenberg & Associates, mechanical & plumbing engineer
CALPEC Engineering, electrical engineer
Gerald Legmer & Associates, shoring engineer
LeRoy Crandal & Associates, geotechnical engineer
Emmet Wemple & Associates, landscape architect
Lindscott, Law & Greenspan, Inc., traffic consultant

Reston Town Center
Client: Mobil Land Corporation
Principal Consultants:
Omni Construction, general contractor
Sasaki Associates, Inc., landscape

Santa Lucia Riverwalk
Client: Consejo Estatal de Rehabilitaccion Urbana
Principal Consultants:
Frontera Associates International, Inc., canal consulting engineers
Arthur Anderson Real Estate Services, market economics
Barton-Aschman Associates, Inc., traffic and transportation

Camden Yards Sports Complex
Client: Maryland Stadium Authority and HOK Sports Facilities Group
Principal Consultants:
RTKL, master planning coordinator and urban design
HOK Sports Facilities Group, architect of record
Wallace Roberts & Todd, landscape and urban design
Rummel, Klepper & Kahl, civil engineering
Wilbur Smith Associates, traffic and parking consultant
Catherine Mahan & Associates, landscape consultant
Sheladia Associates, Inc., architecture and engineering for Camden Station
MEP Engineers, Inc. and Kidde Consultants, Inc., MEP engineering
Delon Hampton & Associates, Chart., structural engineering
The Joiner-Rose Group, Inc., acoustical engineering
TLB Associates Inc., geotechnical engineering
Scharft-Godfrey, Inc., cost estimating
Barton Malow/Sverdrup, construction manager

Centro Oberhausen
Client: Neue Mitte Projektenwicklung GmbH & Co. KG, a subsidiary of the Stadium Group
Principal Consultants:
Architekten RKW, joint venture partner
Bovis International, project management
James Stewart Partnership, mep consultants
HTW, mep consultants
Bingham Cotterell Ltd., structural engineering
Klaus Nühlen, structural engineering
Dorsch Consult IMBH, civil engineering
The SWA Group, landscape
Planungsgruppe Bover Landschaftsarchiteken, landscape
Theo Kondos, lighting
Strabag AG and Heilit & Wörner, contractors

The Entertainment Center, Irvine Spectrum
Client: The Irvine Company
Principal Consultants:
PM Realty Group, project coordinator
Government Solutions, entitlement processing
Burton Associates, landscape architects
CDC Engineering, civil engineering
KAKU Associates, traffic engineering
Musil, Perkowitz Ruth, cinema architects
Ron Mincer, H.C. consultant
Baab & Associates, sign submittal package
Francis Krahe & Associates, Inc., lighting consultant
William M. Simpson, structural engineer
The Keith Company, on-site civil engineering
Snyder Langston, contractor
R.G.I., dry utilities
Zeiser Kling Consultants, Inc., geotechnical consultants

Steven M. Hood Associates, sound and lighting consultant
Store Matakovich & Wolfberg, mep consultants
Contractor: Turner Construction Company

SASAKI ASSOCIATES, INC.

Pusan Harbor Urban Design Plan
Client: Samsung Construction Company
Principal Consultants:
Sasaki Associates, Inc., planning, urban design, architecture, landscape architecture, infrastructure planning
Samoo Architects, design management
GPI Models, model
Curtis Woodhouse, rendering

Capital City Landing
Clients: U.S. Army Corps of Engineers, Louisville District; White River State Park, City of Indianapolis
Sasaki Associates, Inc., master planning, architecture, landscape architecture, urban design, transportation planning, civil engineering, environmental services and other consultants

Cleveland Gateway
Client: The Gateway Economic Development Corporation
Principal Consultants:
Sasaki Associates, Inc., master planning, urban design, landscape architecture, parking and transportation planning, environmental graphics
HOK Sport, Jacobs Field architects
Ellerbe Becket, Gund Arena architects
van Dijk, Pace, Westlake & Partners, parking garages
Richard Fleischman Architects, Inc., service area
Committee for Public Art

SITE

Museum of Islamic Arts
Client: Special Projects Office of Doha, Qatar
Principal Consultants:
SITE, architectural design
Land Design Studio, exhibition design
Polkinghorne Associates, museum planner
Mimar Design, consulting architects
Tourbier and Walmsley, landscape architects
Agassi Consulting Engineers, structural engineering
Jaros, Baum & Bolles, mechanical and electrical engineers
The Hillier Group, environmental design consultants
Quentin Thomas Associates, lighting design
Tillyard, quantity surveyor

Ross's Landing Park and Plaza
Client: The River City Company for Hamilton County and the City of Chattanooga, Tennessee
Principal Consultants:
SITE, architectural design
Robert Seals, architect
EDAW, Inc., landscape architects
Jack Mackie, Stanley Townsend, public artists
Hensley-Schmidt, Inc., engineers
Robinson Associates, consulting engineers
Riverfront Downtown Planning and Design Center, consultants
Turner Construction, project management
Soloff Construction Company, Inc., general contractor

Horoscope Ring Park
Client: Toyama Expo Association
Principal Consultants:
SITE, architectural design
Archinoch Co., Ltd., associated architects
Nomura Co., Ltd., general constructor

Four Continents Bridge
Client: Sea and Islands Expo Association
Principal Consultants:
SITE, architectural design
Signe Nielsen, P.C., Landscape Architect, landscape architect
Geiger Engineers, structural engineer
Quentin Thomas Associates, lighting designer
Takenaka Komuten Co., general contractor

USA Pavilion, Expo 2000
Client: USA at Hannover 2000, Inc.
Principal Consultants:
SITE, architectural design
Weidinger Associates, structural engineering
Tillyard, quantity surveyor

SKIDMORE, OWINGS & MERRILL LLP

State Street Renovation Project
Client: City of Chicago Department of Transportation, City of Chicago Department of Planning & Development
Principal Consultants:
Skidmore, Owings & Merrill LLP, urban design, architectural design
Baker Heavy & Highway, general contractor
Consoer Townsend Envirodyne Engineers, consulting engineer
Greater State Street Council
Rust Environment & Infrastructure Inc., program manager

Riverside South
Client: Riverside South Planning Corporation
Principal Consultants:
Skidmore, Owings & Merrill, master planning
Michael Van Valkenburgh, landscape architect
Mel Chin/Joyce Kozloff/Mary Miss/Fred Wilson, artists
Philip Habib & Associates, transportation engineer
HNTB, civil engineer
Parsons, Brinckerhoff, Quade & Douglas, ventilation consultant
Olko Engineers, marine consultant
Lovell-Belcher, Inc., land surveyor
Tenguerian Models, Inc., modelmaker

Shanghai Waterfront Redevelopment Master Plan
Client: The Shanghai P&K Development Company
Principal Consultants:
Skidmore, Owings & Merrill, master planning and urban design
Shanghai Urban Planning and Design Research Institute, local planning, utilities and transportation
Christopher Grubbs, architectural illustration

G-MEX District Master Plan
Client: Merlin Great Northern, in association with English Partnerships and Manchester City Council
Principal Consultants:
Skidmore, Owings & Merrill, master planning, urban design, architectural design, landscape design
KPMG, project management and financial consulting
Christopher Glaister & Associates, planning/urban design
Alan Baxter & Associates, transport planning and engineering
Beard Dove, cost consulting
Leslie Jones & Partners, architectural design

SMALLWOOD, REYNOLDS, STEWART, STEWART & ASSOCIATES, INC.

Capital Commons Public Plaza
Client: City of Tallahassee
Project Manager: Lincoln Property Company
Principal Consultants:
Barnett Fronczak Architects, architect of record
Post, Buckley, Schuh & Jernigan, Inc., civil engineering
Bliss & Nyitray, Inc., structural engineering
Ardaman & Associates Consulting Engineers, Inc., geotechnical engineering
Hanson Taylor, Inc., landscape design
Transportation Consulting Group, traffic engineering
Project for Public Spaces, Inc., public space planning
B&A Consulting Engineers, M/E/P and fire protection
Broward Davis & Associates, Inc., surveyor

Eleven Hundred Peachtree Street
Client: Carter & Associates, Sunlink Corporation
General Contractor: Hardin Construction Group, Inc.
Principal Consultants:
Stanley D. Lindsey & Associates, structural engineering
Rosser Fabrap International, civil engineering and M/E/P
EDAW, Inc., landscape design
RBA Group, traffic engineering
Law Engineering, soil engineering
JDA Lighting Design, Inc., lighting
Newmont Elevator Analysts, Inc., elevators
Watts & Browning, surveyors

Federal Home Loan Bank
Client: Federal Home Loan Bank
Developer: Lincoln Property Company
Contractor: Pace Construction Corporation
Principal Consultants:
Bennett & Pless, Inc., structural engineering
W.L. Jorden & Company, civil engineering
B&A Consulting Engineers, M/E/P and fire protection
Laubmann-Reed & Associates, Inc., landscape design
Soil & Material Engineers, soil engineering
Watts & Browning, surveyor

The Georgian Terrace
Client: E.F. Howington Company
Client Representative: F.C. Battey Realty Corporation
General Contractor: Hardin Construction Group, Inc.
Principal Consultants:
Stanley D. Lindsey & Associates, Inc., structural engineering
Travis Pruitt & Associates, P.C., civil engineering and surveying
Smallwood, Reynolds, Stewart, Stewart Interiors, Inc., interior design

Hartrampf Engineering, Inc., M/E/P
J.S. Thomas Company, Inc., mechanical engineer
Henderson Electric Company, electrical engineer
Art Plumbing Company, plumbing
Allsouth Sprinkler Company, fire protection
ATEC Associates, Inc., environmental assessment & testing
Dames & Moore, soils investigation
Newmont Elevator Analysts, Inc., elevators
Park Square Consultants, scheduling

IJL Financial Center
Client: NationsBank
Developer: Trammell Crow Company
General Contractor: Beers Construction Company
Principal Consultants:
Stanley D. Lindsey & Associates, structural engineering
W.K. Dickson, civil engineering
B&A Consulting Engineers, M/E/P and fire protection
Smallwood, Reynolds, Stewart, Stewart Interiors, Inc., public space interior design
Hillman DiBernardo, lighting
Smallwood, Reynolds, Stewart, Stewart & Associates, Inc., landscape design
Carter & Burgess, Inc., traffic consulting
Securacom, Inc., security system
Williamson & Associates, Inc., waterproofing
D.S. Atlantic, surveyor

J.W. Marriott Hotel
Client: Robinson-Humphrey
Principal Consultants:
Sedki & Russ Engineers, structural engineering
LRE Engineering, Inc., civil and traffic engineering
Design Continuum, Inc., interior design
Roy Ashley & Associates, Inc., landscape design
Soil & Material Engineers, subsurface testing
B&A Consulting Engineers, M/E/P and fire protection
Newmont Elevator Analysts, Inc., elevators
C.M. Kling & Associates, lighting
Antony J. Gaeta, Inc., food services
Lowe Engineers, Inc., W.L. Jorden & Company, Inc., surveyors

The Mayfair
Client: Laing Properties, Inc.
Property Management Consultant: Trammell Crow Company
Contractor: BCB Company
Principal Consultants:
Nielsen/Uzun Structural Engineers, Inc., structural engineering
The RBA Group, civil engineering and transportation planning consultant
ATEC Associates, Inc., geotechnical/field testing
Law Engineering, subsurface investigation
B&A Consulting Engineers, M/P
Roberds Consulting Engineers, Ltd., electrical
Smallwood, Reynolds, Stewart, Stewart Interiors, Inc., public space interior design
Wilson & Associates, residential interiors
Roy Ashley & Associates, Inc., landscape architecture
Newmont Elevator Analysts, Inc., elevators
Early & Associates, Inc., elevators
Lighting Consultants, Inc., lighting
J.R. Ballentine & Associates, Inc., acoustics
W.L. Jorden & Company, Inc., surveyor

Melville Park
Client: First Capital Corporation, Ltd.
Contractor: Sim Lian Construction Company, Pte. Ltd.
Principal Consultants:
Design Link Architects, local registered architect
Engineers Partnership, structural/civil engineering
Beca Cart Hollings & Ferner (SE Asia), Pte. Ltd., M/E
Northcroft Lim Consultants, Pte. Ltd., contract documentation
JIA Quantity Surveyors & Project Managers, Pte. Ltd., surveyor

The Oaks
Client: Perini Land and Development Company
Contractor: R.J. Griffin & Company
Principal Consultants:
Browder + LeGuizamon & Associates, Inc., structural engineering
Bailey Engineering Associates Inc., civil engineering
Brewer & Skala Engineers, Inc., M/P design
Harold H. Brown Engineers, Inc., electrical
Law Engineering, subsurface testing
Loo-Turley & Associates, P.C., surveyor

THE STUBBINS ASSOCIATES, INC.

Citicorp Center
Clients: First National City Corporation (now Citicorp) and St. Peter's Lutheran Church
Principal Consultants:
Emery Roth & Sons, associate architect
LeMessurier Associates/SCI, structural consultants
The Office of James R. Ruderman, structural consultants
Sasaki, Dawson, DeMay Associates, Inc., landscape consultants
HRH Construction Corporation, construction manager

Treasury Building
Client: The Development Bank of Singapore, Ltd.
Principal Consultants:
Architects 61, associate architect
LeMessurier Consultants, Inc., structural consultant
Ove Arup and Partners, structural consultant
Ewbank Preece Partnership, mechanical consultant
Horton Lees Lighting Design, Inc., lighting consultant
Bolt, Beranek & Newman, Incl., acoustical consultant
John A. Van Deusen and Associates, vertical transportation consultant
Urban Development and Management Co., Ltd, landscape consultant
International Development and Consultancy Corp., Ltd., quantity surveyors

Venetian Casino Resort
Client: Las Vegas Sands, Inc.
Principal Consultants:
TSA (The Stubbins Associates) Nevada, LLP, collaborating architects
WAT&G (Wimberly Allison Tong & Goo), Inc., collaborating architects
Martin & Peltyn, structural engineer (low rise)
MSA Engineering, electrical engineer
AE Associates, mechanical/plumbing engineer
Rissman and Rissman Associates, Ltd., casino consultant
Converse Environmental Consultants Southwest, Inc., environmental consultant
Terracon Consultants Western, Inc., geotechnical engineer
Rolf Jensen & Associates, life safety consultant/fire protection
Lerch Bates, vertical transportation
Lifescapes International, Inc., landscape architect
John A. Martin Associates, structural engineer (high-rise)
Lighting Design Alliance, lighting design
Wilson Associates, interior designer (tower)
Dougall Design, interior designer (casino)

Shenzhen Cultural Plaza
Client: Shenzhen Jinfeng Industry Development Company
Wang International, landscape consultant

The Landmark Tower
Client: Mitsubishi Estates Company Ltd.
Principal Consultants:
LeMessurier Consultants, Inc., structural engineer
Syska & Hennessy, mechanical/electrical engineer
Turner Construction Company, Contractor

SWA GROUP

Capitol Commons
Client: Indiana Convention Center Authority Capitol Improvements Board and the Lilly Foundation
Principal Consultants:
SWA Group, urban design, landscape architecture
Kennedy Brown McQuiston, architects
CMS Collaborative, fountain consultants

Dallas West End Historic District
Client: City of Dallas
Principal Consultants:
SWA Group, urban design, landscape design
Turner, Collie & Braden, Inc., civil engineering

Arizona Center
Client: The Rouse Company
Principal Consultants:
SWA Group, urban design, landscape design
ELS/Elbasani & Logan, Architects, The Shops at Arizona Center architects
HNTB Architects, Communication Center and Sports Arena

TORTI GALLAS AND PARTNERS • CHK

Bahcesehir Phase 2
Client: Emlak Bank
Principal Consultant: Inas, local architects

Ispartakule:
Client: Korkmaz Yigit and Kemal Gulman

Neighborhood Green and Community Building
Client: Trafalgar House, Ltd.
Principal Consultants:
Christopher Consultants, civil engineering
Urban Engineers, civil engineering
Hazel & Thomas, zoning attorney
Callow Associates, transportation engineer

Shot Tower West Entrance Plaza
Client: Maryland Mass Transit Administration
Principal Consultants:
Shemro Engineering Associates, structural engineering
Kaiser/EDA, mechanical/electrical/plumbing engineering
Whitney Bailey Cox & Magnani, civil engineering
S.C. Myers & Associates, cost consultants

Village Center, The King Farm
Client: The Penrose Group
Principal Consultants:
Linowes & Blocher, attorney
Loiederman Associates, civil engineers
The Traffic Group, traffic engineer
McCarthy & Associates, environmental consultant

Old Town Commons
Client: McCann, Inc.
Principal Consultants:
Holland Engineering, civil engineering
Hart & Calley, zoning attorney
BMI, traffic engineer

Arlington Courthouse Plaza
Client: The Artery Organization
Principal Consultants:
Smislova Kehnemui & Associates, structural engineers
Girard Engineering, mechanical/electrical/plumbing engineers
William H. Gordon Associates, civil engineers
Schnabel Engineering Associates, geotechnical engineers

Artery Plaza
Client: The Artery Organization
Principal Consultants:
Smislova Kehnemui & Associates, structural engineers
Silver Associates, m/e/p engineers
Johnson Mirmiram & Thompson, civil engineers
EDAW, Inc., landscape architects
Herbst & Associates, soils engineers
Eric Colbert & Associates, lighting consultant
Stehle Engineering Corporation, fire protection engineer
Francoise Yohalem, art consultant

Hearthstone Mews
Client: Madison Homes
Principal Consultants:
The Mayhood Company, marketing consultant
Alliance Structural Engineers, structural engineering

Courts of Foxhall
Client: Carl Bernstein & Associates
Principal Consultant: Vika, Inc., civil engineering

Lafayette Courts
Client: Housing Authority of Baltimore City
Principal Consultants:
Qodesh Engineering Services, structural engineer
Sidhu Associates, mechanical/electrical/plumbing engineer
Daniel Consultants, Inc., civil engineer
Scharf-Godfrey Associates, cost estimating

Kemer Country
Client: Kemer Yapi ve Turizm

Montgomery Lane
Client: Greenhill Capital Corporation
Principal Consultants:
Alliance Structural Engineers, structural engineering
Macris Hendricks & Glascock, civil engineering

TVS / THOMPSON, VENTULETT, STAINBACK & ASSOCIATES, INC.

McCormick Place
Client: Metropolitan Pier & Expansion Authority
Principal Consultants:
Mc3D, design/construction consortium
TVS/Sthompson, Ventulett, Stainback & Associates Inc., design architect
TVS Interiors, interior design
A. Epstein & Sons International, Inc., architect of record
The Clark Construction Group, sponsoring general contractor
Mesirow Stein Real Estate, developer
Huber, Hunt, & Nichols Inc., contractor
Morse Diesel International Inc., contractor
Walsh Construction Company of Illinois, contractor
Louis Jones Enterprises Inc., contractor
Alex Munoz, contractor
Environmental Systems Design, mechanical, electrical, plumbing
Wiedinger Associates, structural engineer
Alfred Benesch & Co., civil engineer
SWA Group, landscape architect
Schirmer Engineering Corp., fire protection
Sussman Prejza, graphic

Georgia International Plaza
Client: Georgia World Congress Center Authority
Principal Consultants:
Rosser Fabrap, engineering management
SWA Group, landscape architects, design
Leslie Design Group, landscape architects, implementation
Rosser Fabrap: lighting design

Pennsylvania Convention Center
Client: Pennsylvania Convention Center Authority
Principal Consultants:
Vitetta Group, associated architect
Kelly/Maiello, Inc., consulting architect
TVS Interiors, interior design
Design Services, Inc., joint venture interior design
Morse Diesel/Temple, owner's project manager
Hardin/Keating/Kemrodco, Joint Venture, construction manager
Pennell & Witberger, Inc., mechanical, electrical, plumbing
Ross Bryan Associates, Inc., structural engineer
Chilton Engineering, Inc., civil engineer
Synterra Ltd., landscape architect
Grenald Associates, lighting consultant
Noel Mayo Associates, lighting consultant
Schirmer Engineering Corp., fire protection
Cloud & Gresham Associates, graphics

Plaza at King of Prussia
Client: Kravco Company
Principal Consultants:
TVS/Thompson, Ventulett, Stainback & Associates, Inc., architect
TVS Interiors, interior design
E. W. Howell, construction manager
Theo Kondos Associates, lighting consultant
ZMM, Inc., mechanical (design)
John C. Kohler Co., mechanical (construction)
Kelly Lundstrom George, electrical
John C. Kohler Co., plumbing
Ross Bryan Associates, Inc., structural engineer
Robert F. Harsch & Associates, civil engineer
Roy Ashley & Associates, interior landscape architect
McCloskey & Faber, P.C., interior landscape architect
Schirmer Engineering Corp., fire protection
Lebowitz Gould Design, Inc., graphics

URBAN DESIGN ASSOCIATES

Tidewater Community College
Client: Tidewater Community College
Principal Consultants:
Urban Design Associates, urban design, architecture, schematic and design development
Williams Tazwell & Associates, architects of record, architectural design
La Quatra Bonci, landscaping

High Street Landing
Client: City of Portsmouth
Principal Consultants:
Urban Design Associates, urban design
Glenn and Sadler, civil engineering, construction drawings, and landscaping

Diggs Town
Client: Norfolk Redevelopment and Housing Authority
Principal Consultants:
Urban Design Associates, urban design and architectural design
CMSS Architects: architects of record, construction documents, interiors, landscaping

Randolph Neighborhood
Client: Richmond Redevelopment and Housing Authority
Principal Consultants:
Urban Design Associates, master plans, park design, architects, pattern book
Stuart Patz of Hammer Siler George, economics

Pattern Book, Celebration, Florida
Client: Disney Development Company
Principal Consultant:
Urban Design Associates, pattern book (detailed design guidelines)

SMS Engineering Building
Client: SMS Schloemann - Siemag Aktiengesellschaft
Principal Consultant:
Urban Design Associates

VAN TILBURG, BANVARD & SODERBERGH, ARCHITECTS, AIA

Janss Court
Client: Janss Corporation
Principal Consultants:
Van Tilburg, Banvard & Soderbergh, AIA, architects
The L.A. Group, Inc., landscape architects
Group M Engineers, structural engineer

225 Arizona Avenue
Client: Johannes Van Tilburg FAIA
Principal Consultants:
Van Tilburg, Banvard & Soderbergh, AIA, architects
Brian Cochran Associates, structural engineers
Acces Air Conditioning, mechanical engineers
Harold Kushner Associates, plumbing engineers
Dalan Engineering, electrical engineers

Holly Street Village
Client: Janss Corporation
Principal Consultants:
Van Tilburg, Banvard & Soderbergh, AIA, design architects
The Landau Partnership, executive architects
Levin & Associates, Hall of Justice architects

Venice Renaissance
Clients: Harlan Lee & Associates and The Anden Group
Principal Consultants:
Van Tilburg, Banvard & Soderbergh, AIA, architects
Group M Engineers, structural engineers
Harold Kushner & Associates, mechanical engineers
John Snyder & Associates, electrical engineers
Environmental Technology, Inc., civil engineers
The L.A. Group, Inc., landscape architects
Lonnie Gans & Associates, art consultant

Wilshire Borgata
Client: D'Koby Enterprises
Principal Consultants:
Van Tilburg, Banvard & Soderbergh, AIA, design architects
Masoud Dejban, structural engineers
L.A. Group, landscape architects

Villas of Renaissance
Client: Renaissance Villas Association
Principal Consultant:
Van Tilburg, Banvard & Soderbergh, AIA, architects
Group M Engineers, structural engineers
ETI, mechanical, electrical and plumbing engineers
L.A. Group, landscape architects

Oxnard Factory Outlet
Carl M. Buck Building Company, owner
Principal Consultants:
Van Tilburg, Banvard & Soderbergh, AIA, architects
The L.A. Group, Inc., landscape architects

INDEX BY PROJECTS

28 State Street, Boston, MA, **74**
101 Hudson Street, Jersey City, NJ, **32**
225 Arizona Avenue, Santa Monica, CA, **283**
730 North Michigan Avenue, Chicago, IL, **78**
Addison Urban Center, Addison, TX, **202**
Aire Plex, Cass County, NE, **134**
Angle Lake Park Improvements, Phase I, SeaTac, WA, **23**
Apple Computer, Inc., Research and Development Campus, Cupertino, CA, **142**
Arizona Center, Phoenix, AZ, **254**
Arlington Courthouse Plaza, Arlington, VA, **261**
Artery Plaza, Bethesda, MD, **261**
Atlanta Federal Center, Atlanta, GA, **176**
Bahcesehir Phase 2, Istanbul, Turkey, **258**
Barnett Plaza, Tampa, FL, **72**
Bethesda Retail District, Bethesda, MD, **44**
Beursplein, Rotterdam, The Netherlands, **156**
Broward County Library, Fort Lauderdale, FL, **68**
Buffalo Inner Harbor Project, Buffalo, NY, **146**
Camden Yards Sports Complex, Baltimore, MD, **206**
Canal City Hakata, Fukuoka, Japan, **62**
Canal City Hakata, Fukuoka, Japan, **154**
Capital City Landing, Indianapolis, IN, **212**
Capital Commons Public Plaza, Tallahassee, FL, **240**
Capitol Commons, Indianapolis, IN, **250**
Carillon Point, Kirkland, WA, **38**
Centennial Olympic Park, Atlanta, GA, **58**
Centro Medico Integral Hospital Los Angeles, Torreon, Mexico, **130**
Centro Medico Integral Hospital Santa Engracia, Monterrey, Mexico, **132**
Centro Oberhausen, Oberhausen, Germany, **207**
Chicago Urban Entertainment District, Chicago, IL, **90**
Citicorp Center, New York, NY, **242**
CityPlace, West Palm Beach, FL, **80**
Clarke Quay, Singapore, **86**
Cleveland Gateway, Cleveland, OH, **214**
The Colgate Center, Jersey City, NJ, **30**
Conrad International Center, Jakarta, Indonesia, **27**
Coors Field, Denver, CO, **64**
Courts of Foxhall, Washington, DC, **262**
Courtyard Shops of Encino, Encino, CA, **203**
Crosswinds Marsh Wetland Preserve, Sumpter Township, MI, **166**
Dallas Federal Reserve Bank, Dallas, TX, **172**
Dallas West End Historic District, Dallas, TX, **252**

Diggs Town, Norfolk, VA, **276**
Downtown Fairfield Urban Design Plan, Fairfield, CA, **192**
Downtown Livermore Urban Design Plan, Livermore, CA, **190**
Durham Western Heritage Museum, Omaha, NE, **136**
Eleven Hundred Peachtree Street, Atlanta, GA, **238**
The Entertainment Center, Irvine Spectrum, Irvine, CA, **208**
Fashion Show Mall, Las Vegas, NV, **40**
Fashion Valley Center, San Diego, CA, **10**
Federal Home Loan Bank, Atlanta, GA, **237**
Federal Reserve Bank of Minneapolis, Minneapolis, MN, **138**
Fort Lauderdale Beach Revitalization, Fort Lauderdale, FL, **66**
Four Continents Bridge, Hiroshima, Japan, **223**
The Freedom Trail, Boston, MA, **118**
Fremont Street Experience, Las Vegas, NV, **158**
G-MEX District Master Plan, Manchester, UK, **232**
Genencor International Technology Center, Palo Alto, CA, **180**
Georgia International Plaza, Atlanta, GA, **268**
The Georgian Terrace, Atlanta, GA, **236**
Harbor Point, Boston, MA, **116**
Harbor Steps - Phase I, Seattle, WA, **36**
Hearthstone Mews, Alexandria, VA, **262**
High Street Landing, Portsmouth, VA, **275**
Holly Street Village, Pasadena, CA, **284**
Hong Kong Stadium, Hong Kong, **144**
Horoscope Ring, Toyama, Japan, **222**
Houston Street, San Antonio, TX, **168**
IJL Financial Center, Charlotte, NC, **239**
Ispartakule, Istanbul, Turkey, **259**
J.W. Marriott, Atlanta, GA, **236**
Jakarta Financial Tower, Jakarta, Indonesia, **27**
Jakarta Stock Exchange Building, Jakarta, Indonesia, **27**
Janss Court, Santa Monica, CA, **282**
Kaahumanu Center, Kahului, Maui, HI, **12**
Kellogg Company Corporate Headquarters, Battle Creek, MI, **143**
Kemer Country, Istanbul, Turkey, **263**
Kentlands, Gaithersburg, MD, **50**
Lafayette Courts, Baltimore, MD, **262, 264**
The Landmark Tower, Yokohama, Japan, **248**
Langham Court, Boston, MA, **120**
Lehman College Communication Station, Bronx, NY, **151**
Mark O. Hatfield United States Courthouse, Portland, OR, **174**
Massachusetts Transportation Building, Boston, MA, **114**
The Mayfair, Atlanta, GA, **235**

LANDSCAPE CONSTRUCTION
IRRIGATION INSTALLATION
SPECIALTY CONCRETE
WATER FEATURES
TOTAL SITE CONSTRUCTION
LANDSCAPE CONSTRUCTION
IRRIGATION INSTALLATION
SPECIALTY CONCRETE
WATER FEATURES
TOTAL SITE CONSTRUCTION
LANDSCAPE CONSTRUCTION
IRRIGATION INSTALLATION
SPECIALTY CONCRETE
WATER FEATURES
TOTAL SITE CONSTRUCTION
THEMED ENVIRONMENTS

Natural Engineering

24121 Ventura Boulevard Calabasas, California 91302   please call: 818.223.8500   www.valleycrest.com

ARIZONA   CALIFORNIA   COLORADO   FLORIDA   GEORGIA   NEVADA

McCormick Place, Chicago, IL, **266**
Meadowbrook Community Center, Seattle, WA, **24**
Melville Park, Singapore, **234**
Mid-Embarcadero Roadway and Open Space Design, San Francisco, CA, **194**
Midway Airport Exit Toll Plaza, Chicago, IL, **95**
Midway Airport, Chicago, IL, **94**
Mizner Park, Boca Raton, FL, **46**
Montgomery Lane, Bethesda, MD, **263**
Moscow Botanical Garden, Moscow, Russia, **96**
Museum of Islamic Arts, Doha, Qatar, **218**
Museum of Science and Industry, Chicago, IL, **92**
Neighborhood Green and Community Building, South Riding, Loudoun County, VA, **260**
NJT Hudson-Bergen Light Rail Transit System, SOS Phase, Hudson and Bergen County, NJ, **148**
The Oaks, Atlanta, GA, **234**
Old Town Commons, Alexandria, VA, **261**
Oracle Corporate Campus, Redwood Shores, CA, **98**
Oxnard Factory Outlet, Oxnard, CA, **288**
Pacific Avenue Streetscape, Santa Cruz, CA, **200**
Pattern Book, Celebration, FL, **278**
Pennsylvania Convention Center, Philadelphia, PA, **270**
Phillips Place, Charlotte, NC, **122**
Pier 7, San Francisco, CA, **196**
Pioneer Place, Portland, OR, **84**
Plaza at King of Prussia, King of Prussia, PA, **272**
Primera, Lake Mary, FL, **110**
Pusan Harbor Urban Design Plan, Pusan, Korea, **210**
Quest International, Hoffman Estates, IL, **96**
Randolph Neighborhood, Richmond, VA, **277**
Reston Town Center, Reston, VA, **204**
Riga "Ratsnams" District, Riga, Latvia, **96**
Riverside by Post, Atlanta, GA, **56**
Riverside South, New York, NY, **228**
Riverwalk, Fort Lauderdale, FL, **70**
Ross's Landing Park and Plaza, Chattanooga, TN, **220**
San Francisco Lands in the City of Pleasanton, CA, **186**
Sansom Common, Philadelphia, PA, **76**
Santa Lucia Riverwalk, Monterrey, Mexico, **205**
Sears Merchandise Group Headquarters, Hoffman Estates, IL, **164**

Seattle Central Community College Student Activities Center, Seattle, WA, **18**
Shanghai Waterfront Redevelopment Master Plan, Shanghai, China, **230**
Shenzhen Cultural Plaza, Shenzhen, China, **247**
The Shops at Arizona Center, Phoenix, AZ, **82**
Shot Tower West Entrance Plaza, Baltimore, MD, **260**
SMS Engineering Building, Pittsburgh, PA, **280**
South Wells Self Park, Chicago, IL, **95**
Southwest Harbor Project, Terminal 5 Expansion Public Access, Seattle, WA, **22**
St. Louis Union Station, St. Louis, MO, **140**
State Street Renovation Project, Chicago, IL, **226**
Sudirman Central Business District, Gateway Precinct, Jakarta, Indonesia, **26**
SunTrust Financial Centre, Tampa, FL, **42**
Tacoma Dome Transportation Station, Tacoma, WA, **20**
Tent City, Boston, MA, **119**
Third Street Promenade, Santa Monica, CA, **198**
Tidewater Community College, Norfolk, VA, **274**
Tower Place, Cincinnati, OH, **14**
Town of Seaside, Walton County, FL, **52**
Transit Hub Development, Queens, NY, **152**
Treasury Building, Singapore, **244**
U.S. Bank Centre, Seattle, WA, **34**
University of California, Berkeley Silver Space Science Laboratory Expansion, Berkeley, CA, **178**
The University of Michigan, Ann Arbor, MI, **162**
USA Pavilion Expo 2000, Hannover, Germany, **224**
Vallejo Waterfront Plan, Vallejo, CA, **188**
Venetian Casino Resort, Las Vegas, NV, **246**
Venice Renaissance, Venice, CA, **285**
Village Center, The King Farm, Montgomery County, MD, **260**
Village of Windsor, Vero Beach, FL, **54**
Villas of Renaissance, La Jolla, CA, **287**
Vincent E. McKelvey Federal Building, Menlo Park, CA, **182**
Washington Harbour, Washington, DC, **60**
Wells Fargo + Starbucks New Store Prototype, CA, **39**
West Orange Trail, Orange County, FL, **106**
Williamsburg Community Center, Brooklyn, NY, **150**
Wilshire Borgata, West Los Angeles, CA, **286**
The World Bank, Washington, DC, **170**

The Visual Reference Library
of Architecture and Design

Visit

www.visualreference.com

for a World Tour of the Best in Interior Design, Architecture, Visual Merchandising, Graphics, Lighting & Fixtures.

ACKNOWLEDGEMENTS

Thanks to all the great people at ULI whose support and cooperation made this book possible, especially Rick Rosan, Rachelle Levitt, Lloyd Booker, Laura Templeton, Gayle Berens and Lori Hatcher.

John Dixon's editorial experience and knowledge of architecture was essential to the task of successfully presenting and writing about the over 150 projects in *Urban Spaces*. His ability to communicate with the architects and representatives of the participating firms made the copy flow smoothly.

Thanks also to Dan Biederman for his interest in *Urban Spaces* and contributing his insightful lessons on urban development.

The design and production professionals involved with dealing with the many details of the publishing process of *Urban Spaces* were responsible for the very handsome book we have produced. Thanks to Harish Patel, John Hogan, Ken Lee and Avan Lee.

I very much appreciated the publishing advice and expertise of Lester Dundes and Larry Fuersich that guided the progress of Urban Spaces from concept to creation.

The architects, marketing directors and all the personnel of the firms we worked with were terrific. Through our numerous conversations, I made many friends and their responsiveness and enthusiasm made publishing *Urban Spaces* a most enjoyable experience.

Henry Burr
Publisher